The Two Battles of Copenhagen 1801 and 1807

The Two Battles of Copenhagen 1801 and 1807

Britain and Denmark in the Napoleonic Wars

Gareth Glover

Pen & Sword
MILITARY

First published in Great Britain in 2018 by
Pen & Sword Military

an imprint of
Pen & Sword Books Ltd
47 Church Street
Barnsley
South Yorkshire
S70 2AS

ISBN 978-1-4738-9831-8

Printed and bound in Great Britain by
TJ International Ltd, Padstow, Cornwall

Pen & Sword Books Ltd incorporates the imprints of Pen & Sword Archaeology,
Atlas, Aviation, Battleground, Discovery, Family History, History, Maritime,
Military, Naval, Politics, Railways, Select, Social History, Transport, True Crime, and
Claymore Press, Frontline Books, Leo Cooper, Praetorian Press, Remember When,
Seaforth Publishing and Wharncliffe.

For a complete list of Pen & Sword titles please contact
PEN & SWORD BOOKS LIMITED
47 Church Street, Barnsley, South Yorkshire, S70 2AS, England
E-mail: enquiries@pen-and-sword.co.uk
Website: www.pen-and-sword.co.uk

Contents

List of Plates

List of Maps

Preface

Now Denmark Trembl'd to it's deepest base
Tho' conscious valour fill'd its hardy race.[1]

In the city of Copenhagen even today, Nelson's attack on the Danish fleet in 1801 and the 'theft' of the Danish navy in 1807 are often confused and even conflated into one. Many Danes today refer to Nelson as the 'Stealer of the Danish Navy' and wrongly label him with the guilt of the 1807 siege. British knowledge of the operations at Copenhagen is also often poor and patchy, with some knowledge of Nelson's triumph but often little else. This confusion needs correcting, but how has this come about?

Over the years a few books have been published describing Britain's dealings with Denmark during the Napoleonic Wars, but they all concentrate specifically on only one or other of the two major operations carried out by British forces against Copenhagen during the period, as if they were completely unrelated incidents. This occurs for several reasons. Those who concentrate on the Battle of Copenhagen of 1801, the second and perhaps hardest-won success of Admiral Horatio Nelson's trilogy of stunning victories, rightly view it as a naval operation alone and consistently see later events as irrelevant to this episode, taking place when Nelson was no more, whereas those who concentrate on the later siege of Copenhagen in 1807 rarely give much more than a cursory glance at previous events. Again, personalities have a habit of obscuring the bigger picture, much of the writing on the siege concentrating on the first European success of Arthur Wellesley, the later Duke of Wellington, rather than the main events. It is as if the actions of 1801 bear little or no relevance on the largely land-based operations of the latter.

Nothing, however, could be further from the truth. These single-operation accounts fail to follow the connecting thread of relations between Britain and Denmark throughout the period or to adequately explore how the lessons of the first campaign influenced the second. Nor indeed do they often consider

---

1 From the poem *The Battle of Copenhagen* by Thomas Rudd.

what happened after these two momentous episodes, during the remaining eight years of war in Europe, including the consequent loss of Heligoland, the Danish West Indies and indeed the ultimate loss of Norway to Denmark's arch-enemy Sweden and state bankruptcy.

There is much British guilt associated with both of the Copenhagen operations, with many of those involved in them uncertain of the legitimacy of British actions on either occasion, and clearly troubled by the legality of the orders they received from on high. The Danes had then and retain to this very day a profound belief that the British acted illegally and immorally. These are indeed difficult waters to navigate.

The Danes and the British have, however, always shared a mutual respect for each other and both sides in these conflicts displayed not only a great deal of fortitude, gallantry and bravery, but also compassion and sympathy whilst ensuring that the operational objectives were attained, no matter how distasteful they were to the individuals involved. Perhaps the best illustration of this was that the British public received news of these events with mixed emotions and it is certain that victory celebrations were particularly muted on these occasions. It highlights perhaps more than anything, that the British and the Danes recognize kindred spirits, both punching militarily way above their weight, and this short period of conflict is anathema to both sides, an unfortunate episode best forgotten.

But to ignore it cannot be right, as sweeping past events under the carpet rarely helps anyone. It is therefore high time that the fascinating story of Britain's relationship with Denmark throughout the Napoleonic Wars is dealt with in the whole, looking at both the naval and the land operations both in the Baltic and farther afield. This history of the Anglo-Danish war is the first to look at this conflict in the whole, but also to view each occurrence from the viewpoint of both protagonists, to try to understand why it happened and why the British felt compelled to carry out the two attacks on Copenhagen.

It is hoped that this history will help to heal a long-standing and deep open wound between what are ultimately two very similar peoples and to help both to understand the motivations of the other for the events of 200 years ago.

Acknowledgements

Any book of this nature requires the help and support of a host of people to bring it to fruition. I must begin by thanking my commissioning editor, Rupert Harding, who has stuck with me and encouraged me to expand my work beyond my traditional publication of original memoirs. Rupert has now seen me through the publication of *Waterloo, Myth and Reality*, which brings our understanding of the story of the Waterloo campaign right up to date, *The Forgotten War Against Napoleon*, which dealt with the entire conflict in the Mediterranean from 1793 to 1815 for the first time ever in one publication, and now we complete our third, which covers, again for the very first time, the British war against Denmark during the Napoleonic Wars. Where next is anybody's guess!

As always, the required information is scattered everywhere and one of the hardest parts of the task is to bring it all back into one location and for this reason, I have chosen to include no less than thirty-five appendices, bringing the most important and interesting primary material into one place for the ease of further research in the future.

No one man can, however, succeed in such an enterprise alone, and this book has certainly drawn on the help, and almost certainly tested the goodwill of many of those I have corresponded with regarding various aspects of the convoluted story.

Those I must thank wholeheartedly for their great support and sage advice include the staff at the Danish Orlogsmuseet, who were very kind in helping with references and images at a time when they were busy moving home; and the Copenhagen Bibliotech and the Danish National Archives who have patiently tried to help me with all of my varied queries. The Danish historian Rasmus Glenthoj has been particularly helpful and encouraging, as have a number of correspondents on the Napoleon-Series website, who have helped me greatly in identifying a number of obscure titles and sources. I must also thank Charles Fremantle for his kindness in letting me view the Fremantle papers in regard to Copenhagen and to reproduce Captain Fremantle's sketch of the battle.

Finally, closer to home, I must of course thank my wonderful wife Mary, for her unceasing help and support and it is nothing but the truth when I say that I couldn't do it without her. I must finally also thank once again my son Michael who has now become a very useful proof-reader, being very willing to constructively criticize my efforts and the finished result bears much to his efforts and they are deeply appreciated.

Gareth Glover
Cardiff

Maps

Fadden's Map of the Great Belt dated 1807.

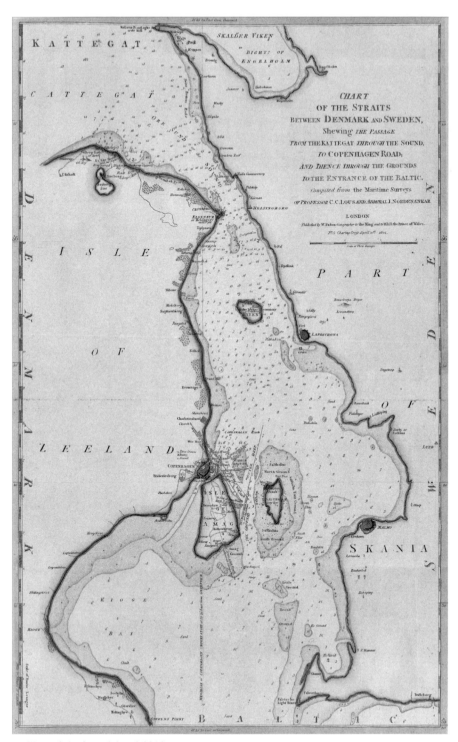

Map of the Sound dated 1812.

Area around Copenhagen from Franz Reilly Map of 1796 (simplified).

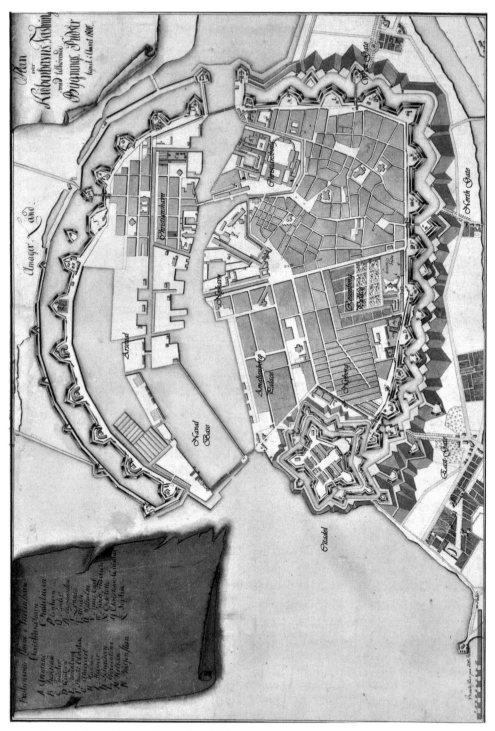

Plan of Copenhagen as it looked in 1800.

Introduction

The night was inky black with few stars peeping momentarily through the thick cloud. The crowd huddled tightly, turning instinctively away from the harsh artic wind which whistled unrelentingly through the grand square of the Amalienborg Palace. They constantly pulled the collars of their thick, fur-lined coats tightly around their throats, in an effort to keep out the icy blast, but the numbing cold still slowly crept up on them, the blackness of the night only pierced by the few flickering flames of the street lamps, lining the square, and reflecting in the inch of snow that carpeted the flagstones.

Few had the strength left to hold any meaningful conversation with those around them; they simply waited in silence, numbed, staring at the great clock, imploring with their eyes for the great minute hand to inch forward one last time, to indicate that the hour had finally come. The soft whirr of the cogs spoke of the imminent final movement and a murmur of expectation arose from the expectant multitude. Suddenly the arm inched into place.

The deep-throated bells of the neighbouring Frederikskirken rang out, only to be drowned by a cacophony of sound as the great cannon lining the grassy walls of the citadel was joined by the guns of the wooden hulls laying in the harbour. The sky violently burst into life as rockets exploded overhead and everyone held forth their carefully preserved glasses of Danish schnapps and cried out with all their might 'Skal' or 'Godt Nytar' and downed the fiery liquid in one to drive out the bitter chills.

Orders bellowed out and the Royal Danish Life Guard, resplendent in their ceremonial deep crimson jackets and black fur busbies, raised their heavy muskets to the shoulder and fired one round high into the night sky in a 'Feu de Joie', whilst the accompanying band struck up national airs.

This was the moment for the Prince Regent Frederick and his wife, Duchess Sophia Frederica of Mecklenburg-Schwerin, to walk onto the first floor balcony of the palace, accompanied by their four surviving children, to acknowledge the masses. The crowd roared its approval, waving the Dannebrog heartily in celebration.

For, as this New Year marked the very dawn of the nineteenth century, Danes had very much to celebrate, the previous century having seen unparalleled peace and great prosperity. Denmark was enjoying a truly 'Golden Age'.

***

That century had not begun well for the city. The Great Northern War had broken out in 1700, including a seven-day bombardment[1] of Copenhagen by a joint Swedish, British and Dutch fleet which quickly forced Denmark to withdraw from the war. However, after the Swedish army of Charles XII was destroyed by Peter the Great's Russian army at Poltava in 1709, Denmark took the opportunity whilst Sweden was severely weakened to re-enter the ring. This costly and largely futile war finally petered out for the Danes with the Treaty of Frederiksborg in June 1720, by which Denmark did gain the northern part of Holstein and Sweden forfeited her exemption from her ships paying dues on passing the Sound.[2]

During these war years, disease had been rife amongst the contending armies and bubonic plague swept through Copenhagen's medieval streets in 1711, in its worst-ever visitation, killing no less than one-third of its 65,000 inhabitants in only a six-month period.

Finally, to complete the ravages of the city, a great fire broke out in 1728[3] which raged for four days, destroying great swathes of the wooden medieval houses. In fact, it is estimated that over a quarter of the city was engulfed in the flames, leaving thousands homeless.

Thankfully, this litany of bad news now finally came to an end.

With the end of the war against Sweden, Denmark had embarked on a new era, determined to remain neutral, whilst Europe continued in a seemingly incessant period of warfare. Denmark managed to maintain cordial relationships with many European countries and signed a great number of agreements with these nations, but cleverly managed to always squirm out of any obligation to fight in support of her allies, so her reputation for loyalty was not always particularly high. Indeed, Denmark had remarkably enjoyed eighty years of unbroken peace since then, studiously avoiding becoming seriously embroiled in the War of the Polish Succession (1733–8), the Russo-Swedish War (1741–3), the Seven Years War (1756–63), the American Revolutionary War (1775–83), the Russo-Swedish War (1788–90) or the wars against Revolutionary France (1792 onwards). This statement must be qualified slightly, as it is true that Denmark did support Russia in her war with Sweden, which included 10,000 Norwegian troops entering Western Sweden, although they were officially deemed to be 'Russian troops'.

The Danish East India Company had been established in 1729, further encouraging Danes to trade worldwide with the Danish trading outposts

---

1 From 20 to 26 July 1700.
2 The thin strip of water about three miles wide at its narrowest between Denmark and Sweden is known as the Sound.
3 It burnt from 20 to 23 October.

in both the West and East Indies, under the umbrella of neutrality. This of course saw their merchant fleet increase rapidly until at its peak it was the second largest in the world. Copenhagen enjoyed a sustained period of great prosperity, which saw the city grow fast. Once the areas devastated by the great fire had been cleared of the remnants of the medieval housing, they were rebuilt to the modern taste, with tall brick houses and wide tree-lined avenues. This then instigated a huge rebuilding programme throughout the city, with the area of Christiansborg being developed between 1733 and 1745, quickly followed by the building of the great elegant houses of the Frederiksstaden district, which began in 1749, including the Amalienborg Palace complex. The city saw the arts flourish, with the Royal Theatre opening in 1748 and the Royal Academy of the Arts in 1754. The first Copenhagen-based national newspaper, the *Berlingske Tidende,* was first published on 3 January 1749,[1] a Free Hospital was built in 1757 for the care of the inhabitants of Copenhagen and the famous Royal Danish Porcelain factory first began production in 1775. The air of improvement and social advancement even led to Denmark being the first country in the world to abolish slavery in the 1790s, although it did not ban its ships from profiting from the slave trade; profit was still king.

Truly Copenhagen was flourishing, and it seemed that things would continue to blossom for the foreseeable future. Even another Great Fire in 1794, which completed the destruction of most of medieval Copenhagen, could not dampen the air of invincibility that permeated the city. The district destroyed was soon rebuilt although the loss of the Christiansborg Palace to the flames forced the royal family to switch its permanent home to the Amalienborg Palace.

The royal houses of Britain and Denmark were of course linked, like all royalty in Europe, George III's sister, Caroline Matilda, being married to Christian VII of Denmark. However, scandal had rocked the Danish throne when it was discovered that the queen had been having an affair with her German-born doctor[2] and this had seriously marred relations with Britain. The king was now, just like George III, suffering some form of mental illness and the Danish throne had effectively been handed to his son, the Crown Prince Frederick. Danish relations with Sweden had improved significantly after the murder of the extremely autocratic and rabidly anti-Danish King Gustavus III, his successor Gustavus IV proving to be a great deal more conciliatory, even leading to joint naval patrols to protect trade.

Denmark not only avoided war, but its success in retaining its neutrality intact allowed its merchant fleet not only to trade and prosper on its own

---

1 The newspaper continues to this day.
2 He was condemned to be broken on a wheel.

account but also to act surreptitiously to safely transport goods on behalf of warring nations. This, of course, was a dangerous game to play, Denmark often sailing very close to breaking its neutrality, by carrying contraband stores, particularly military supplies, under a neutral flag, sometimes right under the very noses of the protagonists' fleets. Denmark utilized its new-found wealth to strengthen its own fleet of warships significantly, helping the country to maintain an international influence well beyond its true weight. A small second-rate European power maintained the fifth largest fleet in the world in excellent condition. The Danes refer to this period as 'The Palmy Days' as their economic boom fed by exploiting their neutrality whilst Europe warred, combined with a massive overseas trade and speculation, won Denmark a huge share of world trade, way beyond their size. Indeed, with the decline of the Dutch, they were now Britain's biggest commercial rival, not a situation any country ever wanted to be in, for very obvious reasons. Peace in Europe led in fact to bad times in Denmark, with their neutral services being in far less demand, leading to large numbers of merchant ships being laid up.[1]

However, as the century progressed and Britain slowly won greater control of the world's oceans, this inevitably brought Britain and Denmark closer to a confrontation on a number of occasions; but a mixture of artful diplomacy, bargaining from strength and sleight of hand had allowed Denmark to successfully avoid such a hopelessly unequal contest. The Danes demanded unrestricted movement across the globe without searches from British ships, but paradoxically Denmark also 'unofficially' encouraged the British searches of others to deter competitors from copying their business model.

But far away, troubles were gathering ominously, the pan-European wars from which Denmark had successfully remained a neutral observer were rolling inexorably towards the Baltic. Soon Denmark's successful policy of neutrality was going to be sorely tested whilst their arrogant contempt for other countries was leading them down the wrong path. One wrong decision had the potential to bring the whole edifice crashing to the ground.

This is the story of how disaster overwhelmed Copenhagen in six short years and how Britain became the harbinger of that doom.

---

1 It is estimated that in 1806 no fewer than 3,500 merchant vessels were sailing under the Danish flag, the Dannebrog.

Chapter 1

Walking the Tightrope of Neutrality

Following the end of the Great Northern War in 1721, Denmark and Sweden had seen their influence wane, with Prussia and Russia becoming the dominant powers in the Baltic. The Danes had not enjoyed much success during the war, but they had emerged with their possession of the north German state of Schleswig now uncontested, but their retention of its neighbour Holstein was still a matter of dispute. These provinces therefore became the soft underbelly of Denmark, bringing her into very close proximity to the danger of becoming embroiled in the almost incessant wars that raged across Germany.

It must first be understood that Denmark in 1800 should not be viewed as simply the Jutland Peninsula and the islands of Zealand, Fyn, Lolland, Falster and Mon, which form the modern-day country. The entire country of Norway formed a part of Denmark, not as a vassal state, but as an equal partner ever since the Kalmar Union of 1397, which had originally also included both Sweden and Finland. The Union had collapsed in 1523, but Norway had retained its ties with Denmark, both continuing as a joint kingdom ruled by the Oldenburg dynasty. Greenland, Iceland and the Faroe Islands were also part of Norway's dowry and they formed a further extension of the Denmark-Norway Union although all were relatively sparsely populated.[1]

Denmark's influence in the Baltic had often brought her into sharp conflict with her neighbours: indeed Sweden was usually viewed as the 'arch enemy'. An emergent Russia also sought to gain influence in the Baltic, leading to interminable squabbles and intrigue between these three states, as they all sought to gain the upper hand. Occasionally, when feeling threatened by outside influences, they had put aside their differences and had tried to work together for the common good of the region. But a severe lack of trust regarding each other's motives, caused by constant intrigues and regular switching of

---

1 Figures show that the populations in 1800 were Denmark 929,000, Norway 883,000, Schleswig 278,000 and Holstein 328,000, giving a total of around 2.5 million inhabitants. Copenhagen was a city of 100,000 people.

allegiances, guaranteed that all attempts at alliances, often termed 'leagues', would soon end in rancour and a return to war.

Like all nineteenth-century European powers, Denmark also possessed an overseas empire, owning the West Indian sugar islands of St Thomas, St Jan (now St John) and St Croix, which had been purchased from France in 1733,[1] and also maintained a number of trading posts and protective fortresses along the Gold Coast of West Africa, including Fort Frederiksborg, purchased from Sweden, Ossu Castle near Accra and Frederiksberg.[2]

Denmark had also established a number of trading posts and small colonies for growing and trading spices throughout the Indian subcontinent, including the colonies of Trankebar[3] in the Tamil Nadu region and Fredericksnagore[4] just north of Calcutta.[5] Both of these enclaves continued until 1845, when they were sold to Britain. They also owned the Frederik Islands or New Denmark (Frederiksoerne)[6] until 1868 when they were also sold to Britain. Danish merchants also maintained regular trade with China.

As can be seen, therefore, Danish possessions abroad were numerous and led to an expanding merchant fleet trading with both the West and East Indies, trading particularly in high-value goods. This trade was of course an irritation to British merchants, but it did not pose a significant threat to British commercial ventures, whilst sailing under a neutral flag ensured them safe and unrestricted passage. This trade grew throughout the eighteenth century, and the coffers of both the Danish merchant houses and of the Danish government grew fat on the proceeds.

Great Britain was of course involved in a very similar business, but on a far greater scale, and a grudging forbearance was granted to the Danes, who were not viewed as a serious military or mercantile threat to Britain's own undertakings. Indeed, the Danes proved that they were willing to cooperate with the British in 1726, when a British fleet under Vice Admiral Sir Charles Wager was sent to sit off the port of Reval[7] on the Baltic coast of Russia and was joined by a significant reinforcement of Danish ships.[8] This combined

---

1 These islands were sold to the United States of America in 1917 and are now known as the US Virgin Islands.

2 The trading posts were abandoned in 1807 and the forts were sold to the British in 1850. The only one of the Danish fortresses still in use today is Fort Christiansborg which now serves as the residence of the President of Ghana.

3 Modern-day Tharangambadi.

4 Modern-day Serampore.

5 Now Kolkata.

6 The modern-day Nicobar Islands.

7 Modern-day Tallinn in Estonia.

8 The Danes sent eight line-of-battle ships.

fleet overawed the Russians and the threatened installation of a Russian prince in Danish Holstein was abandoned and Britain was granted further trading rights. A second British fleet the following year was supported not only by the Danes[1] but also the Swedes this time, but their help was not needed, as Catherine I died, and her successor had no stomach for the fight.

Denmark's location, of course, controls all access into and out of the Baltic Sea, through the narrow channels which run to the east and west of the island of Zealand. Access to the two western channels, known as The Little Belt and The Great Belt, was difficult, with a number of dangerous shoals and submerged rocks, it was passable to ships, but the Danes heavily emphasized its dangers to discourage its use. The eastern channel, commonly known as 'The Sound,' was however commanded by the cannon of Cronborg Castle on the Danish side and Helsinborg Castle on the Swedish side, the channel being only 2.5km wide at this point. Denmark retained the very lucrative rights to levy a charge on every merchant ship passing through the Sound as a percentage of the total value of the cargoes. To ensure that no ship's captain significantly understated the value of his shipment, the King reserved the right to purchase any cargo at the value stated on the customs forms. Major Wybourn of the Royal Marines, aboard HMS *Isis* during the expedition of 1800, records that he was informed that Denmark earned £70,000 per annum from these dues.[2]

Britain had traditionally shown little interest in the Baltic, as long as its own merchants retained free access; but this had become much more of a serious issue as the indigenous supply of wood for shipbuilding was diminishing just as demand soared, as both the merchant and naval fleets grew exponentially during the eighteenth century. New sources had to be secured for the import of naval stores, particularly masts, hemp and pitch to seal the hulls. The best sources yet discovered for these items was Norway and Sweden for general wood supplies, and Russia and Poland for the great masts and hemp for pitch; therefore, Britain became far more concerned about its access to the Baltic and very wary of any suggestion of a combined Scandinavian fleet cutting off these vital supplies.

Britain had secured a fifty-year trade agreement with Russia in 1734 for the supply of naval stores, which had been specifically designed to counterbalance any threat to this supply from Sweden and Denmark, who had at that time traditionally favoured close relations with Britain's arch-enemy, France. This balance of power in the Baltic continued relatively harmoniously until 1756, when the outbreak of the Seven Years War changed everything. Russia and

---

1 This time the Danes sent ten line-of-battle ships.
2 In modern terms that would equate approximately to £2.5 million.

Britain found themselves on opposite sides in this conflict, but they did not come to blows and their mutually-beneficial trade (the ships carrying naval stores to Britain returned fully laden with British wool) continued unchecked.

Sweden and Denmark became increasingly nervous that with this turn of events Britain would challenge their ships on the high seas in search of contraband. The British government had become increasingly aware of the use of 'neutral' ships by their enemies, in an effort to circumvent the British blockades, designed to starve their enemies into submission and destroy their commerce. The Danes saw nothing wrong with this subterfuge which had become a very lucrative trading opportunity. Therefore, Sweden and Denmark came together and sent a large combined squadron[1] into the North Sea, both to protect their merchant ships and to send a very potent message to the British.

This first example of a Scandinavian 'armed response' came to be termed the 'Armed Neutrality' and clearly indicated that they were prepared to fight to ensure that their ships were accepted as neutrals, and were not harmed or captured. This was particularly useful at times when Britain was either isolated or fully stretched, when their naval superiority could not be fully utilized in response.

Britain possessed well over a hundred line-of-battle ships[2] which could clearly overwhelm any of the individual navies in the Baltic. However, the British navy was required for numerous operations worldwide and could not spare much of this huge fleet for any operation in the Baltic. What really mattered was the number of battleships in the area. In 1757, the Russian and Swedish fleets had combined in Kioge Bay, numbering twenty-two ships of the line, defying Britain to enter the Baltic with a superior fleet. Britain could not spare adequate numbers to force the Sound and to bring the issue to a head. The salutary lesson was not lost on either side: the Baltic states were now confident that jointly they could defy the threat from the Royal Navy. The Danes had since signed an 'Eternal Alliance' with Russia in 1773, which had effectively made Denmark into a Russian client state.

The American War of Independence saw the Baltic states resurrect their 'Armed Neutrality' in 1780, including Russia, Prussia, Sweden and Denmark, but the league was not officially limited to just the Baltic states, with Holland at one time proposed for membership. However, squabbling between the individual members meant that it was effectively defunct before any actions

---

1   The squadron comprised of six ships of the line, six 50-gun ships and three frigates, a serious force.

2   'Ships of the line' or 'line-of-battle ships' were ships powerful enough to form part of the line in battle. This was restricted to ships rated with over 60 guns.

could even be agreed. Denmark was horrified by Russian demands for formal ratification of what the Danes had enjoyed 'unofficially' for decades.[1] Indeed, when the Tsarina, Catherine the Great, learnt that the Danish Foreign Minister, Count Andreas Bernstorff, the original instigator of the treaty, had at the same time struck a private deal with Britain to safeguard Danish shipping and trade, she demanded and got his removal from office.

The Dutch West Indian island of St Eustatius was a free port and a magnet for contraband and illicit trade, but when the Dutch allowed American privateers to operate out of its port, which wreaked havoc with British trade in the West Indies, the Royal Navy was sure to react. Therefore, the Dutch, not wishing to lose such a lucrative trade, had looked to join the 'Armed Neutrality' in a bid to stave off any British reprisals, by allying itself with the strength of the other 'neutral' fleets. However, Britain, hearing of Dutch intentions, promptly declared war, effectively blocking their efforts to join the 'league of neutrals', by making her now a combatant. The coast of Holland was blockaded and Dutch trade was soon crippled, sending the economy into crisis; this lesson was not lost on the Baltic neutrals! The Danes secretly continued to help the Dutch, by buying up their ships which were then laid-up and also providing false papers for them, so that they could sail as neutrals under the Danish flag. The Danes even performed the same service for the Spanish, to enable them to bring their South American produce to Europe in safety. This blatant collusion even went as far as having Danish warships acting as escorts for their protection.

The British government did, however, look ambivalently on the Baltic neutrals. It simply wanted to continue its own vital trade with the Baltic without it being in any way inhibited. As long as this remained true, the Royal had much more important business than sending fleets to the Baltic. The 'Armed Neutrality' of 1780 also worked to Britain's advantage, in keeping her rivals out, ensuring that there was no threat of a Spanish or French fleet entering the Baltic.

Things took another turn in 1788, when Sweden attacked Russia, in an attempt to regain its territory in Finland, lost in the Great Northern War. Russia called on Denmark to assist her and a Norwegian force marched into Sweden, in a bid to make the Swedes think again. Britain and Prussia had no wish to see Russia dominant in the Baltic, especially as Catherine was now cosying up to the French, and they brought huge pressure to bear on Denmark. The British Ambassador at Copenhagen, Hugh Elliott, with Prussian support, demanded that Denmark end the war (it had hardly been

---

1 Glenthoj and Ottesen, p. 20.

a war yet, with very little, if any, fighting by the Norwegian troops) and the Danes promptly buckled under the pressure, recalling their forces.

In 1791, Prime Minister William Pitt had rashly got involved in a joint demand with Prussia to halt Russian advances in the Black Sea area, which might have affected naval supplies to Britain, if the Poles had shipped through this new route into the French-dominated Mediterranean, rather than through the Baltic. Pitt arrogantly considered sending a small fleet into the Baltic to threaten the Russian fleet, but this did highlight a very major problem. No officers currently serving in the Royal Navy had ever sailed through the Sound between Sweden and Denmark, and they had no accurate charts or depth measurements for the shoals, the navigation of which channel was so difficult and dangerous. However, all of this was soon forgotten, as the wars against Revolutionary France broke out.

Prussia was initially a leading player in the attempts by the European monarchies to crush the French Revolution in its infancy. Its forces, combined with those of Austria under the overall command of Charles, the Duke of Brunswick, soon made great inroads into northern France, but the mobilization of the French citizens en masse in support of *la patrie* succeeded in halting Brunswick's advance at the Battle of Valmy in September 1792. The Prussians, finding it impossible to finance a continuation of the war, eventually ordered their troops to retire and Prussia withdrew from the war altogether. This had a very positive effect on the Baltic region, as now neutral Prussia, whose lands stretched across the southern border of the region, effectively insulated the area from the fighting. Indeed, Prussia went so far as to declare that it had formed a neutral zone, which lay under its protection. Catherine the Great and her son Paul were also passionately opposed to the French Revolution and all that it stood for, which also further boosted the area's stability. Britain saw advantages in these developments, as it effectively kept the war away from the Baltic and allowed its vital trade in naval supplies to continue uninterrupted.

Denmark had always maintained a fleet well beyond her size, but she also maintained a sizeable army of 40,000 troops on Danish soil, and another 40,000 in Norway. To put these figures into some context, the British regular army numbered around the same figure at the commencement of the war in 1793. Denmark's relationship with France was ambivalent from the start, the Danes broke off official relations with France after the execution of Louis XVI, but they actually still maintained their diplomatic offices in each other's countries.

As the war continued, involving many of the countries of Western Europe, the Danish merchant ships carrying vital trade from both the West and East Indies for France, Holland and even later Spain, who were now Britain's enemies, became ever more threatened. The Royal Navy blockaded the ports of these European states and also sent out swarms of frigates and brigs along the shipping lanes, which decimated the merchant fleets of these nations, severely reducing the supplies of these products and devastating their economies. These countries therefore desperately searched for an alternative method of transporting goods safely to their home markets. The merchant fleets of the neutral Danes, Swedes and the fledgling United States of America were only too happy to provide such a service, becoming 'flags of convenience' to carry both authorized and illicit contraband between the French, Dutch and Spanish colonies and Europe. They even happily allowed merchant vessels of these European powers to sail under their flag to avoid capture, for a fee of course. In their view, this was a legitimate trade as neutrals.

A large number of Scandinavian and American merchant ships were therefore regularly boarded by the British navy and their papers checked, and a sizeable number of these vessels were seized for carrying contraband stores. When these ships were dealt with by the 'Prize Courts', which decided on the legality of the seizure, the value of the ship and cargo, and which ships shared in the prize money pot, it became patently clear that a significant proportion of the ships seized legally for carrying contraband goods were sailing under a neutral Scandinavian or American flag. Britain saw this as a serious and systematic flouting of her blockade, but although aware of and extremely unhappy with this illicit trade, she was forced to turn a blind eye to it, so as to maintain the free flow of her own naval supplies through the Baltic. The British government also did not want to make enemies of the Scandinavian powers, fearing that their sizeable fleets could be added to the already significant fleets allied against her.

This careful balancing act was occasionally threatened, however. In 1794, Denmark and Sweden signed a convention, by which they agreed to mount joint patrols again in the North Sea. Denmark saw this as an opportunity both to reinstate its position as a significant naval power and to scare off the swarms of privateers, under letters of marque,[1] that incessantly raided the Norwegian and Danish coastline. The British, however, also regularly complained that French privateers based in Norwegian ports were devastating their own merchant trade. Britain had always demanded two things of the Danes to retain their neutrality; they must not break an effective blockade and they must not carry contraband supplies for the French. The Danish government was fully aware that the Danish merchant ships were routinely guilty of

---

1 Letters of marque allowed governments effectively to grant licences for private ships to capture enemy merchant vessels and sell the same as prizes. This could be a very lucrative business, but could lead to unscrupulous owners and captains going well beyond the rules of engagement in the pursuit of profit.

breaching the latter requirement and the British now chose to break this time-honoured convention, with the aim of starving France into submission. Britain therefore began to seize Danish merchant vessels on a regular basis, mostly for attempting to break blockades.

This precarious situation now led to a continually awkward balancing act being played out by all sides throughout the remainder of the decade, with everyone afraid of tipping the scales into war, whilst trying to manage the growing discontent in their own countries with the current situation. In May 1799, the British *Naval Chronicle* complained bitterly that no less than 250 British ships had been taken by Norwegian based privateers,[1] whilst Danish merchants clamoured for the Danish government to instigate convoys for merchant shipping to sail with armed escorts for protection.

Sweden had already jumped the gun and instigated convoys in June 1798, with pretty disastrous results. The first Swedish convoy was intercepted by British ships in the English Channel and detained; a second, two months later, suffered the same fate. When the forty-three prizes from these two convoys were jointly brought before the Prize Court the following June, they were all condemned as legal prizes. Sweden was at the time hostile to Russia, who was of course an ally of Britain and therefore there was little diplomatic difficulty for Britain over these captures.

The Danish Foreign Minister, Peter Bernstorff, had consistently refused to sanction the use of convoys, believing them to be very provocative to the British. However, after his death in 1797 he had been succeeded by his nephew Christian, who had soon given way to the Crown Prince's demands and Denmark had also begun to organize similar convoys, although they actually began a little later than the Swedes. Britain was a little more wary, regarding how best to deal with the Danish convoys. This was because Denmark was a staunch ally of Russia and she supplied Britain with a great deal of timber from her Norwegian ports, and they therefore had no wish to antagonize her.

In December 1798, citing the depredations of French privateers, the Danes began to seek British acceptance of their convoying ships bound for the East Indies through the English Channel in 'exceptional circumstances'; however, exception soon became the norm. This, as one modern Danish historian has admitted, meant that the Danes were now 'on a collision course with the world's most powerful navy. This was a signal error of judgement.'[2] The first Danish convoy, escorted by the frigate *Triton* was attacked by two British privateers, who managed to capture one of the merchant vessels, although the Danish frigate then managed to rescue it. The British commander-in-chief

---

1 *Naval Chronicle* II (1799), p. 159.
2 Glenthoj and Ottesen, p. 24.

in the Channel, Admiral John Jervis, Earl St Vincent, soon became aware of the incident, but both he and the Danish Commodore Steen Bille felt unable to decide on such a tricky diplomatic question and both simply wrote to their respective governments asking for advice on how they should proceed. British diplomatic protests regarding the actions of the *Triton*, were to receive a blunt rebuff from the Danish Foreign Minister, Christian Bernstorff.

All calmed down for a little while, but a second, more serious, incident off Gibraltar in December 1798 increased the stakes further. A Danish convoy escorted by the frigate *Havfruen* was intercepted by a small British squadron. A boat sent over to the Danish frigate to inspect the papers of the convoy was fired upon, and although there were no casualties, this was a serious escalation, the Danes denying the British ships the right to inspect their cargoes. It had the potential to become a very serious incident, which neither side really wanted, but it ended in another stand-off without any further hostilities, the Danes even calling in at Gibraltar for water and other supplies without any problems.

The British government finally decided to send a ship into the Baltic, possibly in reaction to the provocation of the *Havfruen* opening fire, or more simply to remind the Tsar who he was allied to. To back the efforts of the British Ambassador, Lord Whitworth, at the court of St. Petersburg, the Admiralty sent Captain Home Riggs Popham in the lugger *Nile* to provide professional expertise if there was any discussion on the projected joint campaign in Holland against Revolutionary France. Popham visited Holstein to view the Eider (or Kiel) canal, as a possible route of entry for British warships into the Baltic and he then travelled on to St Petersburg where he arrived in early June 1799. Popham got on famously with the Tsar, who was fascinated by gadgets, machinery and the workings of warships. It is believed that this was the first British warship to enter the Baltic since Admiral Norris's fleet in 1721. Norris had left a very complete set of surveys with the Admiralty on his return, but these were now eighty years old. Popham did make some new surveys during his passage back through the Sound to update the charts.

The year 1799 had seen some major changes in the political landscape, which caused an alteration in Britain's attitude to these Scandinavian convoys. The Russians and the British had co-operated in a joint invasion of Holland, which had failed ignominiously, although it did achieve one major success, when the Dutch fleet was captured, the Dutch crews having mutinied and refusing to fight. However, in 1800, Tsar Paul withdrew from any further campaigns against the French, even in Switzerland, where General Suvorov had enjoyed great success. In fact, in the Tsar's view, now that Napoleon Bonaparte was in charge as First Consul, the worst excesses of the revolution seemed to have passed and France was on the road to normality, which made it far less threatening to Russia. When Popham was sent into the Baltic once again during the winter of 1799, the ship became blocked by ice in the Kattegat and Popham proceeded to St Petersburg overland, but now the Tsar refused to even meet his erstwhile friend; it was clear that the Anglo-Russian alliance was failing.

Aware that Russia was slowly drifting away from the alliance, the Danish convoys became more of a target, as the Admiralty became less fearful of causing a row with the Tsar. The British government believed that it was in the right over its demands to stop and search merchant vessels, and it now sent out instructions explaining that force, if necessary, was now fully authorized. The Danes were unaware of this new threat to their merchant shipping, but became very concerned when on 3 August 1800 a Royal Navy cutter arrived off Elsinore and promptly ordered the British convoy which had only just arrived from Hull the day before to weigh anchor and to leave immediately. No reason was provided to the Danes, in fact, being unaware of any problems, they naively assumed that the British were in dispute with the Russians, as most of the merchant ships had actually been bound there. In part, the Danes had guessed correctly, but they failed to understand how this would affect themselves, now that Russia's protective umbrella had all but dissolved.

On 25 July 1800, a Danish convoy of six merchant ships was intercepted just off Ostend by a squadron of five British warships[1] commanded by Captain Thomas Baker of the *Nemesis*. The Danish escort vessel was the frigate *Freya* of 40 guns, commanded by Commander Peter Krabbe. The Danish captain had received strict instructions to refuse to show papers and to resist any attempt to board or seize the merchant vessels. Meanwhile, the British ships had clear instructions to conduct the search, using force if necessary. It was a highly-charged situation and it was patently obvious that it could not end well. The two commanders discussed their orders by loudhailer, and eventually Captain Baker sent a launch to board the Danish frigate to scrutinize the convoy's papers as ordered. Unlike the *Havfruen* incident the previous year, it did not end well. The *Freya* fired a shot at the *Nemesis* which killed a sailor, *Nemesis* replied with a full broadside and an unequal battle commenced between *Freya* and the British squadron. After half an hour, the *Freya* struck her colours, having lost two men dead and five wounded, the British having lost four men killed and several wounded. The entire convoy was then escorted into Deal Roads.

On 4 August Lord Charles Whitworth, a veteran diplomat, sailed for Denmark on the *Andromeda* and arrived there on the 11th. It was only on the 7th that Denmark had heard of the *Freya* incident and of the imminent arrival

---

1 Consisting of the *Nemesis* 28, *Prevoyante* 40, *Terpischore* 32, *Arrow* 18 and *Nile* 10.

of Whitworth. The Danes were very wary, as he was a very senior diplomat and this indicated that his arrival meant that something serious was afoot. The Danes, fearing the worst, immediately dispatched messages to Stockholm and St Petersburg, suggesting the formation of a new 'League of Armed Neutrality' and also ordered six of their warships lying in the harbour to be made ready for sea. The Danes always maintained a cadre of 5,000 seamen ready to go to sea, who lived with their families in barracks[1] at Copenhagen, so that they could man the fleet at any time at very short notice. However, additional men were also pressed from the merchant ships in the harbour.

On his arrival, Whitworth was briefed on the latest situation by the British envoy in Copenhagen, Anthony Merry. The British diplomat sought an early agreement to allow checks on Danish shipping, whereas the Danes sought to delay, hoping for a positive reaction to their proposal from the Tsar. Britain had no wish for a war, but Whitworth's diplomacy was to be backed up by a show of force, with the arrival of a British squadron, just to help the Danes come to the right decision and he openly threatened their overseas possessions if they refused.

Vice Admiral Dickson's squadron was organized quickly and sailed from Yarmouth on 9 August.[2] It was composed mainly of lighter warships because their shallower draughts reduced the risk of grounding in the shallow waters of the Sound. The squadron anchored in Elsinore roads, intentionally between a Danish squadron consisting of four ships already prepared for sea that was anchored in the bay, and the safety of Copenhagen harbour, where the main Danish fleet lay. This expedition is also notable for the fact that Home Popham's new signal system for rapid communication between ships was actually tested for the first time on this voyage.[3] It was a success and rapidly became the standard British signal system.

The Castle of Elsinore did not open fire on the ships as the squadron passed and the British fired a fifteen-gun salute, which was then returned by the fortress. After five days of manoeuvring for position, however, the Danish squadron boldly sailed for Copenhagen harbour, passing close to the British squadron, but they were not interrupted in their passage. The Danes, taken

---

1 Known as the area of Nyborg, the sailor's residences are still there today.
2 It consisted of *Monarch* 74, *Polyphemus* 64, *Ardent* 64, *Veteran* 64, *Glatton* 54, *Romney* 50, *Isis* 50, *Waakzamheid* 24 and *Martin* 16, with the gun vessels *Swinger* 14, *Boxer* 12, *Furious* 12, *Griper* 12 and *Haughty* 12, and the *Volcano, Hecla, Sulphur* and *Zebra* bombs. They must have been accompanied by eight transports as Major Wybourn, Royal Marines, counted twenty-six vessels in the entire force.
3 Popham's system used the number flags to indicate a set phrase in his signal book, therefore requiring only three numbers to be hoisted to signal a whole command, such as 'ships are to form line on their squadron leader'.

aback by the size of the British fleet, promptly ordered that a further seven warships be made ready for sea as quickly as possible. The Trekroner (Crown) batteries were still under construction and the guns were unsafe to fire, so a number of gunboats, barges and hulks were armed and moved out to the positions where the forts were planned to be built to defend the harbour. The defence of the city was the main priority, but it was going to take time to get the gun barges ready and in position, and in the meantime the city remained terribly vulnerable. Further batteries were hastily prepared along the coastline and to man them quickly, the Chief of Police was authorized to simply 'round up' 1,400 men, by whatever means necessary.

The British naval officers regularly landed at Elsinore to dine and to make purchases, the Danish infantry looking on with hostile intent, but the local population treating them like honoured guests, although no one was allowed to stay on shore overnight. The officers of the fleet even gave a dinner for the British consul and a number of Danish officers from the castle at a local tavern on shore on 6 September.[1] The British officers were however, extremely unhappy at the slow pace of progress and the extreme caution of their admiral; indeed, Major Wybourn of the Marines recorded in his diary 'I do not think our Admiral a dasher!'[2]

The Danes feared a landing of troops and their own soldiers, who were usually given leave in the late summer to help with the harvest, were urgently recalled to duty. The Danes could muster some 10,000 troops at Copenhagen, whereas Dickson's fleet carried only 800 marines, with a further 300 seamen allocated for a landing. Such a force could not even consider landing and attacking Copenhagen, and it is more probable that they were intended if necessary to attempt the capture of the Trekroner batteries, allowing the bomb vessels the freedom to cause havoc within the naval dockyard. More than anything, Copenhagen feared that the British ships would bombard the city, just like in 1700, and they were fully aware that they still had virtually no defences against such an attack.

Whitworth informed the Danish government that the British were willing to release the *Freya* and her convoy, as long as Denmark agreed to cease dispatching escorted convoys. The Danes indicated that their main area of concern was the Mediterranean, where their ships required protection from the Barbary Pirates of North Africa. Whitworth felt able to agree to this specific exception and agreed that a maximum of two Danish vessels could be based solely in the Mediterranean to ensure the safe passage of their merchant ships in that sea, but that once they passed Gibraltar the escorted convoys

---

1 Major Wybourn, Royal Marines, aboard HMS *Isis* in Petrides and Downs, p. 33.
2 Petrides and Downs, p. 32.

must cease. On 29 August 1800, an agreement was reached on this basis, allowing both to claim victory in the negotiations.

As part of the agreement, further discussions would continue in London regarding the British right to stop and search. But the Danes had only agreed to this clause in the belief that these negotiations could be protracted for so long that the hoped-for renewal of the 'League of Armed Neutrality' would be confirmed. They could then walk away from the talks, safe from reprisals. In fact, the talks in London never happened. But the League brought a whole new set of problems along with it . . .

Chapter 2

The Drums Beat 'To Arms'

Tsar Paul had received the request for the establishment of a new League from Denmark at the very same time that the eccentric Tsar was considering how to react to the recent peace deal signed between Austria and France in June 1800, Napoleon having driven the Austrians completely out of Northern Italy.

Paul had accepted the title of 'Protector' of the Knights of St John and in 1798, the Priory of St Petersburg offered him the title of Grand Master, when it appeared that the current Grand Master, Hompesch, had betrayed the Order and simply handed over Malta to Napoleon without a fight. The Tsar had been angered by the French capture of Malta in 1798, but when his ally Britain recaptured it, he became even more furious when they made it clear that they were keeping it, as it was a strategically important position.

This had driven Paul towards France and when news of the *Freya* incident reached St Petersburg, he ordered that all British merchant ships in Russian ports were to be seized, all British goods sequestered and the crews of the merchant vessels sent far into Russia under arrest. It is estimated that around 300 ships and their crews were caught up in this episode.

Paul was certainly warming to France, now that with Napoleon in charge the excesses of the revolution had been curbed; but he was also well aware that a peace with France would cause a violent reaction from Britain, who would be determined to secure and maintain its supplies of naval stores. The suggestion by Denmark of a new 'Armed Neutrality' therefore held a huge attraction for the Tsar. Unsurprisingly, therefore, Paul grasped the idea with both hands and ran with it.

As soon as Paul began negotiations to set up the League, Denmark felt honour-bound to sign up immediately – having been the instigator of the whole idea, and because they relied on Russian influence to prevent Sweden launching an attack on Norway. But they were also extremely keen to see it come to fruition as a form of insurance for the safety of their merchant trade against hardening British attitudes. Denmark signed to join the League on 4 November 1800.

The Tsar invited King Gustav I of Sweden to St Petersburg to discuss mutual defence matters and he was persuaded to sign up to the League on 9 November and Prussia also soon joined, having been 'invited' to join and feeling that they had no choice but to accept. The second 'League of Armed Neutrality' was finally ratified by all four monarchs and came into official being on 16 December 1800.

This league of four nations was in reality one with only three naval powers, Prussia having no navy to speak of. It was therefore agreed that if called upon to react in a crisis, the league would furnish a set numbers of ships per country to the overall effort. Russia would guarantee to supply fifteen ships of the line and five frigates, Denmark would supply eight ships of the line and two frigates, whilst Sweden would provide seven ships of the line and three frigates. In total, therefore, the league could furnish a fleet of thirty ships of the line and ten frigates, which would be commanded by a Russian admiral, Russia being the largest contributor. The combined fleet was a wholly defensive strategy, designed to dissuade other navies from attempting to interfere in Baltic affairs. Such a fleet was indeed large enough to even trouble the infinitely larger British navy, which would struggle to be able to spare such a large force for operations in the Baltic from its already seriously overstretched fleet. The League therefore inexorably drove them towards war, the Tsar's high-handed attitude pushed the agenda and it was clear that they were in a paradox – to maintain their neutrality it would have to be backed up with a major show of force.

For the Tsar the greatest service the Armed Neutrality did provide was that it put a protective screen in front of Russia itself, because of the geography of the region requiring any potential adversary to deal with the fleets of Denmark and Sweden before they could tackle the Russians themselves. This policy of buffer states has been used consistently by Russia ever since and was effectively used during the Cold War, the Eastern European countries effectively protecting Mother Russia from invasion. This was made abundantly clear when the Tsar immediately 'requested' or more accurately 'asked with menaces' that Denmark would defend the passage into the Baltic from any attack. The League had effectively put Denmark in a 'no win' situation of her own making; now she had no option but to resist against any fleet entering the Baltic. Denmark had simply signed away any hope of avoiding conflict by claiming neutrality in the face of a superior fleet.

The League cannot in any way be viewed as an alliance of equals, nor one of like-minded governments with a concerted goal beyond keeping other naval powers out. Denmark was immediately uncomfortable in its new status as the first line of defence, with little real trust that the others would man the defences in their rear or more vitally, actually come to their aid if attacked.

Russia was seen as overbearing and the real puppet master, but her support was seen as vital to keep Sweden in check.

Sweden was certainly constantly looking in the direction of Norway with avaricious intent. Knowing that Finland was always under threat from Russia, the possession of Norway would be seen as recompense for any losses on their eastern borders, but would also provide greater resources and manpower, allowing Sweden to resist Russian advances more strongly. The Tsar had also noticeably failed to clearly quash Swedish ambitions in Norway, leaving the door of opportunity ajar.

Prussia had only joined the League very reluctantly and had then only bowed to very heavy pressure to carry out the Tsar's seizure of British goods in her ports. Russia, however, wanted the Prussians to go further and seize the lands retained by King George III in Hanover. This they did on 3 April 1801, worrying that what they had already done might cause Britain to react strongly. Prussia was, however, unhappy with Danish claims on the retention of possession of Schleswig and Holstein. The Prussian government under King Frederick William III was therefore keen to drive wedges between Denmark and Russia, in an attempt to eventually win Russian backing for their acquisition by Prussia. Prussian eyes also looked longingly on Swedish Pomerania and even Danish Jutland as future objectives, but quite rightly sought to pursue only one at a time. Ultimately, the League was not one of anything near equals and certainly not one of trusted friends; it offered protection, but really, only to Russia. It was armed in promises, not in actuality, and was certainly far from neutral, effectively all acting as agents of Russia.

The British reaction to the League was expected to be firm, but perhaps not as immediate or as strong as it actually was. Only a few days after Count Bernstorff had signed the Anglo-Danish agreement on armed convoys, William Drummond, the British Envoy at Copenhagen, was already recording hearing rumours of a new League forming. Drummond went immediately to the Danish Foreign Minister, to ask for clarification. Bernstorff readily admitted that the rumours were true, but tried to claim that it was inspired by Russia, and that Denmark's political situation made it very difficult, if not impossible, for her to survive without the continued support of the Tsar. Drummond reported to London immediately, but the initial reaction of the British government was surprisingly mute, afraid of either overreacting or showing weakness, both of which could be utilized by Britain's enemies to weaken her.

What did cause a violent reaction was news of the Tsar's embargo, making the British government realize that the real problem was not their refusal to hand over Malta, but was actually the Baltic League, which seriously threatened Britain's naval supplies and therefore potentially materially weakened her.

Britain's navy was all that stood against a serious French invasion and any weakening of this force might well prompt such an attempt. The British could not allow this to happen and preparations for war began immediately in early December 1800, even before the official declaration of the formation of the League. The Admiralty therefore hurriedly prepared plans for a significant fleet to sail in the spring, to act as soon as the ice had cleared in the Baltic.

Lord Grenville refused to negotiate with Tsar Paul before the embargo was lifted and the British sailors released; the government also began serious attempts to break up the League. Both Denmark and Sweden were bluntly warned to withdraw or to suffer the consequences, and if this was successfully achieved, it was believed widely that Prussia, who was known to be a reluctant member, would soon find an excuse to leave herself, leaving Russia isolated again. The ultimatums were sent to the Swedish and Danish governments on the very same day that the League was officially formed and to prevent any attempt at a coordinated response, both were given a very short time to make their reply.

The courier carrying the ultimatum to the Danish government arrived in Copenhagen on 27 December and Drummond demanded a swift response. He got one, but probably not the one he had anticipated. Bernstorff stated that Denmark was in the League and it was in her best interests to remain so, reiterating that the League was purely defensive and making it clear that no threat would make them leave it. The Danish government were under no illusions what such a refusal would mean. That very night Crown Prince Frederick signed the orders to prepare Copenhagen's defences for the expected attack in the spring.

The courier returned to London on 13 January 1801 with the unequivocal response, which was a surprise to the British government in the level of its belligerency. However, reports had already been received that Russia was making preparations for war, and it now became obvious to the British government that this very serious threat to Britain's navy would have to be dealt with very firmly indeed.

On that same day, the British Cabinet, realizing that further diplomatic approaches would be futile, placed embargoes on all Danish, Swedish and Russian ships in British ports and issued orders for its warships to detain every merchant ship at sea flying the flags of those nations, without exception.[1] Orders were also promulgated for the immediate capture of Danish and Swedish possessions, particularly in the West Indies. Prussia was not penalized

---

1 It is estimated that Sweden alone had 450 ships at sea when the embargo was announced, 200 of which were captured by the British.

in any way, in the hope that this reluctant member might just leave the League of its own volition.

> At the Court at St James's, the 14th of January 1801
> Present, The King's Most Excellent Majesty in Council
>   Whereas his Majesty has received advice, that a large number of vessels belonging to His Majesty's subjects have been and are detained in the ports of Russia, and that the British sailors, navigating the same, have been and now are detained, as prisoners, in different parts of Russia; and also, that, during the continuance of these proceedings, a confederacy of a hostile nature, against the just rights and interest of his Majesty, and his Dominions, has been entered into with the Court of St Petersburgh by the Courts of Denmark and Sweden, respectively, his Majesty, with the advice of his Privy Council, is thereupon pleased to order, as it is hereby ordered, that no ships or vessels belonging to any of his Majesty's subjects, be permitted to enter and clear out of any of the ports of Russia, Denmark, or Sweden, until further order; and his Majesty is further pleased to order, that a general embargo or stop be made of all Russian, Danish, and Swedish ships and vessels whatsoever, now within or which hereafter shall come into any of the ports, harbours, or roads, within the United Kingdom of Great Britain and Ireland, together with all persons and effects on board the said ships and vessels, but the utmost care be taken for the preservation of all and every part of the cargoes on board any of the said ships and vessels, so that no damage or embezzlement whatever be sustained.
>   And the Right Honourable the Lord Commissioners of His Majesty's Treasury, and the Lords Commissioners of the Admiralty, and the Lord Warden of the Cinque Ports, are to give the necessary directions herein as to them may respectively appertain.
>   W. Fawkener

The Danes had a sudden glimmer of hope of a change of policy when Pitt's government collapsed on 14 March over the completely unrelated issue of Irish Catholic rights. The Danes therefore looked towards the new government of Henry Addington in hope, but although the Prime Minister had changed, the government remained full of Pittites and the policy remained unchanged. The main protagonist would appear to be the Minister of War, Henry Dundas, who pushed the project forward against limited opposition.

It would be unfair, however, to say that the British government were now hell-bent on war and that no other option was on the cards. A poorly worded and anonymous letter, believed by the British to have been sent by Prince Karl of Hesse, the Crown Prince's father-in-law, suggested that Denmark still wanted to achieve a diplomatic solution and that Denmark simply needed military support to be able to face up to the threat of Russia in order to change sides. Nicholas Vansittart MP was promptly sent to Copenhagen to see if the letter opened up an opportunity for a peaceful outcome. Prince Karl was visited first, who immediately denied sending the letter. A request for an audience with the Crown Prince was then coldly turned down; but in a conversation on 14 March 1801 with Count Bernstorff, he was informed emphatically that Denmark's position was unbending and the meeting broke up without any hope of an agreement. Vansittart then left for home.

One further attempt was made for a peaceable settlement on the very eve of the outbreak of fighting, but that will form part of the narrative of the next chapter.

What is clear is that Britain felt threatened by the formation of the League and made it abundantly clear that without a compromise deal, which included Denmark's withdrawal from the League, then they felt compelled to react militarily to break up the alliance by force. It was not clear, however, to the Baltic states that her navy would be able to overwhelm the joint forces of the League. It was a huge gamble, but the British government felt that the alternative of doing nothing was certain to lead to even worse results.

Denmark felt that Russia was her only constant ally in her efforts to remain neutral, ensuring that her merchant fleet was protected and that Sweden and Prussia would not be allowed to threaten her territorial integrity. Even this however, was now fraught with danger following the new-found friendship between Russia and France. The French Foreign Minister, Charles Maurice de Talleyrand, had made it clear that if Denmark dared to make an alliance with Britain, then it would simply cease to exist!

The Crown Prince knew full well that the British navy would be sent to attempt to break up the League, and that Copenhagen would be certain to be attacked first as they were in the front line. He could only draw hope and belief from the promises of his allies, that they would support him if attacked. It was therefore a huge gamble for Denmark as well, she simply had to put all of her trust in Russia and hope that it would all turn out well in the end.

Prince Frederick was faced on the one hand with the prospects of a war he certainly could not win alone, or on the other hand, the disintegration of the entire Danish state. He attempted to maintain a balance whilst walking the tightrope between these two extremes, but the problem was that the tightrope continued on into infinity, there was no end in sight.

War was now clearly inevitable to everyone, the only question was when?

Chapter 3

The British Mobilization

The decision by the British Cabinet to go to war with the League of Armed Neutrality might be thought to indicate that they had a plan, but in fact they did not.

The First Lord of the Admiralty began seeking out the few Baltic specialists that the Royal Navy possessed, not an easy task since the last British fleet to have been in Baltic waters had been no less than seventy-five years before. When asked, the Commander-in-Chief of the Channel Fleet, Admiral John Jervis, 1st Earl St Vincent, immediately recommended his second-in-command, Vice Admiral Sir Hyde Parker, as he had played a major part in the plans developed for a fleet to enter the Baltic in 1790, when the last crisis had occurred. He had studied the Baltic but had never been there himself, and this was the best the navy could come up with! He was, however, a sound seamen and he showed himself to be a very good strategist during the discussions that followed his appointment to the command.

There were two major factors that influenced naval forces in the Baltic, which were of great consequence in any deliberations. The first was navigation in its shallow waters, which was of prime importance, especially as it could be assumed that the Danes would extinguish the lighthouses and remove the marker buoys warning of dangerous shoals, so they would need to recruit a large number of pilots experienced in traversing the Baltic. It was also evident that the shallow waters seriously restricted the ability of ships with more than 74 guns to operate in those waters and that shallow-draught vessels were of vital importance. Calms or very light winds were also a feature of this sea, when even the most powerful sailing ships could become very vulnerable to attack by swarms of heavily-armed gunboats and galleys which could be rowed into position. The Danish navy maintained a great number of these gunboats for this very reason. It was patently obvious that besides a sizeable fleet of shallow-draught warships, the fleet would require large numbers of small ships in support, gunships to counteract the Danish gunboats, and bomb vessels to bombard the fleets if they refused to come out of port, or to bombard Copenhagen itself if it proved necessary, just as they had a century before.

The navy, led by the First Lord of the Admiralty and St Vincent, had advocated a major amphibious operation, with the fleet landing a force of up to 10,000 troops ashore, to attack and destroy the Danish naval base at Copenhagen,[1] as they felt a bombardment by a few bomb vessels would be inadequate to break the opposition of the Danes, just as had been found in 1700. The government, however, could not muster or support such a large force and the operation became merely a naval one, severely reducing the likelihood of overall success, effectively tying one hand behind Parker's back.

There was a seemingly inordinate rush to find adequate ships for the expedition, but in fact there was method in the apparent haste. It had become policy to dispatch the fleet to Copenhagen as soon as the seas around Denmark were clear of the dangers of ice. This could be expected to occur in mid to late March, which had the added advantage that the Russian fleet could be guaranteed to remain frozen in their ports in the Eastern Baltic for a few more weeks at least, making it quite possible to knock the Danish and Swedish fleets out of the war whilst the Russian fleet remained trapped by ice.

Serious consideration was given to who should be Parker's second-in-command and the choice eventually fell on the rising star of the navy, Vice Admiral Horatio Nelson, who had already made a great name for himself with the public for his part played in the success at the Battle of Cape St Vincent in 1797, capturing two Spanish warships by his own efforts, and his destruction of the French fleet at the Nile in 1798. Although not admired by all senior naval officers, he was beloved by the ordinary sailors and the British public at large. Parker, a cautious, solid and dependable commander, had been given an impetuous and charismatic second: it would either prove to be a dream team, or a complete disaster. Only time would tell which would be the outcome.

Parker had recently returned from Jamaica, a lucrative station for accumulating prize money, and he came home a very wealthy divorcee indeed.[2] This had made a stolid and elderly man – he was 61 at the time – rather a catch in London society, money turning heads as it always has done. On 23 December 1800, Sir Hyde had married Frances, the 18-year-old daughter of Admiral Sir Richard Onslow. The appointment to command this fleet would appear to have not been to Parker's wishes, as he was still enjoying his

---

1 St Vincent was 'clearly of the opinion that 10,000 troops ought to be debarked to get at the Danish Arsenal'. Nelson told him that the proposal had already been made to Lord Spencer, but the difficulty was who to command it. In the end, the fleet sailed without an army. Pope, p. 115.

2 He was granted a divorce in 1799 for his wife's adultery.

honeymoon far too much at Benhall Manor House in Suffolk, and was clearly reluctant to join the fleet as it mustered at Yarmouth in late February. He travelled from London on 26 March to reach Great Yarmouth two days later, with his young wife, but he did not go aboard ship, despite flying his flag on HMS *Ardent*, setting up home in comfortable lodgings at the Nelson Hotel.[1]

Nelson was certainly not easy to get on with. He was an expert seaman and a daring and brave naval officer, but it cannot be denied that he was also vainglorious and conceited, if not downright arrogant, and often a difficult man to work with, particularly if you were his senior officer. There was also his scandalous private life, which was the talk of the nation. Nelson was oblivious to all this, but he had also had reasons to delay sailing, his mistress Emma Hamilton having given birth to his illegitimate daughter Horatia on 29 January 1801 at Sir William Hamilton's house in London. Nelson was not in London during the birth – his presence there would have confirmed all of the rumours – being aboard ship in the Channel. He then showed some irritation when he was suddenly ordered to move his flag to HMS *St George* for the expedition, as it prevented him from seeing Horatia.

The official announcement of the formation of a fleet, enigmatically assembled according to the national newspapers 'for a particular service' with Parker commanding and Nelson as his deputy, was published on 27 January. By mid-February the warships and transports had begun to congregate at Yarmouth and troop transports at the ports along the north-east coast, but it was not until 7 March that Nelson reached there after his ships were fully prepared at Portsmouth for the expedition, including the embarkation of the 49th Regiment and a company of the newly-formed Rifle Corps[2] to act as marines aboard the ships or to be used to make landings to silence shore batteries which threatened the ships. During this delay, Nelson did also manage to take advantage of a three-day leave to visit Emma and the new-born Horatia in London.[3]

Having finally dragged himself away, Nelson immediately sought to get the expedition going as quickly as he could, simply in order to get it over and

---

1 It is often stated that Parker stayed at the Wrestler's Arms on Brewery Plain in Yarmouth (now Church Plain). This is technically incorrect, as following Nelson's return from the Nile, landing at Yarmouth on 6 November 1800, it was named in his honour as the Nelson Hotel for some twenty years. It then reverted to the Wrestler's Arms and remained as such until it ceased being a pub in 2013. It is now the office of a chartered accountant.

2 In all, 781 men of the 49th Foot and 114 men of the 95th Foot embarked, although seven of the former were landed again before they sailed. See Appendix 1 for details.

3 Letter to his brother, the Reverend Nelson, dated 28 February 1801. Nicolas, Vol. IV, p. 290.

done with, allowing him to return to Emma and Horatia as soon as possible. Nelson sailed from Portsmouth with the dockyard painters and caulkers still on board, dropping them off at St Helens on the Isle of Wight the following morning, when they had completed their work. Arriving with his squadron at Yarmouth in the early hours of 7 March 1801, the Vice Admiral, accompanied by his flag captain, Thomas Hardy, and Lieutenant Colonel William Stewart, commanding the army contingent aboard, attended the lodgings of Sir Hyde, ashore, at 8 a.m. prompt that morning, to find that Parker was still in bed with his young wife, it was an inauspicious first meeting.

Nelson and Parker had no experience of working together, but when they did finally meet, they both seem to have quickly formed a good working relationship. In fact there was some evidence that they got on well in their early encounters. Nelson was keen to sail immediately, fully aware that not all of the ships had yet arrived, but keen to begin operations. Parker insisted that they should wait for the other ships to arrive and made it clear that although his flag would now fly aboard HMS *London*, he would remain sleeping ashore, enjoying the comforts of his wife's bed. Nelson, never the most loyal subordinate, promptly sent private letters both to the Admiralty and friendly politicians, complaining of the unacceptable delay and informing them that Lady Parker was planning to give a ball on the evening of the 13 March.

St Vincent promptly wrote on 11 March a thinly-veiled but still strongly-worded private letter to Parker, as a friend, stating that he had heard that there were delays in sailing and reminding him that speed was of the essence. He advised him, that once the wind was favourable, even one hour's delay would lead to dire consequences for Parker's career. The letter was penned at 2.30 p.m. that day and remarkably, by 10 p.m. the same evening, Nelson recorded in his diary that Sir Hyde was afloat and signals given that the fleet would weigh anchor at dawn. Lady Parker's ball was not to go down in history, like another held by the Duchess of Richmond on 15 June 1815.

The fleet got under way that morning, already comprising seventeen battleships and a large number of smaller craft, but as they made their way towards the Baltic, further ships joined, eventually bringing the total to no less than nineteen ships of the line, six frigates, eight sloops/brigs, seven bomb vessels,[1] two fire ships, eight gun vessels and three hired brigs.[2] This was a

---

1 This was a considerable commitment from the Royal Navy's force of bomb vessels, there being only fourteen of them in service in 1801. The bombs carried one 13in and one 10in mortar each.

2 For a full list of the ships involved in the expedition see Appendix 2.

very impressive fleet already, the largest Britain had assembled since 1794,[1] but was to be reinforced by another squadron commanded by Admiral Totty, which was to sail in mid-April, consisting of a further five ships of the line (although one sank), one frigate, and fourteen lesser vessels.[2] Nelson wrote again to St Vincent on 12 March:

> Time, my dear Lord, is our best ally, and I hope we shall not give her up, as all our allies have given us up. Our friend here is a little nervous about dark nights and fields of ice, but we must brace up; these are not times for nervous systems. I want peace, which is only to be had through, I trust, our still invincible Navy.[3]

The fleet endured some heavy seas as it crossed the North (or German) Sea, icy winds, snow falls and black skies, preventing the ships from taking sightings to confirm their position. On 17 March, the fleet suddenly discovered that it was heading directly for the coast of Jutland and was forced to wear round to safely claw its way into the entrance of the Baltic at the Skaw. Eventually the dispersed fleet found its way individually through the entrance and began to congregate on the coast of Sweden just north-west of the Kullen peninsula on the evening of 22 March. The *Blazer* gun brig was unfortunately blown under the guns of the Swedish fort at Varberg and was forced to surrender and the *Tickler* brig had to be taken in tow by the *Russell* but was saved.

Whilst the weather had been vile, the story goes that Nelson had launched a charm offensive, like only he could, sending a beautiful turbot which had just been caught to the admiral, despite the obvious dangers for his boat's crew, and receiving a warm thank you note in response. Communication channels opened, Parker finally let his second-in-command know the intentions of the expedition and that they were instructed to anchor off the Sound, whilst a final ultimatum would give the Danes only forty-eight hours to reply. Nelson was unhappy that such delay would give the Danes even more precious time to strengthen their defences, he wanted to sail directly up to Copenhagen and to anchor in the roads, applying great pressure on the Danes whilst they considered their final response.

But what was this great fleet actually intended to do? It is clear that Sir Hyde Parker's main aim was to tackle the Danes and their fleet before they could be supported by the other League members. He had explicit orders to take or destroy the Danish fleet. Beyond that, his instructions were pretty

---

1 The fleet of Admiral Howe at the Battle of The Glorious First of June in 1794 numbered no less than twenty-six ships of the line.

2 Details of the ships will be found in Appendix 2.

3 Hounslow, p. 121.

vague, necessarily so, as the British government had no idea what he would have to contend with. Knowledge that the guns of the castles of Danish Cronborg[1] and Swedish Helsinborg controlled the entrance to the Sound was the first obstacle to be overcome, making it potentially a very dangerous passage, which could inflict very serious damage on the fleet as it approached Copenhagen. The lack of a significant force of troops accompanying the fleet also precluded any attempt to besiege the city from the landward side, so it was of necessity purely a naval operation. The reports from Denmark indicated that the Danes were working hard to prepare their defences, utilizing the incomplete Trekroner batteries, armed hulks, gun platforms and block ships to prevent the British navy getting to the Danish fleet itself, which would remain safely ensconced in the harbour. Only having overcome all of these formidable obstacles, could the British navy bombard the city and fleet from the accompanying bomb vessels. Bombardment was however an imprecise art, and the chances of striking individual ships would be a very difficult if not nigh impossible task. Much more likely would be the indiscriminate shelling of civilians, which would test their resolve to resist, but no more.

The option of sailing into the harbour to fight it out with the Danish fleet was not a realistic one. If the British fleet had already had to fight its way through the other defences, they were likely to be in very poor condition to take on an undamaged Danish fleet, even if they retained superior numbers, as the harbour was too restricted in size to allow them to act in concert. It should also be borne in mind that the heavily-armed citadel and other shore batteries would also be able to fire on the British vessels at very short range and would cause havoc amongst them. The fleet also did not carry sufficient numbers of troops or marines to land in an attempt to silence these batteries. The chances of success in such a desperate enterprise were minimal, if not nil.

The only potentially positive outcome against the Danish fleet could only occur therefore if the two fleets met in open water; but given the great discrepancy in numbers, the Danes would have to have been fools to offer such an opportunity. That is why I cannot agree with Ole Feldbaek's contention that Parker's orders were to take or destroy the Danish navy, its stores and base in their entirety.[2]

---

1 Colonel Stewart believed that the castle had 200 guns and was garrisoned by some 3,000 men.

2 Feldbaek, p. 47, effectively claims that the orders were to destroy or remove the entire Danish fleet and its stores, but the terms and size of this operation were not on anywhere near the same scale as the 1807 expedition, which did have these specific objectives in their orders. If they had been so, they had absolutely no hope of success.

The objectives of the British government were certainly aimed at removing Denmark and her fleet from the League of Armed Neutrality, but this was to be done by negotiation if possible, if not then by force. The aim was not to destroy Denmark as a naval power, it was simply to remove them by any means fair or foul, from the League, so as to allow the British fleet safe passage into the Baltic Sea, without leaving a sizeable enemy fleet in its rear, able to contest the passage once again as the fleet attempted to leave. Beyond that, the government had yet to form a decisive policy and had instructed Parker to remain in the Sound and to wait for further orders, a sure recipe for disaster.

Chapter 4

Parker Delays

On 19 March 1801, the *Blanche* frigate was dispatched from the fleet with Lord Hawkesbury's final ultimatum, which included the possibility of forming a defensive alliance against Russia, requiring a Danish answer within forty-eight hours and making it very clear that a refusal would inevitably lead to war. Another attempt to sway the Danes was made the following day, when Lieutenant McCulloch was sent ashore under a flag of truce, carrying a note from Lord Hawkesbury offering to join the Danes in patrolling the Baltic with a joint fleet of ten Danish and twenty British ships of the line.[1] The frigate returned on the evening of 22 March with the diplomat William Drummond and the MP Nicholas Vansittart on board, bearing the Danish refusal to both propositions: it was war.

Whilst awaiting the outcome of the ultimatum, Parker and Nelson had discussed their next moves and both had agreed that the fleet should sail up to Copenhagen as soon as possible. However, Drummond had then spent the entire evening briefing Parker on the Danish defences and the dangers of operating in the shoal waters. Although Parker retired to bed still firm in his resolve to move, having mulled it over during the night in the morning he was less sure. Vansittart reported the dangers of the shoals, but also informed him that the Swedes had promised to send a flotilla of gunboats and five sail of the line to support their Danish brothers, whilst it was also reported that the Russians were attempting to saw through the ice to release their ships, so that they could also support their allies. All of this news, added to concerns regarding the potential cost of sailing past the guns of Cronborg Castle, caused him to waver again. Parker therefore requested a further meeting with Nelson, who was taken aback on his arrival when Parker revealed that he had changed his mind and that they would remain anchored in the Kattegat.

Nelson sought to bolster his superior's resolve by countering the overly pessimistic reports of Drummond and Vansittart and demanding immediate

---

1 Feldbaek, p. 39.

action. They should sweep the Danes aside so that they could move on to the main problem, the Russians. An attack would have to be made and to Nelson's mind, the sooner the better, as time was surely an enemy of the British.

The discussion then proceeded on to how to attack Copenhagen, whether to enter the Sound and suffer the fire of Cronborg Castle, which Nelson argued would cause only minor damage, or to sail through the Great Belt, a trickier navigational problem, but which was undefended by the Danes, who claimed that it was too dangerous to use. Nelson argued that the passage through the Belt offered the best option, as it allowed an attack on Copenhagen from the south which was far less well defended and also had the advantage of preventing any Swedish or Russian ships getting through to bolster the Danish defence. This was a reasonable argument, but in the latter scenario, an attack on Copenhagen, whilst simultaneously fighting off a joint Swedo-Russian fleet in their rear, was far from an attractive alternative. This was a deviation from the Admiralty's orders, but was the boldest option and Nelson always believed that the bold would conquer all. Parker was won over and he advised the Admiralty of his change of plan and the cogent reasons for it, being ever the man to cover himself.

The following morning, 24 March, the fleet prepared to weigh anchor to begin its passage south, but throughout the morning spyglasses constantly inspected the masts of the flagship, vainly seeking the signal that never came. Early in the morning Parker had again allowed his doubts to take control and he wrote to Nelson, listing a number of concerns that he had with the passage via the Belt. Nelson received this note just as he was completing his own record of the discussions of the previous day. Nelson went to see Parker immediately and informed him of what he had written; ultimately, he was providing himself with the evidence to show that he was being decisive and that Parker was being too dilatory, in case it ever went to a board of enquiry. Parker took the point and soon agreed to keep to the original plan. Nelson had bullied his superior into an action he had doubts about: it was bound to come unstuck and it did.

After Nelson returned to his own ship at around 1 p.m. dispatches arrived from England, which informed Parker that the government had now come to the conclusion that the defeat of the Danes was merely a precursor to the more important task of dealing with the Russian fleet. The ultimate aim was to get the British fleet to the eastern Baltic in as good a condition as possible to face the Russian fleet at Reval and to inflict serious damage upon it, making Tsar Paul think again regarding his new-found friendship with France and 'persuading' him to abandon his anti-British policies. In this great game of chess, Denmark was merely a pawn that must be brushed aside to get at the all-important king.

Orders regarding the Swedes were more flexible; having arrived off Karlskrona, he was to attack if the Swedes were hostile, but if they indicated peaceful intentions, then he was to offer them every support against the Russians. These orders emphasized that speed was of the essence. All of this still confirmed Parker's decision to go with Nelson's plan to sail through the Belt, but he decided that they would now have to wait to sail until the morning.

The fleet actually weighed anchor before dawn on 25 March and finally began its slow passage through the Great Belt. However, by 10 a.m. a boat had come alongside Nelson's *St George* inviting him to attend Parker again on the flagship; clearly the admiral was having second thoughts once again. It is not difficult to imagine how deeply frustrating this stop-start indecisiveness was to everyone in the fleet. It soon became apparent to Nelson that Domett, the Captain of the Fleet, had played up the dangers of the passage through the Belt, reminding the admiral that only Captain Murray of the *Edgar* had ever sailed through it. Captain Otway, his Flag Captain, had also chipped in with a long list of problems with an attack on Copenhagen from the south, including the likelihood of favourable winds, the shoals which would restrict the attacking force to the lightest ships only and the fact that batteries being constructed by the Danes would have a severe impact on the ships as they passed them to launch their attack. These two doom-merchants had clearly rattled Parker and Nelson arrived to find the discussion back to attacking via the Sound but, unusually for him, he said nothing. Such silence was ominous: it clearly showed that Nelson was on the edge of an outburst that might well have led to his being placed under arrest on a charge of insubordination and that he remained silent to avoid it. Nelson did not really care which route was taken to get at the Danes: all he wanted was to get there as soon as possible, the inordinate delay rather than the indecision itself was the far greater sin in his eyes. Sure enough, shortly after 11 a.m., the fleet was ordered to turn back and anchored again at sunset off Hornbaek, ready to proceed down the Sound on the first favourable wind. Unfortunately, fate now showed her fickleness: the wind, which had been perfect for the last two days, now blew from the wrong direction to enter the Sound. Further delay was now inevitable, although finally a firm decision on a route had finally been taken.

Now that the method of approach had been agreed upon, plans were now drawn up for the fleet to move close to Copenhagen, having passed the guns of Cronborg Castle, and Parker informed Nelson that he would lead the attack, seconded by Rear Admiral Graves, which now clearly initially entailed the destruction of the defensive line which the Danes were rapidly preparing in Copenhagen Roads. For such an attack amongst the dangerous shoals, it was clear that the warships involved had to be of seventy-four guns or less, which had a smaller draught. Parker therefore ordered Nelson to move his flag from the 98-gun *St George* to the 74-gun *Elephant*, where he would find himself working with his old friend Captain Thomas Foley who had fought alongside him at the Nile three years before.

On 27 March, the wind remained unfavourable, or more accurately non-existent, with a calm which hardly stirred the surface of the water.[1] The day was therefore spent with further planning of the attack, exercising the sailors with the great guns, whilst the gunboats and brigs attempted to carry out manoeuvres. Ominously, that afternoon two bomb vessels accompanied by the *Blanche* frigate moved quietly into position, perfectly sited for the bombardment of Cronborg Castle if that was found necessary, when the fleet did eventually sail down the Sound.

Parker felt that it was now time to begin challenging the Danes on their intentions. The brig *Cruizer* was therefore sent by the admiral to carry a letter to Colonel Stricker, commander of Cronborg Castle, demanding to know what Denmark was intending having expelled the British envoy and whether he had orders to fire on the British fleet as it passed. He also made it abundantly clear that the first shot the Danes fired would be regarded by Britain as a declaration of war.

> Admiral Hyde Parker to Governor Stricker of Cronborg[2]
> *London*, In the Kategat, 27 March 1801
> From the hostile transactions of the court of Denmark, and sending away his Britannic majesty's charge d'affaires, the commander-in-chief of his majesty's fleet is anxious to know, what the determination of the Danish court is. And whether the commanding officer of Cronborg- Castle has received orders to fire on the British fleet as they pass into the Sound, as he must deem the firing of the first gun a declaration of war on the part of Denmark.

Stricker received the note on the morning of 28 March and his initial answer was both courteous and vague. He confirmed that he had received no orders at all regarding the British fleet, which if true was a very strange omission by the Crown Prince, as he formed a key element of the Danish defence strategy. He further informed Parker that he had requested a clarification of his orders

---

1 The author, when a junior officer in the Royal Navy, experienced long periods of absolute calm in the Baltic himself. These calms can often be without even the slightest breath of wind, the sea looking to all intents like glass without a single ripple upon it. It is not like the mild breezes that British readers might assume is meant.

2 These notes passed between Hyde Parker and Stricker were first published in Anon, *Letters to Sulpicius on the Northern Confederacy*.

from Copenhagen and promised to inform the British admiral as soon as he had received a reply.

Colonel Stricker to Admiral Parker
Cronborg Castle 28 March 1801
In answer to the Admiral's honoured letter, I have to inform him, that no orders are given to fire on the English fleet; an express is gone to Copenhagen, and should any orders be sent, I shall immediately send an officer on board to inform the admiral.

The reference to communications with the Prince indicates clearly that the Danes were still stalling for time, as every day strengthened their defences and brought the hoped-for Swedish and Russian fleets ever closer. The delay could not be a long one however, for communications between Cronborg and Copenhagen was kept up by telegraph masts: messages could be sent back and forth in minutes. During the delay, Parker ramped up the pressure another notch, by ordering the remainder of the seven bomb vessels in the fleet to also anchor in position, ready to bombard the castle if deemed necessary, but they remained under strict instructions not to open fire without the admiral's specific orders. Evening came without a reply and as time went on even Nelson suspected that the outcome was not going to be a favourable one.

Just moments before midnight, a Danish messenger arrived aboard the *London* with an answer from Stricker, but clearly worded by the Crown Prince. The note explained that the British envoy had not been expelled, but had asked for his passport and he requested that any political proposals Parker might like to submit would be considered, but it was made very clear that any fleet, whose intentions were uncertain would not be allowed to approach the guns of Cronborg without being fired upon.

From Colonel Stricker to Admiral Parker
Cronborg Castle 28 March
In answer to your excellency's letter, which I did not receive till the following day, at half-past eight, I have the honour to inform your excellency, that his majesty the King of Denmark did not send away the charge d'affaires, but that, on his own demand, he obtained a passport. As a soldier, I cannot meddle with politics; but I am not at liberty to suffer a fleet, whose intention is not yet known, to approach the guns of the castle, which I have the honour to command. In case your excellency should think proper to make any proposals to the king of Denmark, I wish to be informed thereof, before the fleet approaches nearer to the castle. An explicit answer is desired.

By 2 a.m. the Danish messenger was rowed back ashore with Parker's reply. The admiral's patience had finally run out and he wrote to state that such a reply was in his mind tantamount to a declaration of war.

> Admiral Parker to Colonel Stricker
> Onboard the *London* 29 March 1 a.m.
>
> Sir,
> In answer to your excellency's note just now received, the undersigned has only to reply, that finding the intentions of the court of Denmark to be hostile against his Britannic majesty, he regarded his excellency's answer as a declaration of war, and therefore, agreeably to his instruction, could no longer refrain from hostilities, however reluctant it might be to his feelings; but, at the same time, the admiral would be ready to attend to any proposals of the court of Denmark, for restoring the former amity and friendship, which had, for so many years, subsisted between the two courts.

He considered an immediate bombardment of Cronborg Castle, but eventually decided to wait for the next day. March 29th was therefore utilized in making final preparations for the passage of the Sound and at noon the fleet weighed anchor and moved to a position only three miles off the entrance to the Sound whilst the *Edgar* and the seven bomb vessels moved closer, to within a mile of the castle and laid out anchors and springs so that they were fully ready to commence a bombardment at a moment's notice.

During the night of 29/30 March, the wind finally veered to the north-west, which was perfect for the passage of the Sound. Now there was no hesitation from Parker; as dawn broke at 5 a.m., signals flew at every masthead for the fleet to weigh and form line astern as they began to progress down the Sound past the guns of Cronborg. This was the moment that everyone had feared; the heavy 36-pounder guns in the stable shore batteries had a considerable advantage over the warships which found that accurate return fire at distant targets was extremely difficult, as the hulls slowly rolled on the slight swell. The fleet sought to sail down the very centre of the two-mile wide channel, keeping equidistant between the guns of Cronborg and those of Helsinborg on the Swedish coast. Many feared severe damage even at this range, while a few like Nelson were less concerned, but even he expected some heavy damage to the ship's sails and spars.

The *Monarch* led the line down the Sound, the crews were at their action stations, fully prepared to return fire, no matter how futile at such ranges. As the *Monarch* drew abeam of Cronborg Castle, Captain Mosse ordered their colours hoisted, which prompted an immediate response from the castle. A great number of rising puffs of smoke told of the first rounds fired in the war, a few seconds later the cannonballs splashed harmlessly into the sea, well short of the ships and finally the rumble, just like distant thunder, told of the useless barrage fired from the castle. The *Monarch* fired her broadside in an even more futile reply; but what was important was that the fleet had not only realized that they were outside the effective range of the Danish castle, but what made things even better was that there was no fire coming from the Swedish shore. In fact, the Swedish batteries were unarmed, allowing the British fleet to edge further into Swedish waters to sail down that side of the Sound, well outside the range of the Danish guns. After all of the concern, Cronborg eventually proved to be a damp squib. The bomb vessels began a heavy bombardment of the castle, but it soon became clear to all that the firing on both sides was pretty useless. The British ships following the *Monarch* did not even bother firing, preserving ammunitions for the greater challenges that undoubtedly lay ahead.

By 9 a.m. the entire fleet had passed Cronborg Castle in safety, including the bomb vessels, which had abandoned their bombardment.[1] Here the fleet split, Parker's squadron anchoring off Vedbaek, whilst Nelson's attack squadron sailed on to anchor off Taarbaek in battle formation, just in case the Danes chose to test their strength against them. The British ships could now clearly see the spires of Copenhagen, the masts of the Danish fleet inside the harbour and the formidable looking defence line laid out in the Roads; few actually relished the severe task ahead.

---

1 Cronborg Castle recorded losses of two killed and fifteen wounded during this incident; the British fleet reported no casualties at all from enemy fire, but seven men were killed or wounded on the *Isis* after a gun burst. James, Vol. III, p. 45.

Chapter 5

Denmark Prepares

When Vice Admiral Dickson's squadron had sailed out of the Sound following the provisional convention agreed on 29 August 1800, the Danes had breathed a sigh of relief, believing that the great crisis had been averted. They believed that they had won a political victory, achieving much whilst promising very little in exchange, and were very pleased with themselves. This heightened further their belief in themselves as a superior race, who had risen to a level above war; indeed, their ability to maintain their neutrality in the face of so many threats and challenges had begun to make Danes feel invulnerable and that their inveterate neutrality was now inviolable. This self-belief was often misread by visitors as haughtiness and even arrogance, whilst Danish mercantile success had garnered much jealousy. Many in Europe would not be sorry to see Denmark brought down a peg or two, and like most braggarts, they did not recognize how much they had become reviled until it was too late. Paradoxically, the British did not harbour ill-will towards the Danes: indeed they recognized kindred spirits, a people driven by trade, commerce and profit, who had achieved a success and influence in the world far beyond their size alone would dictate. Britain, if anything, viewed Danes, just like the Dutch previously, as a worthy competitor in the world, but they must never be allowed to get too strong or powerful enough to threaten Britain's own success. The Dutch had been driven from the oceans in the last decades and the country had now fallen under the thrall of France, it was obvious that the row between Britain and Denmark would escalate, and that war was inevitable; it was clear that the conflict was very near at hand to all but the Danes still resolutely believed that their superior skills in the art of diplomacy would see them through as they always had done. Perhaps they could have achieved their ambitions, if they had truly retained their position of neutrality. The Crown Prince's decision to maintain an 'Armed Neutrality' had in reality aligned Denmark against Britain and once this happened, the outcome was inevitable to everyone but the Danes themselves, who seemingly could not recognize the new truth.

Contemporary view of Copenhagen.

What the Danes did learn about themselves during the crisis of 1800 was, however, deeply troubling. What had in their minds proven to be a diplomatic masterpiece, had also shown all the signs of a truly disastrous military fiasco. Despite the body of seamen maintained on government pay ready to man the fleet at a moment's notice and the immaculate and inordinately costly store system set up in the dockyards to ensure that ships could be quickly and efficiently made ready for sea, the mobilization of the ships of the line to face the British fleet had failed completely. It had left everyone painfully aware that in a sudden emergency, Copenhagen was completely defenceless and this, everyone agreed, had to be fixed before the next crisis came along.[1]

As soon as the Convention had been signed, the blockships, floating gun barges and converted cavalry transports were ordered to return to the harbour by the Danish Admiralty, to disarm and to return to a 'mothballed' state. With regard to the ships of the line, however, the squadron was now so near to completion for sea that the Danish Admiralty ordered them to complete their fitting-out.

On 16 September 1800, Rear Admiral Wleugel had hoisted his flag on board the 80-gun *Neptunus* and the squadron of nine warships spent the following four weeks carrying out 'working up' exercises in the Sound. The squadron then returned to harbour on 13 October, when Wleugel was

---

1 To pay for the new defences, the Danes increased the tax on all shipping to 2½ per cent of the value of the cargo.

ordered to disarm, unrig and decommission the squadron as quickly as possible, ready for the long winter. This short deployment had been useful as a training exercise, but had been carried out more for the political message it reinforced, that Denmark's Armed Neutrality was very much still in force. Two frigates returning from Mediterranean convoy duties were also rapidly decommissioned in September although the newly-built *Sejeren* of 64 guns and the *Thetis* frigate of 40 guns soon sailed to replace them.

The naval recruiting offices in both Denmark and Norway began their planning for the next sailing season in November, but the demand for sailors for 1801 was already clear, with a commitment to provide eight ships of the line and two frigates to the League; therefore, Crown Prince Frederick ordered that ten line-of-battle ships and five frigates would be prepared in the spring, leaving five ships for all other duties if the League called on the Danes to supply their full commitment. To crew them for active service, but not full-blown war, it was then calculated that the navy would require 4,733 seamen[1] in addition to the 5,000 'maintained' sailors at Nyholm. The orders to recruit to these levels went out. Denmark's recruitment was to be complete by the end of March, Norway's not until the end of April.

The Tsar's imposition of an embargo on British ships and goods was entirely unforeseen in Denmark and it caused a great deal of consternation in diplomatic circles. This soon turned into alarm, when the Danish government received Tsar Paul's assessment in early December that the League could expect to be attacked by the British in the spring of 1801 and even more ominously, that the Tsar expected Denmark to put up a dogged resistance against any such attempt. Suddenly the Danish government had for the first time to contemplate a war between the League and Britain and the realization that they were very much in the front line, but even now it was not seen as a very likely outcome.

This had caused the Danish Admiralty to order that the ships needed for the 1801 season should begin refitting immediately, even in the depths of the Baltic winter, so as to be ready for sea with the first signs of the spring thaw. Initially seven ships of the line were ordered to be made ready. The commander of Holmen dockyard was instructed to expedite the work and to requisition additional carpenters from the city in order to speed up the work and to complete on time. Despite the obvious need, no more ships were ordered to be prepared over the winter, nor were the numbers required to be recruited increased, except in Zealand itself, where the recruiting officer was told to take every man that he could get his hands on. For all of this preparation, there was no real sign of increased anxiety in the Danish government or the

---

1 Feldbaek, p. 66.

people themselves: all that had happened was that the Admiralty had moved their timetable of work forward. Even now, no one in Denmark was seriously contemplating war with Britain.

That was until a few days after Christmas, when the situation began to change very rapidly. When the British envoy Drummond had left the Danish Foreign Ministry on 27 December, with a clear refusal from Count Bernstorff to even contemplate Denmark leaving the League, everything had changed. Bernstorff went immediately to the palace and briefed the Crown Prince, who made his way with great haste to the Admiralty and issued his first set of defence orders that same evening. The 'Permanent Defence Commission' was told to produce a full defence plan for Copenhagen by the spring; the fleet architect, Lieutenant Commander Hohlenberg, was instructed to take a seat on the Commission and they were specifically told to make proposals for 'the defence afloat'.[1]

Nothing had been done regarding the defences since the crisis of the summer of 1800, no more floating batteries had been ordered to be built and literally nothing had been done to complete the construction of the Trekroner Fort, named after the three crowns of Denmark, Norway and Sweden of the old Kalmar Union. This huge fort, built on wooden piles driven into the shoals at the harbour entrance, its stone walls designed to be able to easily withstand attack by the wooden walls of the largest warships afloat, was unfinished and the batteries were not casemated. It was designed to house sixty-six 24-pounder guns, but they were not installed yet, nor had gun carriages even been constructed; no buildings had been constructed to house the projected garrison or magazines to safely house the ammunition for the guns. The projected ten-foot high protective earthen ramparts were also barely two feet high, meaning that the protection for the gun crews was minimal. The nearby Lynetten Battery was old and decayed and of very little use and formed no real part in the defences. Effectively, the defences of Copenhagen were unfinished, ineffective and in fact wholly inadequate.

The other basic problems regarding defending Copenhagen were the perennial ones; that there was only one passage in and out of the dockyard, which could be effectively closed off or blocked by sinking ships in the narrow channel, and that it was open to bombardment, the high-arcing mortar shells having a much greater range than the flat trajectory of normal cannon, no matter how large, therefore the outer ring of defences had to be built far from the city to prevent such a bombardment being able to reach it. These issues had been foreseen and plans to counter these threats by building a number of forts in the channels, to keep enemy ships well away, had been regularly produced

---

1 Feldbaek, p. 68.

and just as readily shelved because of the cost and the lack of urgency felt, because of the absence of a serious perceived threat.

The shoals in front of Copenhagen formed a significant part of the defences of the city from attack by a naval force of large, deep-draught warships. As the Sound narrows directly east of Copenhagen, two relatively deep-water channels formed the only safe passage for such warships travelling north or south. These two channels were divided by a long oval-shaped area of shoals known as the Mittel Grund (Middle Ground), where warships would surely ground in the shallow waters. The eastern channel, known as the Hollander Deep, ran virtually directly north-south and was a few thousand yards wide, allowing ships a relatively clear passage, with a little care. The channel to the west of the Middle Ground, known as the Kongen Dyb (King's Deep), ran initially south-west towards the narrow channel which formed the mouth of Copenhagen harbour. Here the channel running south to the site of Trekroner Fort was even wider than the Hollander Deep, although a small shoal did make the navigation a little more tricky. At the fort the channel turned to the south-east as it ran along the coastline of the Island of Amager and here the channel narrowed significantly to little more than 900m in width, making navigation a great deal more hazardous.

A defence plan had been prepared in 1784, but sixteen years on only the Trekroner Fort had been started and that was far from finished. Further forts planned, called Provestenen and Stubben, had never got beyond the draughtsman's table, because of their inordinate cost and a lack of political will. The Crown Prince, knowing full well the failure to act on previous plans, called for an interim plan within forty-eight hours on a far less extravagant scale, more of an improvised, hasty and cheap defence.

This new plan made it clear that the greatest threat to the city still remained the danger of a bombardment from enemy ships positioned in the King's Deep. Therefore, in this initial sticking-plaster defence strategy, the area around the harbour mouth would be bolstered with fixed batteries, whilst the King's Deep would be defended by the more mobile and less wind-reliant gunboats and gun platforms, with support from the frigate *Hjoelperen*.

As work began in implementing this initial plan, the Commission was ordered to complete a much more elaborate final defence plan by 21 January. This proposed that the work on Trekroner Fort should continue apace, particularly in arming the fort, to cover the northern end of the King's Deep, whilst near the site of an old fort called Provestenen at the southern end of the King's Deep, it was proposed that three old hulks[1] were to be sunk in the shallows there, so as to form an improvised, but still extremely effective

---

1 It was proposed to use the *Christian VII*, *Jylland* and *Wagrien*.

and powerful alternative. The Trekroner Battery and the Quintus Battery on the shoreline nearby were to have their armament further enhanced with a number of mortars. A further fort was planned, to be known as Stricker's Battery, which was to be built on Amager Island, directly opposite the newly-improvised Provestenen Fort. Another fort had been envisaged in the harbour mouth for years, to be known as the Stubben Fort, but as this had never been built, this was also to be temporarily replaced by two further hulks.[1]

A line of floating batteries was also now envisaged, stretching along the channel between the Provestenen Fort and the Trekroner Battery, thus keeping any enemy bomb vessels well out of range of the city and harbour. These ships would be produced by taking out excess decking from old two- and three-deckers and removing their masts and rigging, thus converting them into armed hulks. The hulks would be supplemented by gun platforms, converted cavalry barges and gunboats to form a veritable wall of guns along the western edge of the King's Deep. The big question now, however, was if the Danish defences could be completed before the expected visit of the British finally came?

An early decision had been made that the entire coastline of Denmark and Norway could not possibly be defended by anything apart from local units. All that could be defended was the most valuable and strategically important sites, but beyond Copenhagen these defences were not really in place before the British fleet arrived.

Whilst all of this urgent work was under way, Denmark, rather than concentrate all of its efforts on these projects, had half an eye on other issues at the same time. The bulk of the Danish army was stationed in Holstein, commanded by Prince Karl of Hesse. In late March 1801, these troops advanced virtually unopposed into the German free city-states of Hamburg, Lubeck and Travemunde in order to stop the illicit trade in British merchandise and to confiscate the huge depots of stock already stockpiled in the warehouses there. Having been warned of the impending attack, the bulk of the British stocks had simply been sold to third parties, which therefore meant that they could not legally be touched. The incursion also had the effect of enormously irritating their supposed ally, Prussia, just when they needed all of the support they could muster.

The sizeable portion of the army remaining in Zealand was concentrated wholly at Cronborg or in Copenhagen itself. Six regiments of infantry were stationed in the city,[2] whilst three further regiments were called in to help man

---

1 *Elefanten* and *Mars*.

2 These were composed of the Danish Life Regiment, the Norwegian Life Regiment, the King's Own Regiment, the Crown Prince's Regiment, Prince Frederick's Regiment and the Zealand Regiment.

the naval defences.[1] The latter were needed because the Danish marines had only recruited one-quarter of the men they were expected to find. Along the Danish coastline of the Sound, elements of the Rifle Corps Light Infantry and the 1st and 2nd Battalions of Light Infantry were stationed, supported by troops of the Regiment of Hussars and the Zealand Cavalry Regiment. To bolster the defences even further, a mass of militia units, including the University Corps and the Crown Prince's Own Volunteers, sprang up but were very poorly armed and equipped, many using scythes tied to poles as weapons, having no uniform and wearing clumsy wooden clogs on their feet.

On 11 December, the Crown Prince had ordered three warships to be ballasted[2] and on the 30th he ordered another five prepared[3] and on 19 January he ordered another five[4] to be ballasted and stores embarked, all to form a reserve of warships that could be called upon, some of which were later used to bolster the defence line.

The Danish navy was under huge pressure, not only trying to continue preparations on the eight ships of the line and two frigates required to meet their commitments as a member of the League, but now also completing the defence ships required to line the King's Deep, before any attack could materialize. The Danish Admiralty initially believed that the drafting in of all carpenters in the city would be sufficient to meet these demands, but soon found themselves mistaken.

By the beginning of February, however, the efforts were wholly concentrated on the defences of Copenhagen, the final defence plans agreed on 21 January requiring more hulls in the line along the King's Deep. By 1 March the hulks and floating batteries allocated to the defence line were repaired, but the ships were yet to receive rigging or been stored with provisions. It was actually 14 March before the ships were fully equipped and ready to be moved into position and the laborious process of moving them out of the dockyard into their positions slowly began.

Only now were officers appointed to command the ten ships allocated for duty with the League, but work on the ships remained erratic and broke down completely when news that the British fleet was now at hand set everyone back to the preparation of the defence line. In early April, when everything came to a head at the battle off Copenhagen, the ships of the squadron for the League were still not rigged or manned.

---

1 The regiments allocated to these duties were the Funen Regiment and the 1st and 3rd Jutland Regiments.
2 *Kronprinsesse Marie, Trekroner* and *Ditsmarken.*
3 *Valdemar, Neptunus, Dannebrog, Prinsesse Sophie Frederick* and *Skjold.*
4 *Arveprins Frederik, Odin, Justitia, Prinsesse Louisa Augusta* and *Holstein.*

It may appear strange, but it had never formed part of the strategy of Denmark to use the battle fleet for the defence of the city. Their place in Danish politics was sacrosanct; they had to always remain undamaged and a potent threat, otherwise Denmark would be severely weakened both militarily and politically. It was a superbly equipped navy, which if ever actually used for its primary purpose, would have lost its whole reason for being.

The Defence Commission was established as the nerve-centre of Danish preparations and on 5 January, Commodore Olfert Fischer also joined the Commission, having been appointed to overall command of the defences of Copenhagen Roads. Captain Ole Kierulff, the fiery and strict commander of Holmen Dockyard, became the Commission's 'enforcer', to ensure that everything ordered came to pass.

Trekroner Fort was clearly to be of supreme importance to the defence of Copenhagen. Construction of the current fort had begun on the site of an earlier fortress in 1787, and by the time of the current crisis the walls had been built and the general shape of a large 'D'-shaped structure was complete, with earthen ramparts and an entrance in its rear leading into a large central harbour within, but beyond that, it was far from finished. The armament consisted of fifty-six 24-pounders, eight 36-pounders, one 94-pounder carronade and three mortars, with three furnaces for heating red-hot shot. Major Meyer of the Danish Marines was appointed as commander and a mixed corps of artillerymen and soldiers were drafted in as a garrison, from the Marines, the Navy, the Artillery Corps and Prince Frederick's Regiment. There were, however, a number of basic features which were not in place. There were no barracks for the troops or any protective casemates in which they could shelter; they simply lived under canvas on the slopes of the ramparts – which were only a foot or two high yet, not the 10–12ft planned – and they would be dreadfully exposed in any fighting.[1] But perhaps even worse was that the fort was yet to be supplied with a magazine for the huge amount of gunpowder necessary to supply such a large number of guns. An old Danish East Indiaman, the *Providentia*, was fitted out as a magazine and moored in the relative safety of the internal harbour of the fort, where the walls should protect her from being hit by gunfire. In the case of shelling, however, she was of course dangerously exposed and had she exploded, few if any of the defenders of the fort could have survived. Such an impressive fortification, providing a stable gun platform, held a huge advantage over wooden warships, liable to roll with any swell at all. Trekroner Fort was therefore, on paper at least, a very daunting prospect for the British ships and it did prove to

---

1 It was only after the battle that a protective wall of sandbags was constructed to protect the defenders.

be a very powerful adversary, inflicting severe damage on nearby ships. But in fact it was too weak to sustain a heavy and sustained attack, particularly if the attack included intense shelling. As at Cronborg, its greatest strength lay in the fact that the British had no prior knowledge of its weaknesses and limitations. On the shoreline to the south of Trekroner, the Sixtus Battery now sported five 24-pounders, thirty-nine 18-pounders and two mortars, and just to the east, the Quintus Battery, which watched directly over the King's Deep, had twenty-six guns and five mortars.

At the southern end of the King's Deep, there were of course no defences at all until the crisis called for them to be implemented. The first to be completed was the simplest, a battery on the shoreline near the village of Kastrup. It was armed with eight 36-pounders and two mortars and was of some use during the battle and is usually referred to as Stricker's Battery, after its commander Lieutenant Stricker, a son of the commander at Cronborg Castle. This battery was positioned to give supporting fire to the fort planned for the southern end of the King's Deep, to be known as the Provestenen Fort.

The hulks *Christian VII*, *Provestenen*, *Jylland* and *Wagrien* were to be fitted with two further keels, so that when purposely sunk in position on the shallow shoals, they would sit perfectly level and upright on the bottom, allowing them to be hastily fitted out as powerful gun platforms, forming a wooden fortress. The fleet architect, Hohlenberg, soon realized that it would be impossible to complete this fort before the British could attack and he convinced the Crown Prince to abandon the plans and to simply place the hulks in the defence line already planned.

It might be imagined that placing them in the line was only a minor alteration, as their guns were still fully available for the defence. However, what it did do was to remove the guns positioned in the proposed fort, which had been specifically designed to prevent flanking fire on the Danish defence line; this decision would allow the British ships to manoeuvre to rake the Danish line with impunity, something Nelson did not fail to take full advantage of.

Because of this reduction in the strength of the defences at the southern end of the King's Deep, it was decided to further increase the strength of the defence line; and it was only on 5 February that the *Sjoelland* and the *Holstein* were ordered to be armed with 36-pounders and to be added to the line. Work advanced rapidly, despite their decrepit state[1] and they were actually in position by 23 February. The movement of the hulks into the defence line was severely hampered throughout February by the heavy ice still in the channel, but very slowly and surely the line was formed. The *Elefanten*, which was to

---

1 The fleet architect described both hulls as being 'ancient and decrepit': Feldbaek,
   p. 79.

act as guardship, was not in position until 5 March, one whole month after the orders for her to move out into the harbour were originally issued.

For all of this feverish work to defend the King's Deep, it is also true that hardly any of those thousands of men, working so hard to achieve so much in so little time, ever dreamt that they could possibly win the coming battle. The new commander, Commodore Fischer, even told the Defence Commission that they did not stand a chance and was fully backed in this view by Vice Admiral Wleugel, after the events had unfolded. The Crown Prince and his government also knew that the situation was hopeless, but effectively they had to fight and suffer the inevitable consequences, purely to prove to the Tsar that they had defended the League for as long as they could and thus hopefully retain his support.

The Crown Prince also had other more pressing problems in February, as Norway was starving. Norway was also dependent on shipments of military stores and equipment from Denmark to be able to organize local defences against any attempt at a British landing. Initially a frigate and a brig[1] were prepared to carry the stores, but before the ice broke up, the Crown Prince added two line-of-battle ships[2] to the little squadron. The four ships moved to the outer harbour and continued to fit out ready to sail, whilst Commodore Steen Bille was given command of the squadron on 9 March. The two 74s both ran aground as they left the harbour, but were eventually re-floated and preparations continued. They were close to being ready to sail on 22 March, when the British fleet arrived in Danish waters. The orders to sail to Norway were immediately rescinded; in fact, they never did sail there, but this further increased the number of Danish ships ready for sea when the British arrived and all four would form part of the inner defence squadron in the channel behind Trekroner Fort.

By 10 March twelve assorted vessels attached to the defence line had been warped out of the harbour into position.[3] Warping entailed taking the ship's anchor out by boat for about 100m ahead and then dropping it, and hauling in the rope attached to the fixed anchor, thus moving the ship inch by inch towards its final destination, slow, back-breaking work. Once warped into position and secured in place by four anchors, the real work began, as the ships were only loaded with stores and provisions once in position, most of it rowed out to the ships: this went on day after day without a break. Having completed the stocking of the ships, the crews then turned to incessant practice at the great guns, many of them never having seen one before, let alone fired one.

---

1 *Iris* and *Sarpen.*
2 The 74s *Danmark* and *Trekroner.*
3 *Sjoelland, Holsten, Iris, Sarpen, Dannebrog, Mars, Infodsretten, Hjaelperen, Danmark, Trekroner, Nyborg* and *Rendsborg.*

Between 14 and 16 March a further six ships[1] were brought out of the harbour to join the defence line and ten gunboats also sailed out. The workload on the dockyard had now eased significantly and by 21 March the signal frigate *Elven* and the last of the gunboats moved out of the harbour. With the arrival of the British fleet in Danish waters, the Danish Admiralty put huge pressure on the dockyard to complete the last ships of the defence line and by the skin of their teeth another three ships[2] and barges were rushed through and moved out of the harbour on 25th, with one final ship moving on 31 March, literally with the British fleet in view and the attack expected at any moment.[3]

The ships had all been fitted out with guns, of which the Arsenal was not short of, although in some instances larger-calibre ones would have been supplied if available. The real shortage was in gun carriages for some strange reason, so the carriages available were issued so that each ship could mount all of the guns on one side, many of the cannon for the other broadside simply laying useless, lashed to the decks until provided with carriages. Even when the attack finally came, not all ships had received a full set of carriages as these heavy, solid wooden constructs required skill and some time to build, to withstand the great pressures exerted by a cannon firing.

Manning the Danish defences was a very different problem altogether. The experienced pool of professional seamen maintained by the Danish navy had been required to man the four ships fitted out to sail to Norway and any left were used to man the squadron forming to meet Danish obligations to the League of Armed Neutrality. With regard to the defence line, the ships were expected to remain static at anchor and were not supplied with masts or sails, therefore the crews were merely required to load and fire the great guns, allowing for army and artillery personnel to man many of them. When Commodore Fischer requested lists of the crews from the captains on 21 March, he tellingly only asked for their numbers, not their levels of experience.[4] The entire defence line required a little in excess of 5,000 men to man it fully and it is clear that they were brought together from many different sources and with wildly varying experience regarding the loading and firing of great guns.

First to be appointed were the commanding officers, when a number of junior officers, sailors and marines were added as an experienced core. It must however be understood that the Admiralty had already been required to appoint officers and crews to both the Norwegian and the League squadrons and it is clear that much of the cream of the Danish navy had already been

---

1 *Nid Elven, Wagrien, Jylland, Charlotte Amalie, Cronborg* and *Provestenen.*
2 *Sohesten, Fleet Battery No. 1* and *Svaerdfisken.*
3 *Hajen.*
4 Feldbaek, p. 87.

allocated. The defence line was viewed by them as a lesser role and as such, the crews were appointed from those left; in some cases, great responsibility was put on the shoulders of very young and very inexperienced officers. One commanding officer was found to be so incompetent that he was actually relieved of his position before the battle,[1] but incredibly Sub-Lieutenant Peter Willemoes, who was only 17 and a complete novice, was given command of *Fleet Battery No.1*.

There is no indication that the Danish Admiralty was so cynical as to appoint only those who it could afford to lose, all those in command on the day of battle appearing to have performed well. It is true, however, that there were precious few regular officers in the defence line during the battle, many being 'contract officers' who were employed ad hoc simply on a month-to-month basis. Of the sixty-two officers in the King's Deep during the battle, only eighteen were regulars and forty-four were contract men.[2] This was because the 'regular' service had never been designed to be large enough to man the entire fleet; it was standard practice for regular officers to be bolstered by temporary 'contract' officers to man Danish squadrons.

This small core of officers needed bolstering and the Admiralty looked to recruit as many experienced merchant navy mates as they could find. A register was set up and well over 200 identified across Norway, Denmark and the Duchies; but only the ones in Denmark could be ordered in quickly enough to join, with fifty-four of them joining the defence line by the end of March. There were indeed more available than required and unsuitable candidates were refused.[3]

With regard to the problem of finding men, this was a far more thorny issue and required a great deal of ingenuity to complete. Just over half of the men[4] were experienced seamen of some sort, but with only 300 being regulars, the rest consisting of experienced merchant seamen and naval reservists. The recruiting offices had already been ordered to enlist nearly 4,000 men[5] in the autumn to man the squadrons and 1,000 naval reservists were also called up. Once it became clear that the British were coming, the Crown Prince effectively ordered the recruiting officers to obtain any and every man they could get. The problems of recruiting were exacerbated, however, when easy access to Norway was cut off by the arrival of the British fleet, restricting effective recruitment to only two-thirds of the normal area. This problem was partly

---

1 Commander Runge of the *Provestenen*, who was later discharged from the service.
2 Feldbaek, p. 89.
3 Ole Thomson Dahl was rejected for 'lacking moral character': Feldbaek, p. 90.
4 2,739 out of a total of 5,234 men: Feldbaek, p. 90.
5 Exactly 3,733 were ordered to be recruited: Feldbaek, p. 91.

solved by their ally Sweden allowing Norwegian recruits to march through their territory in groups of up to 100 at a time and then being transported across the narrow straits into Denmark.

The Danish Marines were another obvious source of men, which oddly formed a constituent part of the army, rather than the navy. The number of such troops required for the defence line on top of the 5,000 seamen, was calculated to be around 2,750 men and officers and a further 600 would be required to man the Trekroner and Stricker Batteries. The Crown Prince therefore ordered the infantry to man the hulks and nearly 1,000 men from no less than nine different regiments[1] were aboard the seventeen ships in the defence line during the battle.

Even with all of these methods of recruitment, the Admiralty still did not have anywhere near enough men and a general appeal was launched for volunteers on 18 March, calling on the Danes' patriotism, with the added proviso effectively meaning that if they did not volunteer then they would have to face the ignominy of being taken by the press gangs! Nearly 2,000 did respond to the call and volunteered, but only about 200 of these actually fought on the ships. The appeal was understood by all Danes to be specifically aimed at the lower classes, the upper and middle classes having already formed a great number of patriotic volunteer units. The new volunteers were therefore very much from the young working class and trainee artisans, with many trade guilds supplying a number of volunteers each, although bakers and carpenters were conspicuous by their absence, perhaps their jobs being deemed too valuable to be used in this role. Rather surprisingly, Swedes volunteered in large numbers and apparently made up 17 per cent[2] of the total volunteers recruited; others came from Russia, Germany, Italy, Spain and one from the Cape of Good Hope; even twenty lascars from Tranquebar in India[3] and two slaves from the West Indies volunteered.[4]

Still there were not enough men, they were not coming in quickly enough; therefore, the press gangs were sent out and, as things got more desperate, the Crown Prince ordered that no one was to be spared. Finally, by 2 April, when the fighting took place, enough men had come forward or had been brought in

---

1 They came from the Danish Life Regiment, the Norwegian Life Regiment, the King's Own Regiment, the Crown Prince's Regiment, Prince Frederick's Regiment, the Funen Infantry Regiment, the 1st and 3rd Jutland Infantry Regiments and the Marines.

2 Feldbaek, p. 95.

3 The lascars fought aboard the *Provestenen*.

4 The slaves fought and survived, but unfortunately, they did not gain their freedom for their actions. Property rights still took precedence.

less willingly, that there was in fact a small surplus, but it was only achieved at very much the eleventh hour. Even the Crown Prince himself had to consider what would happen if he fell during the fighting, and decided that on his death command would transfer to the Tsar's brother-in-law, Prince Frederick of Württemberg.

The defences were now fully manned, but were the experienced men spread evenly across the various vessels? There is some variation in the proportion of experienced men in the various crews and Ole Feldbaek has been able to show that this variation was directly related to the ship's position in the defence line. The admiral's flagship *Dannebrog* lay roughly in the centre of the defence line; all of the ships to the south of her consistently show significantly higher levels of inexperienced volunteers and pressed men,[1] whereas the ships to the north, protecting the harbour mouth, show markedly lower levels of inexperienced men.[2] This was no accident. A reserve of men was also established at the citadel under Lieutenant Fasting to reinforce the garrison of Trekroner if they were attacked.

One further issue that Commodore Fischer sought to address before the coming battle was signalling. In the intense noise and smoke of battle, vital communications between the admiral and his ships could only occur via signals flown at the mast stumps. Contract officers and mates of merchant ships had no knowledge of signals and therefore Fischer began regular training sessions on the sending and receiving of them.

The Danish order of battle was also forced to be altered slightly because of specific circumstances. As the *Provestenen* was brought out, it was discovered that she had sprung a major leak. The answer to this was simply to reposition her in the line, where the water under the keel was no more than a few feet deep, meaning that even if she did sink, she would simply rest on the shoal underneath. She therefore became the southernmost vessel in the line and the *Wagrien* filled the next space behind her. Fischer also abandoned the original plan to have the floating batteries set back in a second line, having them move up between the hulks in the main line and filling up the gaps. This had the added advantage of preventing the British ships taking up these positions between the Danish ships and raking them mercilessly from a position where they would also be virtually free from return fire.

As to the gunboats which had been prepared, they were to use their large bow-chasers to fire into the bows of any British ships attempting to break the line to rake the Danish hulks. Eleven gunboats were available, each with two 18-pounders in the bows, but their command structure was oddly arranged.

---

1 Averaging 58 per cent of the total crew.
2 Averaging 42 per cent of the total crew.

They were officially part of a squadron under the command of Captain Steen Bille, who would give them their orders, but they were also briefed to obey direct orders from Commodore Fischer, this made it unclear whose orders they should follow and was a certain recipe for confusion if not a disaster. Steen Bille was a skilful seaman and an officer who led from the front. He was truly loved by his men and he was incessant in his demands for further practice in manoeuvring in unison and gun drills. The Crown Prince wrote directly to Bille on 23 March making it clear that his gunboats were to ensure that the British did not attempt to 'double up' on the Danish defence line as Nelson had so famously done against the French fleet at the Battle of the Nile three years previously.

From the very beginning of the formation of the defence line, it was clear to all that it would be a close-range artillery battle. Commodore Fischer had therefore insisted that as soon as the ships were warped into position, they were to commence regular practice in loading the guns safely at speed and maintaining accurate fire. The vast majority of the crews of all the Danish ships were untrained in these manoeuvres, many being merchant seamen or landsmen, and it was certain that the British ships would keep up an incessant, rapid and accurate fire as they had practised regularly for years. The work was extremely heavy and in action the decks soon became hot, smoke-filled and slippery with gore. The men needed to be proficient enough to go through the operations of loading and firing mechanically, whilst all hell broke loose around them. This hell could not be simulated, but the constant repetition of the routine would drum the basics into their heads and speed the operation up, that was all that could be hoped for. Fischer also increased the number of men in each gun team from six to nine where the guns were mounted on sledge carriages rather than wheeled ones, increasing the physical demands on the crew to haul the guns outboard again before each firing. To help the inexperienced gunners aim, Fischer also had sights fitted to the guns. He ordered that every gun was to supplied with a minimum of thirty cartridges and the *Sjoelland* and *Holstein*, which retained their masts and rigging, were fitted with swivel guns, which were designed to fire down onto the decks of the British warships.

The Crown Prince visited the ships to boost morale and he even offered rewards for damaging shots, with rewards of between 50–100 rigsdaler for diverting or destroying a fire ship, and 50 rigsdaler for shooting away a mast or for striking a ship below the waterline.[1] The senior gunners from the Naval Artillery Company were sent out to the ships to help train the gun crews, but were deemed as too valuable to lose in the battle and were ordered to leave the

---

1 Feldbaek, p. 103.

ships when the fighting began. Despite these orders, many stayed and fought alongside the men they had trained, believing that their departure would not only dishearten them but would be nothing less than dishonourable in the face of the enemy.

The Danes were rightly worried that the British might attack the defence line with fire ships, to which they would be particularly susceptible, being anchored in place. Fire watch duties were a serious drain on resources each night, with boats rowing around the ships all night and others sent to both end of the King's Deep to watch for any ships seeking to enter surreptitiously during the darkness. With the approach of the British fleet, everything was also done to hamper their progress. The lighthouses were extinguished and all of the buoys marking the safe passage through the various shoals were removed. A high level of alert was maintained from 22 March, expecting an attack at any moment and when it did not come immediately, the high level of readiness was ordered to be maintained, no easy task to continue indefinitely.

Commodore Fischer also sought guidance regarding whether a state of war actually existed between Britain and Denmark and how he was to react to any British provocation. The Danish Admiralty sent a very unhelpful response; they were not at war, they did not know the British admiral's intentions and they did not want to be seen to be the aggressor or instigator of the war in the eyes of the world. In the end they left it up to the admiral if he opened fire or not, depending on the position he found himself in!

Last-minute orders continued to be sent out as the British fleet neared Copenhagen Roads: officers and crews were to remain aboard at all times, women were no longer allowed on board at any time, shot and gunpowder should be close at hand to speed the process of reloading, and any boys too young to act as powder monkeys were to be sent ashore. Everything was ready, they were fully prepared to fight to the death, knowing that their chances of success were all but nil, but yet they stood anyway. It was just like the Spartans at Thermopylae and the Danish newspapers portrayed them as such.

To prevent an attack on the harbour itself, huge anchors were dropped in the Kronlobet Channel, designed to catch and damage the hulls of the British ships. Fire watches were also established ashore and fire brigades prepared for the feared bombardment, many wealthier families evacuating to their country estates for safety.

What of Denmark's allies? Denmark was fully prepared and expecting to have to fight alone, but was there any likelihood of support arriving from her allies? Prussia had no ships, whereas Russia had a sizeable fleet, but was physically unable to release any of her ships out of her icebound harbours for a few weeks to come. That is, however, if the Tsar really wanted to send help, as in reality the navies of Denmark and Sweden were there as buffers to protect the Russian fleet. The people of Copenhagen seem to have genuinely expected to see a Russian fleet arrive to their support, but nobody in the Danish military or the government harboured any such hopes.

There was, however, Sweden, her ancient arch-enemy and only very recent ally, which could come to the aid of Denmark. The Danes did not really trust the Swedes, believing that any offers of help would have an ulterior motive. Offering to aid the defence of the Sound was suspected to be simply an artifice in order to regain toll-free status for her merchants and any Swedish army support along the shores of the Sound would only increase fears of a Swedish invasion of Norway.

Crown Prince Frederick had met King Gustav Adolf IV at Helsinborg in February 1801 in order to foster more friendly and trusting relations and as has been mentioned previously, this had helped secure the passage of Norwegian volunteers through Swedish territory. Sweden had promised to equip seven line-of-battle ships and three frigates for the support of the League, to be ready by the end of March. Unknowingly therefore, the delays caused by Parker's uncertainty meant that the British attack could not be made before Sweden's squadron had become active in the League and could therefore potentially bolster the Danish defences. Sweden had also promised to supply a squadron of twenty-four gunboats from Stockholm to bolster Danish defences in the Sound. However, the meeting at Helsinborg merely reconfirmed the previously-agreed joint defensive position south of the Sound at the Drogden Shallows, leaving the defence of Copenhagen a purely Danish affair, just exactly as the Danes wanted it, despite the fact that it condemned them to inevitable defeat.

Things changed, however, with the arrival of the British fleet, which was observed by King Gustav from the Swedish shore. Gustav wrote immediately to Tsar Paul to request Russian support and sent his naval minister, Vice Admiral Cronstedt, to Copenhagen again to liaise. The Crown Prince offered to supply eight floating batteries armed and manned by the Danes and to park them off Helsinborg to aid the defence of the Sound, but Sweden declined, having no shore batteries to support the floating batteries and being aware that their 8-pounders would prove far too small against the British ships. The admiral referred the proposal to Gustav for a decision, which everyone knew meant in all reality, a no. He did however, agree to send a request to the king, which he would heartily support; to send Swedish fire ships amongst the British fleet.

Two days later, however, Gustav offered to send the Karlskrona squadron to aid the Danish defence. The king felt honour-bound to offer this support and it would certainly receive a warm reception from the Tsar.

On 20 March Gustav had speeded-up the preparations of the Karlskrona fleet[1] with orders to sail as soon as possible under the command of Rear Admiral Palmqvist to cover the Drogden Shallows and they would take a number of old hulks with them, which could be sunk in the narrow channels if necessary. The admiral reported that the Swedish fleet would be ready to sail on 1 April.

Receiving this report on the evening of 30 March, Gustav showed an uncharacteristic haste and decisiveness in support of his new Danish allies. He sent a revised order post-haste to the admiral: he was to sail on 2 April and proceed directly to Copenhagen and to join forces with the brave Danes in defence of their city. Cronstedt was ordered to inform the Crown Prince that the Swedish squadron was coming to support them and to help encourage the Crown Prince to maintain sham negotiations with a view to delaying the British. The Swedish offer was a complete surprise to the Danes and as it was under the auspices of the league, it could not come with any conditions regarding dues in the Sound. A number of Danish pilots were therefore immediately dispatched to guide the Swedish squadron over the Drogden Shallows to Copenhagen.

On 31 March, it was also formally agreed that when the Swedish ships arrived, they would attach themselves to the southern end of the defence line in the King's Deep, which would effectively double the number of guns in the defences.[2]

Unfortunately, on 2 April the wind was unfavourable. The southerly wind which allowed Nelson to attack the Danes, made it impossible for the Swedish squadron to get out of Karlskrona. The Swedish fleet had no opportunity to support the Danes and the British fleet had unwittingly escaped having to face a much stronger combined opponent, which may well have altered the balance enough to have prevented a British victory.

---

1 The Karlskrona fleet consisted of the *Gustav III*, *Vladislaff*, *Wasa*, *Dristigheten*, *Tapperheten*, *Forsigtigheten* and *Manlighten* ships of the line and the *Bellona*, *Camilla* and *Froja* frigates.

2 It would increase the number of guns in the line from 690 to 1,264.

Chapter 6

The Die is Cast

Having sailed beyond Cronborg Castle, the British fleet had effectively passed the point of no return: even Parker would no longer brook delay. Had the British fleet not delayed at all and attacked on 23 March, they would have found the defences only half complete, many of the line of ships not yet in position and many of those that were in no condition to fight, with few stores or ammunition aboard and fewer men to serve them. The men that were aboard had at this time never even carried out a single run-through of the gun drill. Parker didn't know it, but he had spurned the chance of an incredibly easy victory.

A week later, as the British fleet lay just to the north of Copenhagen, the prospects of a victory still looked good, but the task certainly appeared to be a great deal more daunting, with a strong line of defence now apparent along the King's Deep and a further defence in depth in the channel into the harbour, all protected by the formidable-looking Trekroner Fort.

A detailed reconnaissance of the defences was required and Parker and Nelson wasted little time in boarding the *Lark* lugger, along with Admiral Graves, Colonel William Stewart and Captains Fremantle, Domett, Otway, Foley and Riou. Escorted by the frigate *Amazon* and brig *Cruizer* the little group made its way slowly down to the northern end of the defence line; Trekroner Fort and a few of the ships opened fire, but the range was too great and Commodore Fischer soon ordered them to stop. The British officers were taken aback by how much stronger the defences were to what they had expected, but Nelson was still confident, writing to Lady Hamilton, 'It looks formidable to those who are children at war, but to my judgement, with ten sail of the line, I can annihilate them.'[1]

With the British fleet now so ominously close, Commodore Fischer ordered that: 'Ships are to prepare for action. Commanding officers are to ensure their

---

1 Feldbaek, p. 118.

people get what sleep they can during daylight hours when duties permit.'[1] Both night and day, half of the crews slept next to their guns, whilst the other half kept a constant watch, fortified by a double ration of Danish schnapps to help keep out the cold.

On the morning of 31 March, Admiral Parker viewed the Danish line a second time aboard the *Amazon*, with the same group of officers as previously, but accompanied this time by seven artillery officers from the bomb vessels to give their professional view regarding bombarding the city and dockyard. The Danes again fired a few shots, but the frigate remained just outside their range whilst the group carried out a second very detailed inspection of the defences. On completion of the reconnaissance, Parker required the artillery officers to make a written report on the feasibility of bombarding the Danish fleet within the harbour. Their report was clear, they could bombard the dockyard, but only once the King's Deep was in their possession.

Parker called a Council of War that afternoon onboard HMS *Elephant*, where he asked for frank and open views on the chances of success and very significantly, he required Nelson, Graves and Domett to provide their views in writing. This would indicate that Parker held some doubts regarding the attack and wanted evidence which he could show to the Lords of the Admiralty to support his position if the attack failed. Worse, it was immediately obvious to his subordinates that he was providing himself with insurance in case of disaster, not a very positive message to promulgate on the eve of a battle.

There were divergent views amongst the group, Admiral Graves being vehemently against an attack, whilst William Domett, Captain of the Fleet, was enthusiastically for it. The views of the other captains present was muted and guarded, not feeling comfortable sitting between the two camps and not wishing to be seen to argue against either Parker or Nelson. During these exchanges, Nelson continued to stride up and down the deck in a very agitated state, clearly exasperated at all of this nonsense and dithering. It was a truth that Councils of War in general were often seen as the refuge of timid and nervous commanders, but worse, that good decisions rarely came out of them.

At a mention of the possibility of the Swedish fleet arriving, Nelson was heard to snap 'The more the better' and when the Russians were mentioned he again cried out angrily 'So much the better, I wish they were twice as many'. Eventually the Council of War ended, with Parker proclaiming himself satisfied and that the attack would go in from the south as Nelson had argued for throughout. Nelson had asked for ten ships of the line; now that he had decided, Parker magnanimously gave Nelson two more, as surety. The *Ganges* and the *Edgar* were therefore ordered to join Nelson's squadron immediately.

---

1 Feldbaek, p. 119.

It was well that he did so, for without these additional ships, given what occurred on the day of battle, it is far from certain that Nelson's attack would have succeeded.

Whilst all of these discussions and reconnaissances continued, the fleet had not been doing nothing. Nelson had already ordered the *Bellona*, *Ardent* and *Elephant* to prepare barrels as danbuoys, which could be anchored by chain shot to mark the shoals where the Danes had removed the buoys. A number of these were laid that night to mark out the Hollander Deep.

The Danes continued their gun practice, urged on now by the British fleet being clearly in view; morale aboard the Danish ships seems to have been good, with everyone showing a firm determination to drive the British ships away. The crews were calm and jovial, Søren Wendelboe, a 25-year-old surgeon onboard *Elefanten*, wrote to his wife 'I am aware that people in the city are more concerned than we are – here there are happy faces and good humour and it is difficult to believe there is an enemy fleet at our door'.[1] Night fell on 31 March, with the Danes still maintaining their high state of alert and confidently expecting an attack the next morning: it was going to be a very long night.

At dawn on 1 April, the Danes watched as Parker's ships, lying to the north, unfurled their sails and manoeuvred themselves down to meet Nelson's larger squadron, meaning that the entire British fleet now lay just north of the Middle Ground Shoal. That morning Nelson boarded the *Amazon* and kept a flotilla of small craft at work continuing to sound and buoy the channel in preparation for his next move.

At about 1.30 p.m. Nelson went aboard the flagship to receive his final instructions from Parker. At this meeting Parker also agreed that three of his warships[2] would weigh at the same time as Nelson's squadron attacked, to threaten the northern end of the Danish defence line and to render assistance if any of Nelson's ships got into trouble. Nelson was fully aware that the current wind from the north was perfect for his squadron to move down the Hollander Deep into its planned position at the southern end of the King's Deep, ready to sail up the channel and to destroy the Danish defence line with the first southerly wind. He therefore avoided any further delays by instantly ordering his squadron to weigh anchor on his return. The squadron weighed anchor at 3 p.m. and immediately unfurled sail in the light winds to make their way down the channel, their way indicated by the *Amazon* which sailed ahead of them. They soon left Parker's eight remaining ships lying at anchor far behind. At 5 p.m. they had reached the southern end of the Middle Ground

---

1 Feldbaek, p. 121.
2 *Defence*, *Ramillies* and *Veteran*.

and came to anchor again, the smaller ships moving later, arrived around 9 p.m. Nelson's ships were now almost within touching distance of the Danes, all they needed was a southerly breeze, but who knew how long it would be before that happened?

Commodore Fischer watched the British manoeuvres with interest. He had declined to attempt to prevent the British ships re-buoying the Hollander Deep, as it might conceivably have indicated that the British meant to pass on into the Baltic without harming the Danish ships; this was clearly unlikely though and Fischer knew it. If anything, he simply wanted the waiting to end; he had made all the preparations that he could, but he could not keep the men on high alert for ever without wearing them down. Better the British came now, as any delay would only reduce the efficiency of his men, it was time.

The Danish crews were determined, eager for the action to come but stoical and realistic as to the probable outcome. Twenty-two-year-old Sub-Lieutenant Wulff of the *Dannebrog*, parted with Sub-Lieutenant Muller of the *Hajen*, that night with the words 'This time tomorrow I shall be either a captain or an angel'; he was to gain his wings literally the next day.

As darkness fell, Nelson's squadron huddled at anchor were a tempting target for the mortars in Stricker's Battery. At 8 p.m. Colonel Mecklenburg commanding the Danish Artillery Corps had spoken to the Crown Prince, regarding Lieutenant Stricker's request to fire on the British ships with his three mortars, and had gained his approval. The mortars fired one round each, but Mecklenburg decided that they could not carry far enough to reach the ships and promptly ordered them to stop firing. However, Sub-Lieutenant Muller aboard the *Hajen* believed that the shells had fallen amongst the ships.[1] It is possible, but none of the British ships note them in their logs, which would be very strange if they had fallen close by. Whatever the truth, the mortars did not fire again, a missed opportunity to cause confusion at night amongst the British in shoal waters.

Danish and British guard boats rowed around the channel all night, both watching and listening for any movement in the enemy ships, any indications of a surprise attack, but nothing occurred. Few on the ships of either side got a good rest that night. Nelson's ships were fully prepared for action, meaning that few could hang a hammock that night and most on both sides hugged the cold damp decks in the vain hope of gaining a few snatched moments of sleep.

From his previous observations, Nelson was confident in his knowledge of the number and position of the Danish ships and the number of guns they carried, but the one piece of vital information that Nelson lacked was how wide the King's Deep was and where exactly the Danish line sat in the

---

1 Feldbaek, p. 126.

channel. Were they sat in the middle of the channel or resting tight up against the shoals of the southern shoreline?

A number of small boats were sent out into the dark, with muffled oars, to attempt to sound the entrance to the channel without alerting the Danish patrols. Whilst Nelson awaited their return and news of a shift in the wind, he provided dinner to a number of his select band of captains. This might have been seen as favouritism by those captains omitted, but Nelson's charisma appears to have overcome such pettiness, as none appear to have ever shown any unhappiness about it. After dinner, they toasted a southerly wind and a fine victory; then they dispersed to their own ships, whilst Riou and Nelson completed his plan of battle.

It was now well past 10 p.m. and Nelson was undoubtedly physically and mentally exhausted, but he was determined to complete the orders so that they could be copied for each captain before morning, just in case the wind changed that night. Nelson's plan as ever was simple and direct;[1] his heavier-gunned ships and his better-trained crews would sail up the Danish line, each ship being allocated a specific point at which to drop anchor and given specific ships to engage. As each ship anchored, those following on would pass on their disengaged side and sail on to their own intended spot further up the line of Danish ships. As they each passed up the line, they were to fire through the gaps between the British ships, engaging any targets in their line of sight. This would effectively double up the fire on each of the Danish vessels and their superior rate of fire and accuracy at close range would, it was assumed, soon break the will of the defenders. The last of the line would tackle the Danish vessels nearest to Trekroner Fort, whilst Parker's three ships would hopefully keep the fort and the ships in the harbour channel fully occupied. Once the Danish ships were defeated Captain Fremantle was to command a large boat attack, using all of the marines and soldiers in the squadron to attack and capture Fort Trekroner.

The smaller ships were also given specific roles. The frigate *Desiree* was to place herself close inshore at the extreme southern end of the Danish defence line, from where she could fire raking broadsides into the bows of the nearest Danish ships, the cannonballs crashing through the hulls and hurtling down the decks, smashing everything in its path. Captain Rose of the *Jamaica* was also to lead six gun brigs[2] into positions where they could rake the four southernmost Danish hulks. This meant that the Danish line south of the *Dannebrog*, which could count on 150 guns for its defence, would be overwhelmed by 262 British guns.

---

1 It can be seen in full in Appendix 3.
2 *Biter, Bouncer, Force, Sparkler, Teaser* and *Tigress.*

The northern section of the Danish line would be tackled by the remainder of the British line and they would be aided by the guns of the frigate squadron of five ships[1] led by Captain Riou of the *Amazon*, but because of the Trekroner Battery they would not be able to get into a position to rake the northerly ships. The two fire ships[2] would be held ready for use as needed and five of the bombs[3] were to take up position ready to shell the dockyard, whilst the other two[4] were sent to bombard Trekroner Fort when wanted. The Danish line of ships was to be destroyed, then the British ships would turn on the Trekroner Fort and the ships in the channel, when the fort was to be stormed by the ship's boats carrying the marines and infantry of the fleet. The plan was well designed and is often discussed at great length to show the genius of Nelson. Here it has been dealt with briefly, simply pointing out the salient points of the proposed attack, because the best-laid plans can easily go wrong and things certainly did go wrong on this occasion when the attack was launched and we must concentrate on what actually happened on the day, not what should have happened in a perfect world.

Shortly after midnight the plan was complete and the writers went fervently to work to make copies for each captain and these were complete by 6 a.m. ready for distribution. At the same time the officer of the watch had reported to the admiral that the wind was altering round, and by dawn the wind was blowing strongly from the south-east, perfect for Nelson to launch his attack. This was it.

The sun rose that Maundy Thursday at around a quarter to six with everything ready for the attack, but Nelson continued to wait. Just before 8 a.m. the captains of the British ships were summoned to Nelson's flagship, to receive their copy of his battle plan and to be given their final orders. The squadron had already cleared for action and an anchor was prepared on each ship, ready to be dropped by the stern to help keep the ships in their intended positions in the currents, with springs attached to the anchor cable, allowing the ships to haul themselves to starboard or larboard[5] as required to engage the enemy ships.

Once everything was cleared for action, the hands went to breakfast, as no one knew when they would next have a chance to eat. By a little after

---

1　*Amazon, Blanche, Alcmene, Arrow* and *Dart*.

2　*Otter* and *Zephyr*.

3　*Discovery, Explosion, Terror, Volcano* and *Zebra*.

4　*Hecla* and *Sulphur*.

5　'Larboard' was still used in preference to the modern-day 'port' for the left side of a ship until officially changed by the Royal Navy in 1844, reputedly to avoid errors as 'Starboard' and 'Larboard' sounded too similar.

9 a.m. the squadron was fully ready to proceed into battle and everyone was on their mettle. The Danes were also full ready and expectant, everyone was inwardly nervous, contemplating death and thinking of family. The silence was the thing most people remarked on as individuals contemplated the next few awful hours, many making peace with their God and silently praying to be one of those who survived uninjured. No one looked forward to what was about to happen with glee, those who tried to crack a joke to relieve the tense atmosphere found that they failed to get much of a reaction and soon gave up the attempt, knowing inwardly that it was only false bravado, to try to mask their own fears. Most simply wanted to get it over with and they looked anxiously to the *Elephant* eagerly looking for the signal to weigh, for the sooner it began, the sooner it would all be over. The signal did not come, however, was Nelson thinking again?

Nelson worried that the squadron might not have sailed far enough south to fully clear the Middle Ground and he ordered a flotilla of small boats out to sound the channel and the gun brig *Cruizer* was ordered to anchor, so as to mark the southern tip of the shoal. As to the King's Deep itself, that was too close to the Danish guns to be able to be sounded. The pilots who had been specially sent to aid with the navigation in these shoals, were understandably unable to agree where exactly the channel was, for they had made their passages through the Sound when it had been buoyed. Nelson was furious with frustration and ungenerously castigated them for having 'no other thought than to keep the ship clear of danger and their own silly heads [clear] of shot', which to be fair was their job, their necks being on the line of they didn't. At length Alexander Briarly, who had previously been Master if the *Audacious* at the Battle of the Nile, bravely, or foolishly, offered to guide the squadron in. Briarly was immediately sent to the *Edgar* which was to lead the line.

It was now 10 a.m. and finally Nelson felt confident enough to signal for ships to weigh anchor, to form in line and to proceed into the King's Deep. The Danes were clearly able to see the final flurry of signals and the British ships beginning to move into formation; everyone now knew that it would not be long before the bloody mayhem began.

A view of Copenhagen drawn from the British fleet by Robinson Kittoe in 1801.

Chapter 7

The Battle of Copenhagen

April 2nd had begun in a frustratingly difficult way for Nelson and his squadron, and as the ships sailed slowly towards the Danish line, he must have felt great relief, knowing that at last it was simply down to a straight fight. However, worse was yet to come and very soon Nelson's entire battle plan would not be worth the paper that it was written on.

As the ships began to move into their assigned positions, the *Agamemnon* made haste to take up her allocated spot as fifth in the line. Because she had anchored as the most northerly ship of the squadron overnight, she needed to beat up against the wind in an effort to clear the southern tip of the Middle Ground before she could enter the King's Deep. However, even with all sail set, the ship could still not make enough headway against the wind which was combined with a strong current. She was forced to put her anchor out again and to try to warp up to it, but effectively the ship was unable to pass the shoal and participate in the battle. Nelson had lost one of his twelve ships of the line even before the two opponents had opened fire.

The *Jamaica* and her flotilla of six gun brigs were also positioned near the *Agamemnon*, but as they had much shallower draughts, they did not face the same danger of grounding on the shoals. They also struggled, however, to beat up against the wind and current and they only began to reach their assigned positions singly from early afternoon. The seven bomb vessels also struggled, of the five assigned to bombard the dockyard and fleet, only four finally arrived at their station around 2 p.m. and the two assigned to bombard Trekroner Fort never did arrive.[1] These further losses were not so significant, with the majority getting to their stations later than desired, but at least they got there.

---

1 *Hecla*, *Zebra* and *Sulphur* failed to get round the Middle Ground at all, while *Discovery*, *Explosion* and *Terror* managed to get into position and open fire before 2 p.m. and were joined by *Volcano* at 2 p.m. *The Journal of the Royal Artillery* (October 1953), p. 309.

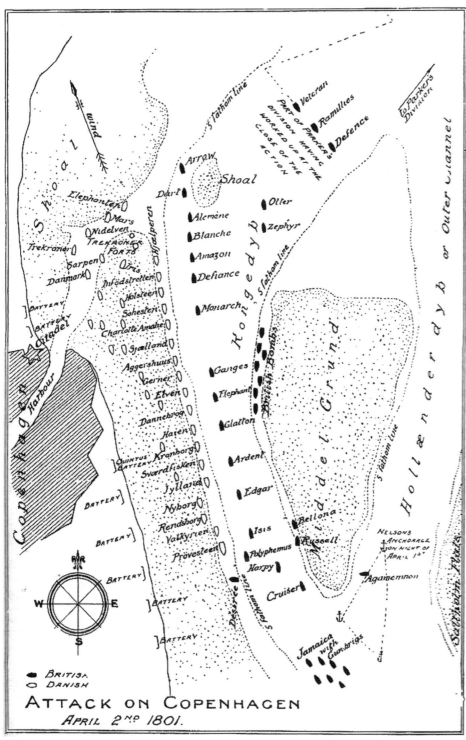

The Attack on Copenhagen, April 2nd 1801.

As the *Agamemnon* was planned to be the ship that tackled the southernmost ships of the Danish line, Nelson immediately reallocated her role to *Polyphemus*, 64, which had originally been allocated to tackle the most northerly of the Danish ships, just before the Trekroner Fort. She was now ordered to anchor astern of *Isis* to engage *Provestenen*, the first Danish ship in the defence line. Thanks to Nelson's prompt action, this first minor crisis had been swiftly and effectively dealt with. Worse, however, was still to come.

The 64-gun *Edgar* led the squadron and she successfully sailed up the Danish line, firing into each of the ships whilst receiving in return the first fire from each of them as she passed, as well as being favoured with the initial fire from Stricker's shore battery. She shrugged off all of the attention and moved into position beautifully, anchoring perfectly to engage the 48-gun *Jylland* in a firefight and trading shots with the two floating batteries *Nyborg* and *Rendsborg* lying next to her.

Ardent, another 64, followed immediately behind her and when *Edgar* dropped her anchor, she passed down her starboard side and anchored in a position to take on the next three ships in the Danish line, the 22-gun brig *Cronborg* with the two 20-gun floating batteries positioned on either side of her, *Svaerdfisken* and *Hajen*.

Next, as per the original battle plan, was the 54-gun *Glatton*, commanded by Captain William Bligh, the very same who had been so famously involved in the 'Mutiny on the Bounty' some twelve years ago. She sailed past the two previous ships, as planned, anchoring to trade broadsides with the larger 62-gun *Dannebrog*. Well behind her, the 64-gun *Isis* anchored perfectly in place to exchange broadsides with the 48-gun *Wagrien*.

Next should have been *Agamemnon*, but in her absence, *Bellona*, 74 followed. This was the moment when the position became infinitely worse for the British. Believing that the Danish line was anchored tight to the shoals along the southern edge of the deep, the pilots on the British ships constantly edged their ships further away from the Danes to maintain their position – as they imagined – in the centre of the channel. Colonel Stewart witnessed Nelson's 'distress at the pilot's refusing to take the ship closer to the enemy was very great & and he called me down at the beginning of the day from the poop to tell me the indignation he felt at the fellow's refusing to go nearer to them ¼ less 5 – which is within a fathom [6ft] of what the *Elephant* draws.'[1]

Nelson signalled to *Bellona*, warning her not to stray too far across to the right of the channel, but it was too late. As she passed *Isis*, she strayed way too far eastwards and was soon run firmly aground on a finger of the Middle

---

1 Letter from Colonel Stewart to Sir Henry Clinton dated 6 April 1801. NMM AGC/14/27.

Ground shoal. Nelson's 74-gun *Elephant* was fortunately next in line and the admiral was therefore in the perfect position to recognize the problem and to instantly react to it. The *Bellona* instantly hoisted signals warning that she was aground and Nelson, realizing that the ship had strayed far too far to the east, instantly ordered the ship to pass *close* down the starboard side of the engaged ships rather than attempt to pass to the east of *Bellona* as had originally been ordered. Nelson has been roundly praised for this swift decision, but with *Bellona* clearly way off course, lying aground far to the east, he took the only sensible course open to an experienced sailor. He would have thought little of the decision himself. Nelson then ordered Captain Foley to anchor *Elephant* in the position previously allocated to the *Bellona*. The ship therefore anchored opposite the 24-gun floating battery *Grenier* (or *Fleet Battery No. 1*), and the converted horse transport *Aggerhuus*, with 20 guns, whilst also taking on *Dannebrog* in support of *Glatton*. Whilst the ship began to engage these three enemy ships, Nelson stood on the quarterdeck to watch the rest of the ships pass and shouting orders to each redirecting them to new targets now that the *Bellona* was no longer in the line.

Following *Elephant*, came *Ganges*, commanded by his friend Thomas Fremantle. He ordered the 74-gun *Ganges* to engage the Danish *Sjoelland* which also carried 74 guns and which *Elephant* had originally been paired against in the plan. Next up, the 74-gun *Monarch* was then allocated the *Charlotte Amalie* of 26 guns and the 18-gun floating battery *Sohesten*. Behind her, Admiral Graves in the 74-gun *Defiance* was now tasked with engaging the 60-gun *Holstein*.

Russell was following *Defiance* as one of the last of the line, but in the smoke-laden atmosphere, Captain Cuming lost sight of the mastheads of *Defiance* in the smoke and mistakenly sailed towards the masts of the stranded *Bellona* instead. Before he realized his mistake, the *Russell* was also firmly aground, Nelson had now lost three of his ships of the line from his original plan, fully 25 per cent of his attack squadron.

Polyphemus, which had brought up the rear of the line, had already anchored off the southernmost ship of the line in place of *Agamemnon*. She faced the 56-gun *Provestenen*, which had already been in action for over an hour and had received a broadside from every British ship as they had passed.

The British line was now fully engaged, but because of their losses, Nelson's squadron were not able to stretch to engage the two most northerly Danish vessels in their line; these were the 64-gun *Infodsretten* and the 20-gun frigate *Hjaelperen*. Captain Riou recognized the situation and bravely, if foolishly, led his frigate squadron into an unequal contest with these vessels, which also brought him under the fire of the formidable Trekroner Battery.

Nelson has been praised to high heaven for these rapid tactical changes, shoring up his disorganized forces when he had lost such a significant portion of his battle line, but does he deserve all the praise he gets? The grounding of *Agamemnon* and his rapid decision to replace her in the station at the southern tip of the Danish defence line with the ship originally destined to be the northernmost ship, tackling the very last vessels in the line, was the right one, made with commendable speed and firmness of action, but was also perhaps the obvious one, choosing not to tackle the last Danish ships before the front of their line had been overcome; reducing the length of his own line and therefore maintaining his superiority in cannon.

However, Nelson had already been unwittingly guilty of a major error in his method of attack. He and his pilots had assumed that the Danish line was anchored along the southern edge of the King's Deep with the shoals lying very close by, thus denying the opportunity to pass their ships on both sides. In fact, the Danish fleet was anchored virtually along the centre of the deep, with a sizeable expanse of navigable water to either side. Had Nelson realized this, he could have acted exactly as he had done so inspirationally at the Battle of the Nile three years previously, passing his own ships up both sides of the Danish line and overwhelming each enemy ship in turn by doubling up on them, firing on them from both sides at the same time. He does, however, have some excuse for this error, as the Danish ships were anchored fore and aft and therefore fixed in position, unlike the French ships in Egypt, which were only anchored by the bow and as an experienced sailor would realize, they therefore had to be far enough away from the shoals to be able to swing round with the tides without grounding. In many accounts of Nelson's deliberations, however, they fail to mention one very pertinent fact. Captain Hardy had approached the Danish line the previous night, in a small rowing boat with muffled oars, accompanied by only a couple of men in dark boat cloaks. They had silently rowed around the first ships in the Danish line without causing an alarm and had established by a number of soundings that there was deep water on both sides of the vessels. This invaluable discovery must have been communicated to Nelson by 11 p.m. the night before the action, so why did he choose not to double up the line by sailing half of his ships to the west of the Danish ships and why did two British ships keep such a distance from the Danish ships that they ran aground, when there was clear evidence that the Danes were not anchored tight to the edge of the deep? It can only be that Nelson either distrusted the information (unlikely as he had a high regard for the professionalism of Hardy), or that he did not feel able to take such a gamble, perhaps unable to believe that the Danes would not be so foolish as to fall into the same trap as the French ships had at the Nile. We will probably never know why on this day, the most adventurous and daring admiral in the Royal

Navy felt unable to take such a gamble, but if he had it would almost certainly have meant a far more decisive victory at much lower cost to the British ships and would certainly have meant that *Bellona* and *Russell* would not have run aground, significantly boosting the strength of his attacking force. It was certainly a very significant omission, which would have a great influence on the final chapter of the battle. The decision to curtail the length of the line after the two British 74s drove onto the shoals was an obvious one, to avoid the possibility of the last few British ships having to tackle too many of the Danish ships and being overwhelmed by their greatly superior firepower.

The British ships had sailed majestically into the heart of the Danish line, shrugging off the fire from each of the ships as they passed unflinching, moving on to their assigned station, whilst pouring in a violent reply before anchoring with precision alongside their chosen opponent. Soon a great pall of smoke hung over the battle, occasionally obscuring the view and making accurate fire much more complicated. The fire from the British ships was impressively rapid, deadly accurate and incessant, as was to be expected from a professional and superbly-trained force. The great guns fired solid iron shot which tore through the oak hulls as if they were made of matchwood, the iron sphere macerating any flesh it impacted with, but infinitely worse was the shower of wooden splinters which fanned outwards in a great arc, causing horrendous injuries to anyone unlucky enough to be struck by the jagged fragments, which sliced through flesh like butter and ripped through limbs, leaving dreadful injuries and often embedding bacteria deep within the wounds which would go septic a few days later. But the surviving men, often reinforced by new hands rowed out to the defence line from the city, refused to cower and continually replied with gusto, causing similar scenes of horror aboard the British ships. For those stationed on the open upper decks, there was a violent hail of bullets of all sizes emanating from the enemy carronades which spread deadly showers of small iron balls far and wide, just like a modern machine-gun burst, decimating the gun crews and the marines who lined the ship's sides, attempting to pick off their opponent's officers and crew with their muskets and grenades. Soon the decks were slippery with gore, with blood sloshing around despite the sand purposely strewn about to help absorb it. The thick acrid smoke, the suffocating heat, the deafening thunder of the guns, the slippery gore, the crushing exhaustion, the awful cries and groans all around and the sheer terror, that was what it was like to be aboard a warship in battle. For those lucky enough to be killed outright, their still-warm corpses were unceremoniously pushed overboard, whilst those dreadfully wounded, screamed with the agony and shock and were carried to the relative safety of the lower decks where the surgeon and his untrained mates butchered their remains further, removing limbs with astonishing speed from patients who were fully awake and with no pain relief or infection control to avoid gangrene and sepsis taking hold. Soon many of the ships on both sides were simply charnel houses: the devil himself would struggle to envisage a worse hell. Some on both sides are sure to have sought ways to get away from the carnage on the lower decks, but it was usual practice in all navies that every ladder to the upper deck was guarded by a soldier or marine with a loaded musket and bayonet fixed.

By 11 a.m., within half-an-hour of the action starting, fifteen of the eighteen ships of the Danish line were fully involved in the fighting; the northern three ships, the *Holstein*, *Infodsretten* and *Hjaelperen* were still waiting until after 12 noon to begin the action, no ships having yet approached them out of the smoke billowing around to the southward.

After only three-quarters of an hour, some ships had already suffered greatly. At 11.15 a.m., the *Rendsborg* floating battery was so damaged by the fire of *Edgar* that she had to abandon her position. Lieutenant Commander Egede recorded that he had little choice but to abandon his place in the line, the *Edgar*'s second salvo having holed her below the waterline and another shooting away her anchor. This caused the ship to swing round so that her stern was facing the *Edgar* and she was raked mercilessly. By loosening a few sails, she was able to make headway into a position where she could run aground, but which allowed her to continue to fire on the British ships. The nearby *Nyborg*, a converted cavalry transport, came under similar intense fire, which only increased with the withdrawal of *Rendsborg*. The number of killed and wounded was soon nearly as high as on *Rendsborg*, but it continued to fight valiantly until about 12.30 p.m., when Lieutenant Commander Rothe decided that enough was enough and rigging a sail on her foremast, he pulled out of the line, further increasing the gap. *Nyborg* sailed slowly northward towards the safety of the harbour along the inshore, or disengaged side of the Danish ships.

This gap would have been quickly pounced upon by *Jamaica* and her six gunboats, allowing them to fire raking shot into the Danish ships to either side. However, these boats were still struggling to get into the action against the wind and current and they failed to take advantage of the opportunity. Neither Nelson nor his captains felt confident enough that there was sufficient deep water to allow them to manoeuvre into this gap with the line-of-battle ships, another opportunity lost.

Commodore Fischer continued to defiantly fly the signal for the Danish ships to engage the enemy as soon as they came into range; whereas Nelson flew signal No. 16, 'Engage the enemy more closely': it was to be a slugging match. On board *Elephant*, Nelson turned coolly to Colonel William Stewart as the splinters flew, exclaiming with a slight smile, 'It is warm work, and this day may be the last to any of us at any moment. But mark you, I would not be anywhere else for thousands.'

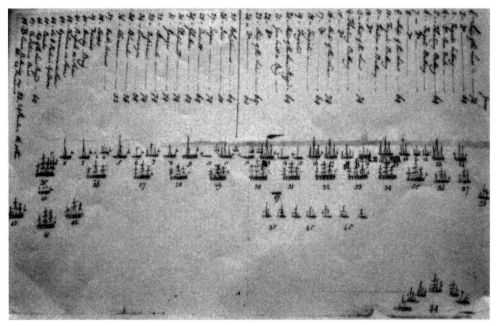

Captain Fremantle's own sketch of the battle, 1801.

By 11.30 a.m., the Danish flagship *Dannebrog*, was suffering severely under the concentrated fire of both *Elephant*, whose great firepower had quickly overwhelmed her two small opponents, and Bligh's *Glatton*. The gundecks of *Dannebrog* were already largely swept clear by the British guns, her hull was shattered and a number of fires had broken out, which despite a supreme effort could not be got under control. Up to a third of the crew had been killed or wounded. Commodore Fischer was among them being struck by a large splinter striking his brow, which caused him to suffer from a terrible concussion headache as the day progressed. Soon it was clear to Fischer that the ship could not continue much longer and he decided to leave her and to fly his flag in one of the other ships. The commodore and his staff took a boat to *Holstein*, which he now chose as his new flagship. Despite having one officer killed and four wounded, including the captain, who lost his hand,[1] the ship continued to fight on, although fewer and fewer guns could be maintained in action by the dreadfully diminished crews.

---

1 Sub-Lieutenant Wulff was killed and Captain Braun had his right hand blown off, Lieutenant Lutzen was hit in the leg and arm, and Lieutenant Kornbeck was wounded in the right arm and face, whilst Lieutenant Mollerup received serious burns on his hands.

Crowds of Danes assembled along the shoreline to watch the battle unfold on their very doorstep. Soon however, the wind blew the smoke from the cannon fire across the waters and eyewitnesses could see very little. One young student remembered that:

> In fact none of the ships out there could properly be seen, only the impression of the enemy guns and cannon balls which were skimming across the water towards the Customs House. All that the crowd could see was smoke and the occasional flashes of the guns. They stood there without a thought of going home for food or water for five or six hours. They all wanted to experience the mood of this unforgiveable attack and bloody butchery.[1]

The signal boat *Elven* had been situated in the lee of *Dannebrog*, but had therefore suffered heavily from the shot which passed through or over the flagship. At one point her ensign was shot away but quickly raised again, causing some confusion in the British ships as to whether she had struck or not. By this stage her captain, Lieutenant Colonel Holsten, mistakenly believed that the *Dannebrog* had struck so he cut his two anchor cables and sailed to safety at about 12.30 a.m.; his ship had never been intended to fight in the line.

Elephant had also rapidly destroyed the converted cavalry barge *Aggerhuus* with just a few of her guns. Having come into action at 11 a.m., by noon her captain, Sub-Lieutenant Fasting, recorded that he had only three guns left which could be fired. The battery continued to fight valiantly for another hour, but when a spring on the stern anchor was shot away, the vessel swung round to present her bow to the enemy and she was soon decimated by raking shot. Fasting decided to cut his moorings in an effort to save those of his crew that remained, but she hardly moved. The dead and wounded now amounted to more than a third of the crew; the injured were ferried ashore and then preparations were made to sink her. However, the damage was so severe that the barge floated rudderless until her sister-ship *Nyborg* appeared from the south. *Nyborg* passed a rope and setting more sail, towed *Aggerhuus* into safety behind the Trekroner Battery. However, it was discovered that *Aggerhuus* was taking on water and eventually she was scuttled, whilst *Nyborg* was taken under tow and passed the harbour boom but sank just off the Customs Quay, a local newspaper report stating that only one gun had still been serviceable and that the deck was strewn with dead bodies and severed limbs.[2]

Another of the smaller gun batteries to suffer in the early exchanges, was *Fleet Battery No. 1* (also known as *Grenier*), which was under fire from *Elephant*

---

1 Pope, p. 365.
2 Feldbaek, p. 156.

and occasionally *Ganges* which, however, was more interested in *Sjoelland* as her main opponent. This raft-like structure had the advantage of lying very low in the water and therefore difficult to hit, but also had the serious fault of offering virtually no protection to the Danish crew and they suffered severely. The 17-year-old Sub-Lieutenant Peter Willemoes was forced at around 1 p.m. to pull his battery out of the line. In the first hour and a half, the crew had suffered forty-six casualties, some one-third of their number, and seven of her twenty guns were unable to fire. *Dannebrog* appeared to be no longer flying the admiral's pennant and therefore Willemoes ordered the anchor cables to be cut and she slowly drifted out of the line. The battery collided with the next ship to the north, *Sjoelland*, and many of the crew, wading in ice cold water on deck, took the opportunity to scramble aboard the 74 before they parted again, fearing that the battery would soon sink. The battery was however supported by the boats of the ships anchored in the Kronlobet Channel and was warped back into the safety of the harbour.

Monarch came under a sustained and heavy fire from her lesser opponents, the *Charlotte Amalie* brig and the *Sohesten* floating battery, but also had to fight, along with the *Ganges*, a very worthy opponent in the *Sjoelland* of 74 guns. During one of the early Danish broadsides, as *Monarch* came to rest at anchor alongside them, a cannon ball killed Captain Mosse instantly and another smashed the helm and killed or wounded most of the helmsmen. Lieutenant John Yelland immediately took command, calling to the other officers to inform them of their captain's death and demanding that they declare their loyalty to him. This position, against the strongest opposition, had originally been earmarked by Nelson for his own ship. However, when *Bellona* and *Russell* had gone aground, they had inherited the 'point of honour'. *Monarch* was to suffer the heaviest casualties during the battle, amounting to 56 dead and 164 wounded, more than one-fifth of the total British casualties. The soldiers of the 49th Foot on board lined the deck and fired on every conceivable target on the upper deck of the Danish ships with their muskets, but they suffered for their temerity as their bright red uniforms made them an easy target; they were eventually sent below to reduce their losses. The infantry officers sought something useful to do and they raised their spirits by starting cheers throughout the ship and occasionally helping to command the gun batteries. The ship took casualties particularly in the forward part of the ship, where it also received occasional deadly raking shots from the Trekroner Battery. Midshipman William Millard recalled having to pass across the main deck from the mainmast to the foc'sle: 'When I arrived on the main deck, along which I had to pass, there was not a single man standing the whole way from the mainmast forward, a district containing eight guns on each side, some of which were run out ready for firing; others lay dismounted; and others remained as they were after recoiling.'

Monarch was suffering, but so was her main antagonist, *Sjoelland*. The quarterdeck had suffered a great deal of damage during the early exchanges where the guns were soon dismounted and the red-coated soldiers of the Norwegian Regiment were ordered to go below, just as the 49th had done facing them. As the battle raged, the fire from the two British ships cleared the upper deck of almost every living soul, her masts were shot away, hundreds of shot holes had been driven through the hull and splinters by the thousand tearing harshly through the flesh of those they struck. But most dangerous of all were the twenty to thirty shot which had penetrated the hull below the waterline causing flooding and taking the efforts of all of the carpenters and their teams to stem the ingress of water, whilst the pumps were employed constantly to keep her afloat. By 1 p.m. all fire from the upper deck had ceased and only a few guns aft on the two gun decks showed that *Sjoelland* was still putting up a fight. Looking around, *Dannebrog* could be seen in flames and *Fleet Battery No. 1* had cut her moorings and was about to crash alongside, destroying all of her boats. At this point, First Lieutenant Schultz lost all reason, ran down to the lower gun deck and left the ship via a gun port; he then ordered the ship's boats with about fifty men and a number of wounded to Trekroner Battery. By the time Schultz had arrived at the battery, he realized what he had done and returned to the ship to carry on fighting, but it was too late, many of the crew having witnessed his flight. In the confusion of *Sjoelland* crashing alongside and much of the crew clambering aboard, another officer who had fought bravely throughout the day now lost his mind as well. Captain Westerholt, who commanded the contingent of the Norwegian Regiment, left the ship via a lower-deck gunport with a number of his men and found a boat to transport them to Customs Quay. It is easy to be critical of these men, but they had endured hours of a living hell and who can tell how much death and exhaustion anyone can take before they finally break?[1] Captain Harboe had seen enough and he ordered the anchor cables to be cut, hoping to be carried by the current behind Trekroner Fort. However, the ship drifted directly towards the battery, restricting its arc of fire. Harboe therefore ordered his last anchor to be dropped, hoping that the ship would then swing out of the fort's line of sight, whilst avoiding getting in the way of the guns of the next ship, *Hjoelperen*. This unfortunately did not take him out of range of the British guns and he finally had to admit defeat and lower his colours, to save what was left of his crew.

Just after the centre of the Danish line had collapsed, consternation ran through the British fleet when Admiral Parker, nervous as to the result of

---

1 The two officers were subsequently tried by court martial and sentenced to be executed by being shot in the back, but both were reprieved at the last minute at the place of execution.

the battle, having seen three of Nelson's ships run aground and signalling for assistance, saw that the odds were not good. Because of the thick canopy of smoke enveloping the contending ships he could not judge how the battle was going, and the fact that the plan for his own ships to move up to attack the Trekroner Battery and the Danish ships in the Kronlobet Channel was proving impossible to achieve against the current, Parker lost his nerve and called the attack off. At 1:15 p.m., with signal 39 being hoisted on board *London*, ordering the fleet to 'Discontinue the Action'. Nelson's ships signalled that they had received and understood the order, but no ships left the battle, except for Captain Riou's frigate squadron which lay nearest to the admiral. The warships looked to *Elephant*, expecting to see the order repeated, but it wasn't, Nelson maintained the signal 'Engage the enemy more closely' at his masthead and they simply continued the battle. Nelson, loving a theatrical display, famously turned to Captain Foley and with a shrug of his shoulders, said, 'You know Foley, I have only one eye and I have a right to be blind sometimes' and putting his telescope to his blind eye, continued 'I really do not see the signal'. Captain Riou turned his ships away from Trekroner Fort to sail down the channel to join the admiral; in doing so his ships presented their sterns to the battery, which took full advantage and fired a number of brutal raking shots, which tore through the length of these ships, killing and maiming many, including Riou himself, who was killed outright.

Still the crowds lined the shoreline and tried to peer through the dense smoke to try to ascertain how the battle went. One 12-year-old boy recalled how he climbed a crane in the dockyard and shouted reports down to the crowd below:

> As a result of my good practise in climbing I was immediately halfway up the crane, and I could look over the buildings at Nyholm and see most of the battle.
>
> Higher up the crane above me sat an old sailor, and he reported to me because he could better see what was going on, and then I repeated everything down the crane to the masses of people below.[1]

Dannebrog had continued to valiantly withstand the storm of British shot, although the length of time between each of her rare shots in reply gradually got longer and longer. At one time the colours had been shot away, but they had been rapidly replaced to correct any British impression that she had surrendered. The British shot had eventually started a number of fires on board and by 2:30 p.m. it was clear that the fires were now raging out of control and finally her colours were lowered and she fell silent. It was clear to all that there was an imminent danger of the crew being overcome by the

---

1 Pope, p. 366.

flames and smoke and an even greater danger of her blowing up. The British ships nearby sent their boats to help the Danish boats remove the crew as quickly as possible, as an act of humanity. She floated out of the line, drifting slowly to the north, billowing smoke and forming a silent sepulchre for those who had been cut down. The British ships manoeuvred away from her as the danger of an explosion continued to grow.

During the early part of the action, the *Hajen* artillery barge had found herself largely ignored, in fact during the first hour the ship only received four casualties. However, once the *Elven*, *Aggerhuus* and *Grenier* had been battered into submission and the *Dannebrog's* fire began to slacken, the British guns finally turned on her. The low profile of the barge meant that it was difficult for conventional cannon to depress their guns enough to strike home, but the carronades on the upper deck suffered from no such problem and could rain down showers of balls, which decimated the poorly-protected gun crews. Murmurings of mutiny began to be heard, but Sub-Lieutenant Muller succeeded in keeping them at their guns with free-flowing akavit and exhortations to their patriotism. They were however, exhausted and close to running out of powder and signals were flown asking for more to be rowed out. With the weight of guns against her, she could not last long and eventually at 2:45 p.m., Muller ordered the colours to be hauled down. This wasn't perceived by the British, however, who continued to rain shot onto the deck. The men were ordered below whilst a few spiked the guns and attempted to build a raft on which to escape. Eventually the British perceived that *Hajen* was not firing back and two longboats took the ship as a prize and carried the crew as prisoners to *Elephant*. When Muller was taken on board *Elephant* he was escorted to the captain's cabin where he met Foley who declared that 'the English had never had such a warm day as this, neither against the Dutch, the French or the Spanish' and Admiral Nelson announced 'It pains me what has happened today, and as proof I have already sent an envoy to negotiate a cease fire. Should it transpire that this is not acceptable, I will have to take Trekroner Fort and burn the Arsenal.' Muller did reply that the fort would not be an easy nut to crack, at which the short interview came to an end.

Just before 2 p.m. Nelson had decided to write to the Crown Prince of Denmark in an effort to end the fighting. The reason consistently given by the admiral for this action was simply one of 'humanity', to save the useless loss of human lives. The centre of the Danish line had been smashed, but at the northern and southern ends, the battle continued to rage; the Danish ships, although their colours had been lowered, still refused to allow British boats to come alongside to take them under control and even fired on them. Nelson was all too aware that the battle was far from won yet.

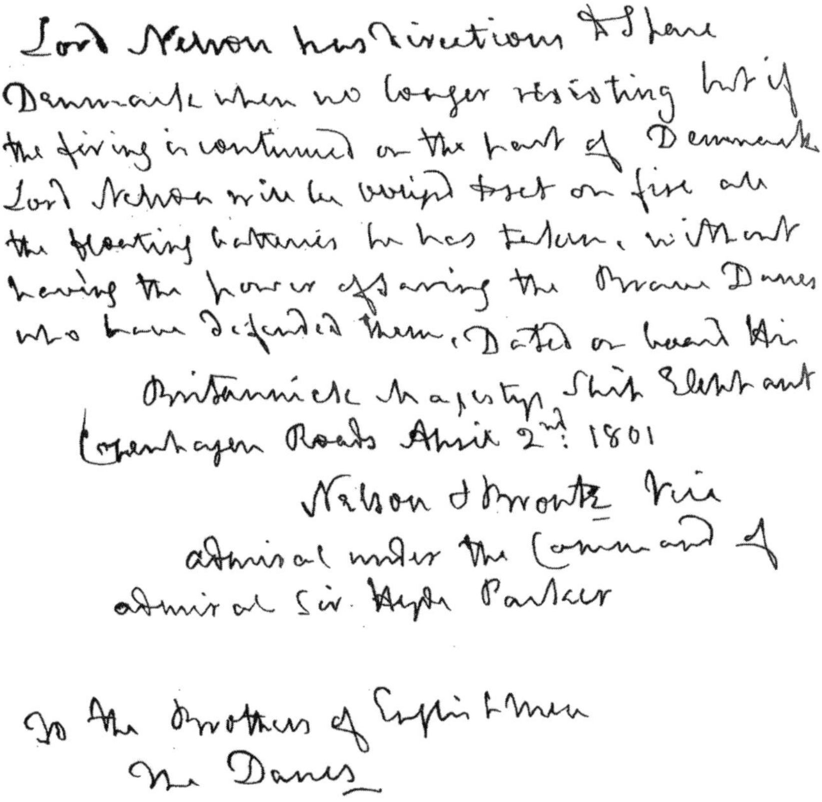

[Handwritten letter in facsimile:]

Lord Nelson has directions to spare
Denmark when no longer resisting but if
the firing is continued on the part of Denmark
Lord Nelson will be obliged to set on fire all
the floating batteries he has taken, without
having the power of saving the Brave Danes
who have defended them. Dated on board His
    Britannick Majesty, Ship Elephant
Copenhagen Roads April 2nd 1801
        Nelson & Bronte Vice
    admiral under the Command of
    admiral Sir Hyde Parker

To the Brothers of Englishmen
    the Danes

The letter was hastily scribbled but properly sealed with wax to avoid the appearance of a desperate appeal and then carried ashore by Captain Frederick Thesiger. The boat reached the *Elefanten* blockship in the Kronlobet Channel around 2:30 p.m., when Captain von Thun forwarded the boat to the Prince at Citadel Point. It was a hard pull for the oarsmen against the tide and they finally arrived at the jetty around 3 p.m., where Thesiger handed it to the Prince. It simply stated:

> To the Brothers of Englishmen the Danes,
>
> Lord Nelson has directions to spare Denmark when no longer resisting, but if the firing is continued on the parts of Denmark, Lord Nelson will be obliged to set on fire all the floating batteries he has taken without having the power of saving the brave Danes who have defended them. Dated onboard His Britannick Majesty's Ship *Elephant*.
>
> Nelson & Bronte Vice Admiral under the command of Admiral Sir Hyde Parker.

Chapter 8

Battle Continues

The southernmost ships of the Danish line had been in action from the very beginning of the battle, having exchanged a broadside with each of the British ships passing to the north. When the first two ships of Nelson's line had entered the King's Deep, they had manoeuvred into position, the *Edgar* engaging the 48-gun *Jylland* and *Ardent* tackling the gun platform *Svaerdfisken* and the frigate *Cronborg*. Both sides began a hard-fought exchange of broadsides which continued with great fury without intermission for a number of hours. *Jylland* soon suffered heavy damage to her aftermost guns and her crew was decimated, but the surviving gunners simply moved to the remaining pieces and continued the action. Before long the intense and accurate fire from the British guns took such a toll that only a couple of guns could still be fired on each deck. *Jylland*'s colours were shot away, but soon replaced and it was some four hours into the battle before she finally struck at 2:30 p.m. to spare any further useless blood-letting, having only four guns still serviceable. The ship had also suffered a number of shot below the waterline and was slowly sinking; therefore, Captain Branth ordered the anchor cables to be cut to allow her to drift onto the shoals to prevent her going down.

Despite their surrender, First Lieutenant Wleugel and the remnants of the crew still capable of fighting, who were now technically prisoners of war, were sent by boat to aid the ships still fighting to the south. They rowed to *Rendsborg*, only to find that she was a wreck, so they rowed to the north to Trekroner Fort. A British boat then approached *Jylland* and the remaining officers were conveyed onto *Ardent*. Whilst the British boat was arriving on one side, boats were still transferring the crew ashore on the other side, in direct contravention of the rules of war.

Svaerdfisken and *Cronborg* still continued the fight with the same determination. Aboard *Svaerdfisken* Sub-Lieutenant Sommerfeldt saw almost all of his guns destroyed and his crew mowed down mercilessly and he finally struck at the same time as *Jylland*. *Cronborg* had lost Captain Bohne with the very first broadside, but the crew fought on valiantly under First Lieutenant

Søren Bille. After two hours of hard fighting, Bille was severely wounded by splinters in the right leg and Lieutenant Haunch took command, but he lost an arm moments later and command devolved on Lieutenant Helt, the last officer standing. Gunner's Mate Petersen described the carnage on board: 'the piles of dead bodies on the deck were growing so fast that we could barely get to our guns'.[1] Eventually *Cronborg* ran out of serviceable guns entirely, no less than three shot had gone through the magazine, the ship was taking on water and finally the crew lost heart and she also struck at 2:30 p.m. With all three ships here beaten, there only remained *Rendsborg* which had run aground and continued to annoy the British ships with her fire. Now the British ships in the area concentrated their fire on this last annoying little ship and with shot constantly drilling holes through the hull, Captain Egede threw his signal books over the side and hauled down his colours at 3 p.m. Here again half of the crew were transported ashore by boat before a boat came from *Jamaica* and took her as a prize.

There still remained the two southernmost of the Danish ships to account for. *Wagrien* and *Provestenen* had exchanged fire with each of the British ships as they had progressed towards their stations further north. *Desiree* had also placed herself in a position where she could rake the two Danish ships mercilessly, whilst remaining safely out of their arc of fire, but she was not completely protected from enemy fire, her position being bows-on to the Stricker Battery on the shoreline. Four of the British gunboats had finally manoeuvred into a position to support her and used their guns to annoy the Danes without being under return fire from anything more than the bow chasers of the Danish vessels. The losses in all of these British ships was noticeably light, they were clearly not taking many casualties from the shore batteries, which looked so formidable, but failed to have any serious impact on the fighting.

Isis had followed the original plan and had anchored so as to exchange broadsides with *Wagrien*, but she also suffered from the fire of *Provestenen*, who had no regular opponent until *Polyphemus* eventually arrived, replacing *Agamemnon* which had originally been given this station. The crews of *Wagrien* and *Provestenen* were particularly effective against *Isis* which suffered one of the highest losses of any British ship that day, but with the arrival of *Polyphemus*, the contest was more even, although the latter did not suffer as much as *Isis* as the Danish fire was now divided against two targets. The two Danish ships began to suffer heavily, *Edgar* using a spring to fire into *Wagrien*'s stern whilst *Desiree* and the four gunboats raked her bows, having already destroyed her bow chasers. This, coupled with the devastating broadsides of the *Polyphemus*,

---

1 Feldbaek, p. 182.

tore the ship apart, but the Danes continued to give as good as they got. By 2:30 p.m. all but three of her guns were rendered useless, numerous shot had pierced the hull and more than half of the crew was killed or wounded, whilst those still living were utterly exhausted after four hours of continuous fighting. Captain Risbrich therefore ordered as many of the crew as possible to leave in the ship's boats and he then lowered his colours in defeat. The guns facing the Danish shore were spiked to prevent their use against the shore batteries and the powder thrown overboard to render it useless. Captain Risbrich went ashore with the other survivors near the Quintus Battery and immediately reported to the Crown Prince, who received him with a 'gracious welcome'.

This now left *Provestenen* fighting alone to the south. The ship was struck repeatedly and fires had broken out on three separate occasions, but had been successfully extinguished each time. Lieutenant Michael Bille, son of Captain Steene Bille, commanded the lower deck guns enthusiastically. At one point, the seaman standing next to him had a hole literally bored through him by a cannonball and Bille had to be led away from the terrible scene. The upper deck crews were ravaged by grapeshot whilst those below were shredded by the raking shots flying the entire length of the ship, destroying everything in their path. Captain Lassen ordered the surviving upper-deck crews to go below and help the lower-deck gun crews work the few guns that were still in a serviceable condition. The constant heavy losses, the alarming regularity of fires breaking out and the unrelenting fire from the British ships, all concentrated on this last remaining defender, finally broke the will of the crew and some men were seen to be retiring from their posts. No other ships of the defence line could still be seen firing and to prevent further useless slaughter, the captain eventually ordered the ship to stop firing at 3 p.m. It is believed that a Norwegian seaman by the name of Jacob Hansen on board *Provestenen* fired the last Danish shot that day. Captain Lassen took as many men as could fit into the ship's boats and rowed ashore. British boats soon appeared and they took command of the shattered hull; Michael Bille had remained on board with the wounded and was taken to *Russell*, where he was treated with great respect.

The grounded *Bellona* and *Russell* had taken serious casualties, laying as they did like sitting ducks. Captain Sir Thomas Thompson of the former had his left leg carried away by a cannonball. First Lieutenant Wilkes took command and he recorded his admiration for the Danes in his report: 'I will do them the credit to say that they fought well, far better than I have found the French or Spaniards; not a vessel surrendered till nearly all her men were either killed or wounded.'[1] Their losses were however, not all caused by the

---

1 Feldbaek, p. 185.

Danes, two cannon exploding on board *Bellona* and devastating their gun crews, most likely owing to human error.

The northern range of Danish ships had not been involved in the early fighting as Nelson was forced to truncate his battle line. It was, however, the most powerful part of the Danish line, if the guns of the Trekroner Battery were included. The two most northern ships initially engaged by Nelson's line were *Charlotte Amalie* and the *Sohesten* floating battery. *Holstein*, *Infodsretten* and *Hjaelperen* were not immediately engaged and were forced to largely see out the initial fighting as reluctant spectators.

Initially *Charlotte Amalie* was spared a heavy fire, the British *Monarch* and *Ganges* concentrating their efforts on destroying the ships just to the south of her; but by noon, most of these had retired and she began to receive a very heavy and destructive fire from both warships. The intense fire caused horrific scenes, so reminiscent of all of the other Danish ships, but soon it became obvious that the ships to the south had surrendered and to save the ship from further devastation, Captain Koefoed formally surrendered his ship at 2:45 p.m. As normal, much of the surviving crew was transported ashore. *Monarch* had also suffered in the exchanges, particularly from raking shot fired from the Trekroner Battery. Further disaster was only narrowly averted when a garbled message to cut away the spring, led to a seaman wrongly believing that he was to cut the anchor cable, but he was luckily stopped at the last minute.

The *Sohesten* barge was to receive the dubious honour of contending with the British 74-gun *Defiance*. They began to exchange broadsides at around 11 a.m. and in no time the *Sohesten* had lost two of its nine-gun broadside to direct hits, killing most of their gun crews. Around 1 p.m. having taken a severe battering for two hours, the forward cables were cut by British fire and the barge swung so that her bow faced straight on to *Defiance*. The ship took a terrible battering until by about 2:30 p.m. Lieutenant Middelboe recorded that only two guns could still be manned and he was devastated to observe that *Monarch* and *Ganges* were using their springs to bring their guns to bear to rake her. Before she was overwhelmed by the fire of three 74s Lieutenant Middelboe concluded that further resistance would only result in seeing the massacre of the remaining crew and he therefore surrendered.

Holstein, one of the strongest vessels in the Danish defence line, had remained almost an observer of the action for much of the day. In fact, before she fired their first cannon in anger Commodore Fischer came alongside in a boat, having abandoned *Dannebrog*, and transferred his pennant to her.

The most northerly ship of the revised British line, *Defiance*, had originally anchored to take on *Sohesten* and *Charlotte Amalie*, but with their rapid demise certain under the broadsides of the *Ganges* and *Monarch*, Rear Admiral Graves ordered at around 12 o'clock, that the cable on the stern anchor was to be paid out as far as possible and used his springs to maintain the ship's broadside facing the Danish ship. By this clever manoeuvre, *Defiance* was carried northwards by the current, into a position to take on the impatiently-waiting *Holstein*.

The Danes fired a broadside, but the reply from *Defiance* was particularly destructive. Captain Arenfelt stated that 'The enemy shot was raining down like a hailstorm and almost all the men at the first three guns were killed. At the fourth gun at this time Lieutenant Haas informed me there was only one man remaining.' The speed and accuracy of the British 74's fire quickly overwhelmed the Danish 60 and in less than two hours, with few men left manning the guns, Commodore Fischer realized that the ship would soon have to strike her colours and he departed from his flag ship for a second time, taking himself this time to the Trekroner Battery. At 2:15 p.m. *Holstein* struck, having received a devastating raking fire from the north, which had effectively ended all organized resistance. The gundecks of the Danish ship had received over 150 shot, which had breached the wooden sides and at least thirteen shot had struck below the waterline, causing serious flooding. Few men could be sent ashore as two of the ship's three boats had been smashed by a Danish ball fired from one of the ships in the Kronlobet Channel. Captain Arenfelt and his officers surrendered to the British boarding party and were transported over to *Elephant*. Boats sent to take her as a prize were, however, continually fired upon and she was not formally captured; in fact, Nelson wrote to Parker the following morning asking him to demand the Danes relinquish her immediately. Captain Otway again attempted to gain possession that morning, but the Danes still insisted that although the colours had been shot away, their pennant remained flying at the masthead. On arrival on board *Holstein* Otway's coxswain managed to remove the said pennant unperceived whilst they were all in conversation on the deck and when the Danes pointed to the pennant and finding it gone, they were obliged to finally cede the ship.[1]

When it had become obvious that Nelson's truncated line would not be able to engage the most northerly ships, Captain Riou had used his frigate squadron to fire on *Holstein*, *Infodsretten* and the Trekroner Battery in an effort to form a distraction, well knowing that their fire-power was well capable of destroying his squadron with ease.

The last two vessels in the Danish line were strong opponents, but each acted very differently to the evident sight of the destruction of the Danish centre. The northernmost ship, *Hjoelperen* – a custom-built defensive frigate with wooden walls 5ft thick at the waterline – had exchanged a few shots with *Defiance* and *Monarch* and then Riou's frigate squadron, but she had

---

1 *A Naval Biographical Dictionary*, Vol. 2, p. 843.

suffered very little damage before Captain Lillienskjold ordered the cables cut at around 1 p.m. and the ship sailed into the harbour, 'to avoid needless sacrifice'.

The commander of the 64-gun *Infodsretten* made a decision which was poles apart from this. Being moored so near to the Trekroner Battery, she was not seriously engaged until all of the other opposition had ended at the northern end of the line. Because of the thick smoke, the officers on board were unsure of the course of the action, but the steady stream of ships passing, having abandoned their position in the defence line, did not augur well. It was 1 p.m. before *Infodsretten* began to come under heavy fire from *Defiance* and within half an hour Lieutenant Commander Thurah, the commanding officer, had been killed. At 1.30 p.m. the Danish ships in her vicinity noted that her ensign had been lowered in surrender, but further reinforcements sent out in boats boarded the vessel and the colours were re-hoisted. Lieutenant Lutzen, one of the recently arrived reinforcements went below to find 'a situation of utter confusion – many men drunk, and only a few guns had been fired'.[1] It was clear that with *Defiance*, *Monarch* and *Ganges* now concentrating their fire on her and the crew incapable of offering a defence, the reinforcements were simply being slaughtered for no good reason and at 3 p.m. the last Danish ship in the defence line surrendered. But nothing had really been settled.

---

1 Feldbaek, p. 177.

Chapter 9

Winning the Peace

The fighting had largely come to an end, but there was now a pregnant pause, whilst everyone awaited the outcome of Nelson's communication to the Crown Prince. Because of this, a number of the Danish ships were left without a British boat having arrived to claim them as a prize: everything seems to have been in limbo.

There has been constant debate for the last two centuries over the issue of whether Parker and Nelson had concocted the raising of signal No. 39 in advance, thus allowing Nelson to withdraw with honour only if necessary. How this claim has ever been allowed the oxygen to continue for so long is a mystery and it is about time that it was finally laid to rest. There is absolutely nothing in the correspondence of either admiral, or of any other officer who was present at their discussions, to support this theory. We know that Parker tolerated rather than loved his second-in-command, whilst Nelson had at times shown clear frustration at Parker's inability to stick firmly to decisions and had even shown some contempt for his superior. He had also not been afraid to write to his friends in government and the Admiralty to bypass his superior and to get his way. There is therefore no earthly reason why Parker would be prepared to fall on his sword merely to preserve the reputation of his junior.

Parker was undoubtedly thinking of the greater goal: the main task of the fleet was to attack the Russians. If the fleet was so heavily damaged at Copenhagen as to be unfit to face the Russians, then the expedition would be a failure: that is why he called the attack off. The order was peremptory and mandatory and all ships were to obey it directly once received, not to wait for the confirmation of their squadron leader. This again proves that the signal was not pre-arranged, as the reaction of the individual ships' captains could not be predicted: many or all could have followed Riou's example and sailed away, no matter what signal flew from *Elephant*.

Nelson's reasons for refusing to follow this order are understandable, but he knew that by ignoring such a direct order he was guilty of blatant insubordination and would undoubtedly be court-martialled if he lost the battle. Nelson was, therefore, not ignoring the order lightly, but was confident that he was better informed of the situation at that moment, being aware that a number of ships had just pulled out of the Danish line and confident that many more were close to surrendering. He was confident in his decision, but he could not personally be certain as to the consequences of his actions.

Having ignored Admiral Parker's order to disengage from the battle, Nelson began to contemplate his options. He needed a swift and successful termination to the battle; failure would almost certainly ensure that he would face a court martial, but just as importantly, he himself realized that the fleet still needed to be in a state capable of facing the Russians. The stubborn defence put up by the Danes had clearly been a shock: these virtually untrained crews had stood up manfully against the superbly professional crews of his own squadron and had given almost as good as they had got for a considerable period of time. The damage to his ships would undoubtedly be heavy, but the losses yet to come, if as planned the Trekroner Battery was assaulted by the boats of the fleet, would be much greater still.

Nelson, like all great military heroes, was a multifaceted and complicated individual. The son of a parson and deeply religious, he could also live a life way outside the moral code of his own beliefs and be guilty of great harshness and spite, as in the case of the Carracciolo affair in Sicily in 1799. The reasons for Nelson's letter to the Crown Prince are therefore bound to be multi-layered, as with his personality, despite his protestations to the former. The Prince was rightly suspicious of the British admiral's motives and delayed his response, he questioned his reasons, suspecting a *ruse de guerre*.[1] So, what did prompt Nelson to send the note?

The possibility of the letter being written purely on humanitarian grounds, as claimed by Nelson himself, can be discounted: his motives may have included a humanitarian aspect but it was certainly not the only one. Nelson was aware that his refusal to acknowledge the order to retire meant that he had to win a convincing victory without such a heavy loss to his own fleet that it might render it incapable of facing the Russians. It was certainly in Nelson's nature to strain every sinew to gain a comprehensive victory and not to let up halfway through a fight, when the outcome of the contest was still far from certain. At both the Nile and at Trafalgar, his mantra had been simply to gain a comprehensive victory by totally crushing the enemy and only showing humanity after the last gun had fired; but the fight at Copenhagen does not fit that profile. It is therefore almost certain that the letter was, as the Danes have

---

1 Even his friend Thomas Fremantle recorded in a letter to the Marquess of Buckingham on 4 April, 'At this time he [Nelson] was aware that our ships were cut to pieces, and it would be difficult to get them out'. Quoted in Hounslow, p. 138.

always suspected, a *ruse de guerre*, to persuade them to end the battle swiftly so as to preserve his own fleet and to maintain his own reputation.

The Danish line was showing signs of collapse, but Nelson knew that it would take another hour or two of punishing fighting to break them completely, and then there was still the Trekroner Battery to be stormed and even the possibility of having to face a fresh Danish fleet sailing out of the harbour to continue the battle, and or a Swedish fleet appearing to swing the balance against the British fleet.

It is obvious that Nelson was confident of a localized victory, but was unsure that his squadron would be left in any sort of condition to win the continuing war. A hollow victory followed by an enforced retreat from the Baltic would not be viewed well at home and his reputation would be severely tarnished. The letter to the Prince was simply sent in an effort to end the fighting quickly, with the intention of persuading the Danes to stand aside, whilst the British moved on the Russians. It betrays Nelson's fears that a protracted battle would cause them to fail in the ultimate aim of the expedition. The exact meaning regarding his intentions for the captured Danish vessels is unclear, but what it clearly is, is a threat to the safety of the wounded Danes still onboard. It all simply shows that when needed, Nelson was also an arch schemer. Nelson, however, was pretty indignant in his letters after the battle, when claims began to emerge as to his real motives for writing the letter; but his indignation cannot hide the facts as they stood when he wrote it. Even the great majority of the British officers who fought with him were of the clear opinion that it was a ruse, because the battle was far from won with any certainty. Colonel Stewart described it as 'a masterpiece of policy'. Humanity was quite possibly one factor, but it certainly was not the only one, as Nelson later claimed.

The Crown Prince responded to the letter by sending Commander Lindholm out to HMS *Elephant* to request a full explanation of Nelson's motives for the approach. However, the situation had altered dramatically since Nelson had written the note. The Danish line was now completely defeated and the battle was clearly drawing to a close, with the guns falling silent and the smoke clearing to reveal not one Danish flag flying beyond Trekroner Battery. Admiral Parker's squadron had also finally moved up close to the harbour channel and *Ramillies* and *Defence* were now firing at long range, on Trekroner Battery and the nearby *Elefanten* and *Hjoelperen* ships in the Kronlobet Channel.

The British boat was therefore required to row back again with Lindholm onboard, passing a message on the way for the Trekroner Battery to cease firing, which caused the British to stop their firing as well. Lindholm listened to Nelson's reasons for the offer of a cease fire, but asked him to put it in writing. Nelson obliged–cleverly assuming that hostilities were at an end and offering diplomatic discussions with Admiral Parker – writing:

Elephant April 2nd 1801

His Royal Highness the Prince Royal of Denmark, has sent Adjutant General Lindholm, on board His Britanick Majesty's Ship Vice Admiral Lord Nelson, to ask the particular object of sending the Flag of Truce.

Lord Nelson's object in sending on shore a Flag of Truce is humanity, therefore consents that hostilities shall cease till Lord Nelson can take his prisoners out of the prizes, and he consents to land all the wounded Danes & to burn or remove his prizes. Lord Nelson with humble duty to His Royal Highness, begs leave to say that he will ever esteem it the greatest victory he ever gained if this flag of truce may be the happy forerunner of a lasting and happy union between my most gracious Sovereign & His Majesty the King of Denmark.

Nelson & Bronte

Whilst these events unfolded, Nelson sought the advice of Admiral Graves and Captains Foley and Fremantle regarding what he should do next. They unanimously agreed that an attack on Trekroner would be suicidal and that while the guns were silent and the truce in place, they should seize the moment to sail out of the King's Deep whilst the wind was still favourable for such a manoeuvre. A white flag was raised and all but *Ardent*, which was ordered to help release *Bellona* and *Russell* from the shoals, were ordered to sail out of the restricted channel. The difficulties of this passage, even when not under fire, was clearly illustrated when *Monarch* and *Ganges* promptly ran aground, but luckily got clear again, whereas *Elephant* and *Defiance* were soon stuck fast. All four would have been severely mauled, if not lost, if the Trekroner Battery had still been firing. To the south, *Desiree* also grounded whilst trying to help free *Bellona*.

Work began immediately on repairs to the battered hulls and masts of the British ships, whilst parties were also sent to remove the wounded from the Danish prizes and to assess the chances of repairing the shattered Danish hulls. During this lull, the abandoned *Dannebrog*, which had slowly floated into a position about 300–400 yards north of Trekroner, suddenly disappeared in a huge explosion, the final poignant incident of the battle.

The Prince accepted a truce for twenty-four hours and for diplomatic talks to proceed with Parker. At 7 p.m. Lindholm went on board *London* and began the negotiations, Denmark still believing that they could win the peace. Whilst the political negotiations progressed, the British fleet turned to, the ships which had run aground were re-floated and a huge effort was made to repair the damage suffered as quickly as possible, in order to allow the fleet to sail on for the Russian coast. Within two days Captain Fremantle could declare, with his tongue quite possibly firmly in his cheek, that *Ganges* was in as good a condition as when she had left Yarmouth. *Monarch* and *Isis*, however, had suffered extensive damage, including a number of their own guns exploding, requiring them to be sent back to Britain for major repairs.

The Danish vessels which had surrendered were boarded and brought out for inspection, after the wounded had been landed for hospital care. However, the only Danish prize deemed to be in a state worth keeping, was *Holstein*. She was therefore repaired and then sailed to Britain in company with *Monarch* and *Isis*, acting as a hospital ship for the British wounded, she then entered the Royal Navy and was renamed HMS *Nassau*.

On 2 April 1801, there was no confusion over who had won the Battle of Copenhagen and the Danish government went into the talks knowing that the city was defenceless from any threatened bombardment. The outcome had not been a surprise to the Danish military, but that did not make the bitter pill any easier to swallow. During the afternoon of 3 April, the people of Copenhagen could clearly see the British bomb vessels moving into a position where they were out of range of the Danish shore batteries and Trekroner Fort, but easily capable of shelling the city. The Danish government still felt awkwardly placed, feeling bound to show her loyalty to the League and Russia, whilst negotiating to avoid the destruction of their own capital. Failure to keep Russia on side could allow Sweden to snatch Norway away and might even tempt Prussia to invade Holstein. The Danish Prince and his government therefore began to attempt to nimbly unpick the Gordian knot, rather than to simply cut through it. The Danish public were righteously enraged, however, Surgeon Peter Cullen recording in his diary: 'The Danes were very much enraged against us, and none of our people were allowed to go on shore.'[1]

The Crown Prince and his brother-in-law Prince Frederick Christian believed that the situation was so desperate that they actually contemplated the destruction of their fleet lying within the harbour by launching a desperate attempt to reverse the outcome of the battle. This suicidal attempt was abandoned eventually on humanitarian grounds. The defences of the harbour were however strengthened wherever possible by Steen Bille, who had taken command from a wounded Commodore Fischer in order to deter a landing by British troops. The Kronlobet Channel was defended in greater depth whilst earth and even wet manure was laid on the upper decks of the Danish ships to help prevent the incendiary shells setting them alight. During the battle, the ship serving as a magazine for Trekroner Fort had been sunk[2] and a replacement was moved into position. By 5 April *Fleet Battery No. 1* had

---

1 *Navy Records Society* (1951), p. 111.
2 It is unclear how this loss occurred, but it would indicate that if attacked that afternoon, Trekroner Battery may well have run out of powder and been forced to surrender.

been re-floated and repaired and was back in the harbour under the command of Sub-Lieutenant Peter Willemoes.

The Danes even held a large ceremonial funeral for the majority of the victims of the battle, attended by the admirals and their staff. Forty coffins were taken on carts from the Infirmary at Christianhavn to Holmen Churchyard, where they were buried in a mass grave, watched by a great throng singing patriotic hymns. But no one could ignore the plumes of smoke still rising from the roads, where the British were burning the useless prizes, reminding them all of the defeat. The Crown Prince was not present as he was attending the Privy Council to discuss what to do next, the discussions went on for hours, and the ministers split into two equal camps, forcing the Crown Prince to decide their strategy for the talks. He decided that delay and a determination on a negotiated settlement that would appease Tsar Paul were to be Denmark's goals. The Crown Prince therefore eventually replied to Parker's demands by offering to be an intermediary between Britain and the Armed League, but because of the huge the gap between the British and Danish negotiating positions, Nelson was sent ashore to continue the discussions face to face with the Crown Prince.

Therefore, at 4 p.m. on 3 April Nelson landed and walked through the restrained and brooding crowd to the Amalienborg Palace, only to find that the Crown Prince was absent, but the British admiral remained and the Prince eventually arrived back a few hours later. Nelson expressed his admiration for the strong Danish defence and his hope of bringing hostilities to an end. His private audience with the Crown Prince, attended only by Lindholm, was apparently frank and far reaching, but the Prince's offer to be a go-between with Russia was unsurprisingly rejected. Parker's counter-offer was that Denmark should either leave the League and join forces with Britain or disarm the Danish fleet entirely. The Crown Prince rejected the first proposal but he wanted to know more regarding a decommissioning of his fleet before making his decision. Nelson therefore offered a ceasefire until 5 April if the British navy were allowed to re-stock their supplies whilst at Copenhagen and the prince agreed to a suspension of Denmark's obligations to the Tsar during the negotiations.

The Prince reconvened his Privy Council on the morning of 5 April when he found the two camps in his council were still as far apart as they had previously been and could not agree on a strategy. Two negotiators were however appointed, Lindholm and Major General Walterstorff, and sent to talk to Parker aboard *London*. The discussions were not particularly productive, both sides proving to be too firmly entrenched to give much ground and finally Parker issued an ultimatum which would expire at noon on 6 June, requiring Denmark to declare in writing that she was not obliged to support the navies of Sweden and Russia. The delegates returned to *London* an hour before the deadline, with a verbal statement regarding her Baltic allies which Parker found unacceptable. After further discussions Parker and Nelson jointly presented another ultimatum, capitulate or hostilities would resume in twenty-four hours. The admirals had finally lost all patience with the procrastination and diplomatic shuffles of the Danes, they would no longer brook further delay. That day Parker eventually sent his victory dispatch off to London: he would no longer hold it back waiting for a political treaty.

Count Bernstorff, ever the diplomat, discovered a minor error in Parker's ultimatum and he turned it to his advantage, saving Copenhagen from the threatened bombardment and bringing the admiral back to the negotiating table. The Privy Council had met again on the morning of 7 April and had sent the two negotiators back with a letter full of diplomatic nonsense, but when Parker inadvertently admitted that he did not have a copy of Vansittart's proposals delivered in February, which was stated as the proposed basis of the current negotiations, everything fell apart. The experienced Danish negotiators brought the discussion back from a political treaty to a military armistice, despite this being completely contrary to Parker's orders from his own government. The Danes categorically refused an alliance but agreed to discuss a long-term armistice and not to do anything further to prepare their fleet for sea. Parker and Nelson were going way outside of their orders, which required the removal or destruction of the fleet. The two were however both in agreement that a bombardment of the harbour, if even feasible, was likely only to alienate the Danes further and was unlikely to destroy the Danish fleet and dockyard.

Parker appointed Nelson and Colonel Stewart to negotiate further on this armistice with Alexander Scott acting as their Secretary at the Amalienborg Palace on 8 April. The discussions began immediately, but were intense and intricate, with Denmark desperately trying to do the impossible and make a deal acceptable to both Britain and also to Russia as well. The length of the armistice was in fact the biggest stumbling block, Britain wanting a period of four months with a two-week notice period of a break; the Danes wanted only four to six weeks as a maximum. One awkward moment occurred when a Danish official whispered to a colleague that if there was no movement by the British, they might have to renew hostilities. Nelson understood enough French to realize what had been said and exploded with rage and retorted that if the Danes wanted to renew hostilities, then the British vessels would bombard the city that night. Apologies were instantly offered and accepted but the two sides were as far apart as ever. During an interval, the British representatives dined with the Crown Prince affably and Nelson and the

Prince eventually retired to another room for private discussions, but these still dragged on without any agreement.

All seemed useless, the two sides as far apart as ever, when Commander Lindholm interrupted with a message containing just four simple words, that changed everything instantly: 'The Tsar is dead'. With Tsar Paul gone, although no one could know how the new tsar would react, Denmark was no longer threatened by immediate reprisals for coming to an understanding with Britain.

The Crown Prince now felt comfortable agreeing to a fourteen-week armistice with a full two-week notice period of a break. Nelson tried to persuade the prince to change the agreement from a simple armistice into a peace treaty, but the Prince still felt unable to go that far. When Nelson reported to Parker on board *St George* late that night; it was purely a military armistice; exactly what the Danes had hoped for, even if it would last much longer than they had wanted. The representatives met on the morning of 9 April aboard *London* to sign the document, Parker ratified it and Nelson took the documents ashore to get the Prince's ratifying signature, which he duly did. Parker sent Colonel Stewart to London with his dispatches, but he was sent overland for speed.

The British ships were able to fully provision at Copenhagen and the British released some 1,800 prisoners of war and put them safely ashore at Tarbaek. Once fully supplied, the squadron moved through the Hollander Deep and over the Drogden shallows on 12 April, where the lightened *London*[1] still only just scraped over the shoals. Once in deeper water, the ships prepared to meet the Swedish squadron which was known to be at sea, but could not intercept them before they scuttled back into the safety of Karlskrona harbour, where the British squadron arrived on 19 April.

Before the British ships could proceed on towards the Russians at Reval, a Danish naval cutter *Le Petit Diable* appeared on 5 May carrying Colonel Stewart who had returned from London, having been sent home with news of the armistice. He brought the good news that Russia and Britain were now in dialogue and therefore the fleet was to delay any proposed actions and he also brought confirmation that Lord St Vincent had congratulated Parker on his victory at Copenhagen and that Parliament had passed a vote of thanks both to him and the fleet. However, he also brought an order from St Vincent, ordering Parker to return home immediately and to hand his command over to Horatio Nelson.

The Admiralty had already been concerned by reports coming – mostly, it has to be said, from Nelson – regarding Parker's procrastination and although

---

1 All of her guns were removed so that she floated over the shallows.

they fully appreciated the victory at Copenhagen, Nelson gained all the laurels. As commander-in-chief, Parker alone was blamed for what was considered in London as a very weak armistice following such a significant victory, which did not achieve anything like what he had been ordered to achieve. Parker was effectively called home in disgrace and never was employed on active service again. The fact that Parker was certainly past his best and needed to be retired cannot be denied; however, Nelson and Stewart carried out the armistice negotiations and neither felt that they could have achieved anything more in the way of concessions from the Danes. In this regard, Parker was the scapegoat for a thoroughly unsatisfactory expedition. Indeed, the reaction to the victory in Britain was distinctly muted, for beyond the thanks of Parliament, Nelson and any heirs were made Viscounts and Admiral Graves became a Knight Companion of the Bath, but no official medal was produced and the City of London did not vote its customary thanks to the fleet. The British public generally did not see the Danes as a threat nor as enemies and the whole event was largely seen as simply unfortunate.

Parker left for home the very same afternoon on the frigate *Blanche* and he arrived in England on 13 May when he wrote immediately to the Admiralty demanding a Court of Enquiry, but his letter was ignored and he was simply ordered to 'strike his flag'. Parker considered putting his defence in print, but Nelson wrote to him advising him not to continue with the plan; but he also assured him that 'I shall always consider myself as your old friend'.[1]

On 6 May Nelson took his fleet across the Baltic, leaving a small squadron to watch the Swedish ships in Karlskrona whilst he proceeded to Reval to make a demonstration off that port. He arrived there on 12 May, but being informed that the new Tsar – Alexander – was friendly towards Britain, but would not negotiate whilst his territory was threatened, Nelson quickly retired towards Denmark again. On 19 June Nelson handed his fleet over to Rear Admiral Pole and he sailed for home too.[2] Eventually, the fleet passed through the Sound and sailed for England on 21 July, their work done.

Sweden had broken with Denmark on news of the armistice, in a play for power with St Petersburg; in fact, the Swedish king even contemplated – if he was in receipt of Russian agreement – a sudden invasion of Denmark or more likely an attack on Norway; but he abandoned the idea, having failed to gain any meaningful support. Such antics did not play well in Denmark, where the great majority of the populace already suspected that the failure of the Swedish ships to arrive on time to support the Danes had been a deliberate ploy.

---

1 Howarth, p. 24.
2 Nelson sailed home on the brig HMS *Kite*.

Prussia had abandoned the League immediately on hearing the news of the Tsar's death; and Russia signed a convention with Britain on 17 June ending the Armed Neutrality and copies were sent to Denmark and Sweden demanding their immediate and unconditional ratification of the agreement. Both did ratify it, without much fuss, and the League of Armed Neutrality was no longer.

But who was the true victor of Copenhagen? Both Britain and Denmark viewed the outcome differently then and still do to some extent to this very day, both believing that they were the victors. In fact, Nelson became very angry when he read the official report of Commodore Fischer, who claimed that two British ships had struck their colours and that Nelson's humanitarian plea for a ceasefire was actually a ploy to save his ships from destruction as so many had run aground – depriving the Danes of their victory – although conveniently forgetting that many of these ships ran aground hours after the letter had been sent ashore.

Two Danish historians admit that 'the First Battle of Copenhagen can only be regarded as a British victory'.[1] Any Danish claims to the contrary are nothing less than preposterous. Danish poetry even described the battle in a classical context as the Greeks against Xerxes. Despite these unfortunate events, the view of the Danish general public remained generally positive towards the British until the later events of 1807 changed things. High ranking Danish generals and politicians were now almost openly pro-French but the populace remained ambivalent to both sides in the wars. Crown Prince Frederick is often mistakenly portrayed as a lover of Napoleon, in fact his personal view of the French Emperor would seem to be that he was indeed a great general but that he was also a dangerous usurper of power and a threat to the entire stability of Europe.

The reality is however, that Nelson's victory had been over the Danish reserve fleet,[2] and many of these vessels had been incapable of safely sailing out into the open sea. The victory had not destroyed the Danish seagoing fleet, nor did it force Denmark to abandon the Tsar or the League of Armed Neutrality. The Danish fleet had effectively been taken out of the League temporarily for the best part of four months, but if the new Tsar had finally proven to be equally anti-British, then the British fleet in the Baltic would have been in a very dangerous and challenging position, with a larger Russian

---

1 Glenthoj and Ottosen, p. 25.

2 Even Nelson was very aware of this, in his letter to St Vincent on 5 April 1801, he states in his defence 'It is true, our opponents were in hulks and floats only adapted for the position they were placed in; but that made our battle so much the harder, and victory so much the more difficult to obtain', Nicolas, Vol. IV, p. 336

fleet before them – although of a lesser quality – and with the possibility of another just as large joint Swedo–Danish fleet in their rear, blocking their safe passage out of the Baltic. With no friendly countries from which they could get supplies, the position of Nelson's fleet would have been very precarious at best.

In fact, the armistice should really be seen as a diplomatic failure for the British and had Tsar Paul not died, it is far from certain that Nelson's victory at Copenhagen would be seen as anything of the sort today. The Danes saw the battle as a moral victory and celebrated their brave defence with a Danish Defence Medal, which was inaugurated by Christian VII on 31 July 1801. This Danish medal was not universal; all officers who were present and had received no criticism of their conduct received a gold medal, the other ranks receiving a silver version – only if they had distinguished themselves – and the silver medal came with a pension for life of 15 rigsdaler per annum. This was the first-ever gallantry medal issued to Danish other ranks. In time, the British Naval General Service Medal, which was only inaugurated in 1848, had a bar issued, which participants who were still alive could claim.

The British fleet undoubtedly won the naval battle, but Britain lost the political war and they are only seen as the victors today because of a technical knock-out. In fact, the failure of the British fleet to achieve anywhere near what it was sent to accomplish, can be seen to be the root cause of why Britain felt compelled to send a much bigger fleet, this time with a large army in tow, back to Copenhagen, only six years later.

Chapter 10

Five Years of Relative Harmony

Denmark had lost a great deal more in 1801 than just her reserve fleet at Copenhagen. Much further afield, the British government had sent orders for a force of ships[1] in the West Indies, under the command of Rear Admiral John Duckworth, to liaise with Lieutenant General Thomas Trigge[2] at Barbados to obtain troops to deprive both Sweden and Denmark of their possessions in that part of the world. The squadron carrying 1,500 troops sailed on 16 March, without awaiting the arrival of expected reinforcements from home, in an attempt to overawe the islands before they had time to make any preparations for their defence.

Their first objective was Swedish St Barthelemy, as this was the furthest out and prone to variable winds. The squadron arrived off Grand Saline Bay on 20 March, a summons was almost instantly sent ashore and just as immediately accepted by the governor. A number of Danish and Swedish craft were captured and a small garrison left on the island.

At this juncture, a large fleet of sail caused some momentary consternation, until it was identified as the expected reinforcements from Britain under the protection of the *Proselyte*. With such an augmentation of their forces, they were emboldened to go beyond their instructions from government. They therefore progressed to the neighbouring French/Dutch island of St Martin on 24 March, having been joined the previous day, by the *Coromandel* carrying the 2nd West India Regiment. Immediately on arrival, the troops began landing and by early afternoon some 3,500 troops were ashore. After some brief skirmishing, the defenders were overwhelmed and the garrison of 400 men capitulated and were transported to Martinique.

1 This force consisted of *Leviathan* 74, *L'Unite* 38, *Diana* 38, *Andromeda* 32, *Southampton* 32, *Amphitrite* 28, *Hornet* 16, *Drake* 14, *L'éclair* 3, *Alexandria* (tender) and *Fanny*.

2 The troops involved were the 64th Foot, and the 8th West India Regiment

The troops immediately re-embarked and proceeded on 26 March directly to Danish St Thomas, arriving there on the 28th. A summons was again sent ashore and the governor immediately agreed to surrender, not only St Thomas, but the neighbouring St John and their dependencies. They did not rest there however, moving on immediately to Danish St Croix, which again capitulated without resistance on 31 March 1801. In May, some of the Danish East Indian possessions, namely Dansborg and Frederiksnagore, were also captured and were retained by the British until August 1802. However, within the year, France and Britain had signed a treaty of peace at Amiens on 27 March 1802, by which the Danish possessions were returned to their previous owners.

The uneasy peace only lasted just over a year, when because of seemingly irreconcilable differences, Britain declared war on France on 18 May 1803 and Europe was plunged into another dozen years of war. Denmark successfully avoided any involvement in these wars for four more years, by maintaining a scrupulous neutrality and avoiding further clashes with the British navy by abandoning the ill-fated policy of 'armed neutrality'. In fact, Denmark attempted to avoid antagonising either side, in the hope that her neutrality and her newly-assumed low profile might allow her to avoid becoming involved in the wars once again. Indeed, so desperate was Denmark to avoid conflict by assuming a mantle of anonymity, that the Danish government even banned her merchant ships from operating directly between Asia and Europe under the Danish flag, therefore avoiding a repeat of one of the biggest causes of the previous conflict with Britain. They had hopefully returned to the golden days of the 'prosperous neutrality of Denmark'.[1]

The Danes began to canvas the idea of a renewal of the union of the three kingdoms as 'Scandinavia', and a committee was even set up in Paris to consider the possibilities, but it was soon suppressed by Napoleon who saw it as a particularly inopportune moment; the idea was raised again occasionally between 1807 and 1814, but it never garnered any serious French support.

1805 saw the destruction of the Franco-Spanish fleet at Trafalgar, driving the final nail into the coffin of Napoleon's naval ambitions, but it also saw the complete destruction of an Austro-Russian army at Austerlitz, forcing Austria to sue for peace. The following year, saw the Prussian army, which had rested its laurels for far too long on the memory of Frederick the Great, humiliated at the joint battles of Jena and Auerstadt and their country overrun.

The only other major military power in mainland Europe, Russia, now found itself cornered in Poland and following an inconclusive battle at Eylau in February 1807, they were comprehensively defeated at the Battle of

---

1 Fortescue, Vol. VI, p, 49.

Friedland on 14 June 1807. Five days later, Napoleon met Tsar Alexander on a raft anchored in the middle of the River Niemen at the tiny village of Tilsit and a peace treaty was duly signed.

To all intents and purposes, these changes in the great-power blocks held little concern for neutral Denmark, but as with all such treaties, the devil was in the detail. Britain watched the rise and rise of France's Empire on mainland Europe with alarm, as Napoleon had begun to wage economic warfare on Britain, following the publication of his Berlin Decree on 21 November 1806, which forbade all correspondence or commerce between Britain and all areas of Europe which were under French control or influence. All ships having goods from Britain, or even ships having simply put into a British port, were deemed lawful prizes and were to be seized, as were all stocks of British goods held in warehouses in the areas of French influence. With the defeat of Britain's allies in Europe, the area under direct French control or allied to France, now stretched from the coastline of Spain to the Russian ports and from the heel of Italy to the Prussian ports on the Baltic coast. This left Denmark, Sweden and Portugal as the only countries in mainland Europe which remained open to continued trade with Britain and the only obstacles preventing the blockade from being complete.

If Napoleon was to ensure that the economic war was won, he would now have to assert his influence on these three states to complete his aim of preventing Britain trading with the entire European continent and thus ruining her economy, forcing the dominant sea power to finally bend to the dominant power on the Continent. Pressure was immediately put on Britain's long-standing ally Portugal, but it soon became obvious to Denmark, that Napoleon was now looking directly at them as well. On 6 August 1807, the Danish envoy in Paris was called in by Napoleon and an ultimatum was issued, either to join the blockade, go to war with Britain, or France would go to war with her. This unexpected demand caused consternation within the Danish government, but worse was to follow.

Britain's spies had quickly learnt of the Treaty of Tilsit, but they were soon sending further reports to London, with worrying information of a second 'secret treaty' signed by Napoleon and Tsar Alexander regarding the extension of the 'Continental Blockade'. The British government was also painfully aware that Napoleon's ambition was still not sated, indeed the ultimate aim of his economic war was not only the destruction of British commerce, but the end of its naval dominance and ultimately, the break-up of the fast-expanding British Empire. Napoleon had already announced a huge warship-building programme, with the aim of overwhelming the British navy, but the accession of the fleets of other maritime nations within Europe would also greatly increase the number of ships available to Napoleon in a very short timescale.

This further increased the advantages for Napoleon in exerting pressure on Portugal, Denmark and Sweden, all of whom of course also retained sizeable fleets, particularly Denmark. Britain also began to view these navies as vulnerable, fearful of these ships falling into French hands and thus significantly boosting the size of the French navy overnight. Whether they liked it or not, Denmark was now suddenly placed centre stage again, caught between the great warring nations and not clear what to do next for the best. What was clear however, was that the great era of Danish neutrality was about to come to an abrupt end no matter what she did.

Since the Battle of Copenhagen in 1801, Britain had looked upon Denmark as a friendly power and was very content to see the Danes revert to a true and strict neutrality. British exports continued to land at Tonningen without interruption and British ships continued to sail in and out of the Baltic without hindrance, in fact no less than 6,000 merchant ships had sailed out of the Baltic on route to Britain in those years.[1]

In 1806, Benjamin Garlike, British Minister to the Danish Court, had been ordered to challenge the Danes over rumours of Denmark closing its ports to British goods, particularly Tonningen, and closing the Sound to British shipping. However, Garlike was able to quickly dispel these fears, having obtained assurances from the Danish Foreign Minister, Joachim Bernstorff that the French had made no demands and that Denmark would defend her neutrality and independence against any aggressor. The minor crisis passed, but it did highlight how fragile the situation with Denmark remained.

With the Prussian defeat of that year and the subsequent arrival of French troops in the Prussian territory and the Hanseatic towns including Lubeck, Bremen and Hamburg, Crown Prince Frederick's army encamped in Holstein to protect their borders now appeared insensitive, if not provocative and he decided to withdraw his main force into Schleswig behind the protection of the River Edjer and from where a further retreat into the island of Zealand was much more practical if necessary. The war had then moved further eastwards into Poland and the Danes gave a collective sigh of relief, little thinking that the problem would soon return to haunt them. Britain looked on with little concern, but plans were prepared for the capture of the island of Heligoland as a base for their trade, if Tonningen was closed to British goods.

The Danish navy still remained a considerable force, but the army had other ideas, with plans to build up to 300 oared gunboats which could more easily support the army in their operations and they suggested a gradual reduction in the number of ships of the line to just twelve, which was accepted by the Crown Prince. Garlike heard of the plans in late 1806 and he reported to the

---

1 Munch-Petersen, p. 46.

British government that France might attempt to purchase any spare ships, despite acknowledging that the Danes would prefer to sell them to Russia.[1] In fact, the Danish plan had never envisaged selling off any ships, but this was the only version of the plan that the British government received and it understandably caused a great deal of concern.

The Baltic waters were further muddied by claims of King Gustavus IV of Sweden that the Danish withdrawal from Holstein had been co-ordinated with the French, to put the Swedish enclave of Pomerania under greater threat and he also claimed that the Danes might land troops in Sweden in support of the French. At the same time, the Danish government saw these Swedish troop movements as a threat to themselves and the defences of Copenhagen were prepared, just in case. The problem was, that Lord Howick, the Foreign Secretary, was convinced that these preparations, although purportedly against Sweden, were actually for use against British interests.

Sweden had enjoyed a large British subsidy for a number of years to maintain its army; she had thus remained extremely loyal, but had achieved virtually nothing for all the expense. Sweden was offered other extensive territories by Napoleon, in recompense for the loss of Stralsund, Gustavus refused to countenance such an exchange, but his refusal was nothing more than mere passive defiance.

When Pierrepont, the British envoy to Sweden, suggested that the Swedish army should be increased in size, King Gustavus simply refused until he received a larger subsidy from Britain! The British government however, refused further subsidies purely to see it spent for Sweden's defence of her own backyard.

On 28 January 1807, Marshal Mortier marched a French army into Pomerania and swiftly forced the Swedish troops to fall back into Stralsund, where he began a formal siege. Suddenly Gustavus changed his tune, offering to attack in Pomerania if supported by British troops rather than receiving a subsidy. Further Swedish troops were sent to Stralsund to bolster the defence and another 5,000 were planned for that coming March. These troops were retained deliberately in southern Sweden to seize £80,000 in gold, a shipment being sent as part of the British subsidy to Russia – supposedly owed by Russia to Sweden since 1791, or so he claimed. A large part of Mortier's corps had been called elsewhere and with his increased numbers General Essen, commanding at Stralsund drove the French out of Pomerania temporarily.

However, Mortier returned and the Swedes were soon holed up in Stralsund and under siege once again. On 20 April Prussia had agreed to supply 5,000 troops to aid the defence of Stralsund and it was not long before

---

1 Munch-Petersen, p. 51.

they arrived under the command of General Gebhardt von Blücher. Gustavus renewed his request for British troops and specifically mentioned the King's German Legion (KGL). By an agreement signed on 23 June, Britain agreed to subsidise another 16,000 Swedish troops, to send 10,000 muskets for the use of the Prussian army and to send General William Schaw Cathcart – a man described by Francis Jackson as better 'making bows in the drawing room . . . than commanding an army'[1] with 10,000 KGL troops to Stralsund, where they would be under the command of King Gustavus, although George III reserved the right to call his troops away for other uses at any time. Cathcart and his troops duly arrived and disembarked on Rugen Island on 8 July where the waters were so shallow that it took an entire week to land his force by boats. Cathcart was alarmed to find Stralsund close to defeat and kept his troops on Rugen, where they were safe from the French.

This mild paranoia in London regarding the Baltic grew even further in January 1807 when Howick received Garlike's report on the state of the Danish navy. Garlike was not a sailor, therefore he employed Captain James Dunbar, the commander of HMS *Astraea*, which was in Copenhagen for repairs having run aground. Dunbar reported that all of the ships of the Danish fleet were in excellent condition and that all of the material required to make the ships ready for sea were in the dockyard stores for them. He therefore felt that the ships could be made ready for sea within a month in the season, although he did admit that the want of adequate seamen might delay them some time. Dunbar had simply reported on the standard preparation of the Danish fleet and gave no indication that preparations were actually under way to send the Danish fleet to sea. Howick, however, saw the preparedness of the Danes as a specific threat

At this point, the British government ordered Vice Admiral Sir John Duckworth to return home as soon as he could from his present station in the Mediterranean. Meanwhile, Thomas Grenville, the First Lord of the Admiralty, ordered that ten or twelve ships of the line should be prepared to sail for the Baltic in late February. By the end of January, however, the Foreign Secretary had calmed down a little and now believed that Danish preparations were genuinely defensive against the Swedes and the fleet was not sent, allowing tensions to ease a little.

The British government had, however, finally reacted in January to Napoleon's Berlin Decree, with their counter Orders in Council published on 7 January 1807, which declared that any vessel trading between two ports which both specifically banned British ships, was liable to be taken as a prize, but it did not ban trade between French and neutral states, such as Denmark.

---

1 Letter from Francis Jackson to Lord Hawkesbury, dated 28 August 1807.

The Danish envoy in London, Johan Rist, was relieved to learn how reasonable and understanding the orders were regarding neutrals and he wrote home quite pleased at the British attitude. The government in Copenhagen viewed things very differently however, vehemently demanding that Rist should deliver a strongly-worded protest to the British government, pointing out that they would have dire consequences for the Danish merchant fleet and claiming that they had complained equally against the Berlin Decree – a claim the British government did not believe.

Although the Grenville administration fell in late March, Thomas Grenville remained at the Admiralty until early April and one of his last actions was to order Commodore Keats to proceed to Yarmouth to take command of a squadron of sixteen of the line that was assembling there, until Duckworth could arrive to take overall command.

With the German coast now in French hands, the British navy renewed its blockade of the coastline and when Denmark requested as usual for concessions for the Danish ports of Gluckstadt and Altona, they were readily granted. Despite the French occupation of the German coastline, it appears that the local French commanders were easily bribed to look the other way and British exports into Tonnigen were at an all-time high.

George Canning took the post of Foreign Secretary and his initial decision was to maintain the relatively friendly terms of his predecessor and the ships ordered for Danish waters continued to wait at Yarmouth for orders to proceed. In fact, Rist would appear to have taken a liking for Canning, judging that he would continue a liberal approach to the Orders in Council; but Canning had deep seated suspicions that the Danes were in reality much more inclined towards the French, but that there was no benefit in causing a dispute whilst the war had played out in Poland.

But now things had changed dramatically . . .

Chapter 11

Rapid Escalation

The British had regularly used the small port of Husum in Schleswig as their entry point into the European postal system and a regular packet service plied between Harwich and Husum. This post carried amongst other things, illicit trade deals, correspondence with British agents and reports on French operations. This of course put the Danes in a very awkward situation when France sent repeated demands for these packet boats to be refused access to Husum. The Danes however, did not want to close the port to the British for fear of reprisals, but at the same time, a blank refusal might lead to the French forcing the issue. As usual Denmark found herself in a very awkward position, trying to placate both British and French demands, an impossible and ultimately hopeless task. Joachim Bernstorff, the Danish Foreign Minister, made the suggestion of landing the mails at Danish Heligoland and that Danish ships would actually land the correspondence in Europe; however, this suggestion soon foundered with the realisation that the French would soon see through this subterfuge. Garlike was fully involved in putting these concerns to the Danish government, but ultimately, he was reassured by the fact that the Danes were under no illusions: war with Britain would lead to the total loss of their commerce and the utter devastation of their economy. Garlike reported to London that the Danes had no wish to break with Britain, but he did foresee that France might ultimately force them to do so. Canning, who already held a negative view of Denmark's stance, seems to have read enough in Garlike's reports to confirm his suspicions of Danish perfidy; it is certain that Garlike had not intended such an impression, but that unfortunately was how they were construed. Indeed, reading the correspondence of Christian Bernstorff, the Danish Prime Minister, to his envoys abroad, he clearly betrays a dislike of French dominance and rejoices in any French reverses; these comments in his official correspondence must betray the honest views of the Danish government. Denmark hoped that Napoleon's star would wane, but they would never admit this publicly or join any coalition against him, as they felt themselves very vulnerable to attack. What Canning saw as Danish fawning and obsequious behaviour towards Napoleon, was truly borne out of nothing more than abject fear. The Crown Prince's letters to his brother-in-law, Duke Frederick Christian of Augustenburg, betray a very similar view.[1] On 30 December 1806 the Danes had even declared that if Napoleon demanded the closing of Danish ports to British ships, that it would then regard Britain as 'its natural ally', but this bold statement seems to have gone unnoticed in London. Sweden had even offered to set up a joint Scandinavian army based in Holstein, but Denmark refused, not trusting her neighbour's real objectives. This again caused real anger within the British government. Indeed, when French troops entered Danish Holstein whilst pursuing fleeing Prussians in 1806, the Danes had instantly taken up arms and forced the French troops to withdraw, although this does not appear to have seriously harmed Franco-Danish relations. Even demands from Paris for the British mail route to the Continent, which passed through the Danish duchies, to be closed, were ignored.

The question of the detention of neutral ships unfortunately soon raised the temperature once again. In 1805, thirty-five Danish vessels were taken, but all but three released by the prize courts. In 1806 however, the figure reached over 150 and the prize courts began to regularly declare them as valid prizes; the levels of seizures therefore remained just as high in the early months of 1807.[2] The Danes protested vehemently, but their recent history of selling false papers and concealing prohibited cargoes did not help their cause one bit. Rist wrote a protest after each batch of detentions and each letter became progressively more abusive in its tone. This situation came to a head when two vessels were detained whilst on route to Tunis and Algiers, carrying the year's 'tribute money' to the Barbary Pirates, to buy safe passage for their ships. Canning then wrote to Garlike, not to demand Rist's removal, but merely to suggest it to the Danish government; but he also wondered if it was being done under higher orders, to give a cause for a rift in their relations. Canning therefore sought to force Denmark to show their true hand.

Rist continued to receive the support of his government and British representations were only tardily and inadequately answered. The poor atmosphere generated, did not cause the crisis to come, but it certainly ensured that relations were already poor and very strained when the real crisis did occur, making it very difficult to prevent things escalating very quickly.

The crisis began relatively innocuously in early June 1807, when Canning received a letter from Lord Pembroke, the new British Ambassador to Vienna,

---

1 Munch-Petersen, p. 75.
2 The numbers detained were eighteen in April and thirteen in May 1807.

who had landed en route at Memel[1] and had proceeded to Copenhagen on the *Astraea* before travelling south towards Austria. He toured the Danish dockyard and wrote to Canning that same night, that the Danish defences were fully prepared and as many as twenty Danish ships of the line were 'fit to go to sea with all their stores &c named and numbered'. This backed up a report previously received from Captain James Dunbar of the *Astraea* in December 1806 and a second from him, written a little later, confirmed his views. Pembroke, a professional soldier, had clearly been influenced by Dunbar to believe that the Danish fleet was actually ready to sail, but the evidence is clear that what he actually saw was the Danish ships 'mothballed' with all of their stores ready to be embarked in quayside warehouses as previously described in 1801. Canning read this – as Pembroke had clearly intended – as a warning that the Danish fleet and defences were fully prepared for war, but nothing could be farther from the truth. In fact, the Danish naval records show that in the first six months of 1807 that only three ships of the line, two frigates and three brigs had been fitted out for sea service.[2] This was standard Danish practice, when two ships were sent to Norway each year for the summer months, two more routinely sailed to the Danish West Indies; whilst two other were used to keep up the skills of the naval reserve corps kept permanently at Copenhagen. The only slightly unusual feature of the preparations for this year, was the fitting out of a third ship of the line and an additional brig, but, this had been authorized specifically to convey the Grand Duchess Maria Pavlovna, Tsar Alexander's sister and married to the Prince of Saxe-Weimar, from Copenhagen to St Petersburg. This voyage did not eventually happen, as Tilsit changed the diplomatic situation so as to make the passage unnecessary, when both ships were promptly decommissioned once again.[3] There is also no evidence at all that naval reservists were being called up to man more ships, a clear indication that Denmark had no intention of arming its fleet. Such a report of serious naval preparations could only mean one thing to Canning, the Danes were planning to break with Britain and were preparing their defences, in order to avoid a repeat of what happened six years before.

---

1 Modern-day Klaipėda in Lithuania.
2 The author has been struck quite often, in his research of the build-up to the crisis of 1807, how remarkably similar they are – due to the masses of misinformation received by government and their own tendency to read into the reports they received, the worst possible predictions – to the Blair government and their decision to enter the Iraq war in more recent times.
3 Munch-Petersen, p. 79.

Two other naval officers made reports to Garside around this time, Lieutenant Hanchett of the *British Fair* and Captain Francis Beauman of the *Procris*, both professional mariners and both concluding that the Danish ships were 'in ordinary' with almost all of their guns and stores ashore in warehouses, Beauman in particular stating that 'there is not at present the shadow of appearance for the equipment of a fleet'.[1] Unfortunately such evidence from these professional men did not arrive until far too late to influence things, but in all honesty Canning would probably have still chosen to believe the previous alarming reports. Things were to escalate quickly with the news of the Treaty of Tilsit.

The British government remained blissfully unaware of the crushing Russian defeat at Friedland on 14 June until the end of that month, when news of it arrived from Lord Granville Levenson-Gower, who had been sent out again to Tsar Alexander's court to try to ensure that Russia and Britain remained on friendly terms. However, the first snippets of news of a peace treaty having been signed, came from the British government's man in Altona, Edward Thornton, who had been forced to flee to Danish Holstein, when the French took Hamburg. Here he had met and formed a friendship with the exiled Duke of Mecklenburg-Schwerin, whose son just happened to be brother-in-law to the Tsar. Napoleon had made the gesture at Tilsit of reinstating the dukedom and Alexander had written to the Duke to convey the good news. The Duke shared his letters with Thornton, who thus obtained early news of the Franco-Russian peace and sent this information on to London. Peace between these two giants quickly led to renewed rumours of French expansion into Schleswig and Holstein and that their ports would soon be forced to shut to British ships. This rumour was apparently given legs by Alexander Cockburn, the British consul at Tonningen, who apparently wrote to Canning warning of an imminent French invasion, which simply increased the alarm in London. Cockburn panicked to such an extent that some forty British merchant ships sailed immediately, many unladen, to escape the supposed invasion. The French newspaper reports from the end of April had talked openly of 50,000 troops being sent to the area around Hamburg, these were clearly designed to influence the Danes. However, later letters from Cockburn and Thornton continually talk of troops being removed to other theatres and of the non-arrival of the expected troops. Napoleon had clearly encouraged these rumours to keep Central Europe quiet whilst his forces were marching ever further eastwards into Poland. Soon the initial scare subsided a little, and British merchant shipping returned to their normal operations, Thornton reporting that the rumours appeared to have been

---

1 Munch-Petersen, p. 80.

started by French merchants at Hamburg, who had snapped up the British goods already in storage incredibly cheaply as merchants sought to offload their stocks before they were confiscated.

However, Thornton did continue to expound his belief that if France and Russia had indeed signed a peace treaty, then it was highly likely that France would invade Holstein and even possibly take control of all of Denmark, threatening not only Britain's last remaining opening for landing their goods on mainland Europe, but even securing access into the Baltic, so vital for Britain's general trade and more specifically for naval stores. He therefore ventured to advise the government to consider the use of force to occupy and hold the island of Zealand. All of these rumours and warnings were actually premature, but what they did do, was to convince Canning that the British government needed to act and act quickly.

Reports from British spies in France were full of peace deals with Russia and rumours that a Spanish force in the Hamburg region would be sent into Denmark. Some of them went further however, with agents such as Louis Michel Danican, a former soldier in the French Royalist army, reporting that once Denmark was captured, the Danish navy would be used to land Spanish troops in Northern Ireland, whilst the south of Ireland would be invaded by French troops sailing from Bordeaux. Britain was always particularly nervous of French attacks on Ireland, which would be supported by the United Irishmen; and any such rumours caused an immediate reaction.

There is in fact no evidence at all, in Napoleon's correspondence, of any intention by him of launching such an invasion of Ireland at this time, but it certainly helped Napoleon's designs to keep Britain nervous of such a threat whilst he dealt with Russia. Napoleon did write to Admiral Decres in late April 1807, instructing him to order naval preparations at Brest and to communicate with the United Irishmen regarding a descent on Ireland. The rumours were however, merely that, they were clearly designed to keep the British occupied whilst he was far away in Poland and he expected the British to react defensively, retaining large numbers of troops in Ireland to counter any supposed threat of invasion, rather than landing troops on the Continent, in order to provide a diversion for their embattled allies. What he did not anticipate was that the British government would conclude that offensive action was the best form of defence. Canning had already been convinced of the need to act and needed little more excuse to do so.

Chapter 12

The Cabinet Deliberates

The British Cabinet had begun to discuss the option of sending a fleet to the Baltic on 10 July, but over the ensuing eleven days, their deliberations led to a hardening in attitudes and by the end, the decision had been made to send a very large fleet with a specific goal in mind.

The various deliberations can only be guessed at now, but certainly the arrival of dispatches from Levenson Gower informing them of the telling news that he had been excluded from contact with any of the Russian statesmen at Tilsit, certainly had its effect. The obvious conclusion was that Russia and France were drawing closer together and that Britain was to be excluded from the Continent.

For months, all of the reports, rumours and conjectures had indicated a French advance into Denmark in the near future and although British support would be offered to help defend Denmark in such a scenario, it was far from clear that the Danes would actually welcome or accept it; nor was it clear whether they would really resist such an attack by the French at all. Either way, the loss of Husum and Tonningen were almost certain and the capture of the Danish fleet and closure of the Sound to British vessels very likely. The rumoured plans to use the Danish fleet in an invasion of Ireland was simply the icing on the cake. The invasion of Denmark by the French would have dire consequences for Britain and although it was impossible for Britain alone to prevent it, they could certainly soften the blow by taking the initiative in the only way they could.

The Cabinet therefore began serious deliberations on the possibilities of successfully preventing the Danish fleet from being utilized by Napoleon. This could be achieved in a number of different ways, depending on the forces deployed, but one thing cannot be ignored at this point. The entire operation now planned, would entail the removal or destruction of the Danish fleet, the very same fleet which Parker and Nelson had signally failed to remove or destroy six years previously. It needs to be understood that the operation of 1807 only became necessary because the job had not been completed in

1801. Such a scenario is not unusual in history, one example being the two Gulf Wars in the recent past, but this has usually occurred when the military are prevented from finishing the job by politicians, all too eager, perhaps understandably, to bring the fighting to an end. On this occasion, the military themselves were too eager to end the fighting, almost certainly due to the uncomfortable position they found themselves in, but also because they did not feel that it was a 'just' war and they were too keen to bring the fighting to an end themselves, without achieving their ultimate goal. That is why the two British attacks on Copenhagen must be seen as one whole and indivisible event.

A fleet attack alone would not succeed: the last attempt had shown that only too clearly and the Danes had improved their defences further since then. There was also now a very high risk that the Russian fleet would arrive in support. Nelson had been unable to enforce the destruction or removal of the Danish fleet, so what could mere mortals achieve against stronger defences?

Canning therefore sought every way in which to present the evidence to the Cabinet in a form that supported his views; that a pre-emptive attack was not only desirable but essential. A British fleet in the Baltic would, he claimed, ensure the safety of British merchant shipping and therefore would not be a declaration of war in its own right, but it could deter the Danes from continuing their rumoured preparations for their fleet to sail. These supposed preparations were, as we have seen, actually non-existent, but Canning and his Cabinet colleagues were, to be fair, not aware of this during their deliberations. Canning had worked hard and he had manipulated the evidence in order to gain Cabinet support, but he still could not be certain of it. In the event, the Cabinet proved unanimous in their decision to send a fleet to the Baltic with a sizeable army on board, fully ready to deal with the Danes if they would not comply with British demands.

On 14 July Lord Mulgrave, First Lord of the Admiralty, wrote to King George III asking for his acceptance of the proposal to send between twenty and twenty-two ships of the line to the Baltic. The fleet would have three specific aims; to observe the Danish fleet, to counteract any French moves on Schleswig and Holstein and suitably vaguely 'to execute such prompt and vigorous operations as the circumstances of the moment may point out'.[1] The King readily approved and agreed to Mulgrave's suggestion that Admiral Sir James Gambier would command the fleet.[2]

---

1 *Correspondence of George III*, Vol. IV, p. 604.

2 It seems that Gambier was third choice for the expedition, Admirals William Young and Sir Charles Cotton having been approached earlier, both declining the position: *Naval Chronicle*, Vol. IV, p. 75.

Canning had got his way and the wheels quickly began to turn for getting the expedition under way, but he still looked to clear any potential obstacles out of the way. Garlike was regularly writing frantically from Denmark in an attempt to correct Pembroke's observations and he needed to be silenced. Canning took the opportunity of using the age-old government device of removing a problem by promoting him, swiftly removing Garlike from the scene and replacing him with Brook Taylor, who came with the added benefit of having the King's ear – his brother, Sir Herbert Taylor, being the King's private secretary. Taylor was sent out with instructions to counter Danish protests regarding the size of the British fleet now openly sailing for Baltic waters, by explaining the need to support Britain's ally Sweden, to help support troop movements between Sweden and Pomerania, to protect the British troops on Rugen and to protect British merchant shipping in that sea.

Until 16 July, all deliberations centred around a purely naval expedition, but things soon changed dramatically. On 17 July Lord Castlereagh, the Secretary for War, wrote to the King, reiterating the proposal already approved by the king, but then expanding further on the deliberations of the Cabinet. The sea defences at Copenhagen had been greatly improved since 1801 and it was obvious that a purely naval attack would be one of great hazard – just as the first one had proven to be. Therefore, he added to the proposal that a sizeable force of soldiers were also carried, with the intention of 'a conjoint operation' to take possession of the Danish fleet. If the fleet carried an army with them, there was a decent possibility of landing troops on Zealand, which was weakly garrisoned and besieging the city, whilst the navy prevented the Crown Prince and the bulk of the Danish army, which lay in Holstein, from interfering by closing the Great Belt.

Providentially, Britain actually had an army available and ready to be utilized in such an expedition, a rare event indeed. A force of 10,000 troops of the King's German Legion commanded by General Cathcart, had sailed to Swedish Pomerania.[1] They were to aid the troops of the King of Sweden to retain Stralsund. The first division of these troops were landed on the island of Rugen on 8 July, with the remainder not far behind. A further 16,000 troops had been assembled in England in preparation for a projected landing in Germany or Holland, designed to cause a diversion and relieve the pressure

---

1 It is often stated that the force under Cathcart consisted of the entire KGL, except for the heavy dragoons. This is incorrect, as it actually consisted of 1st and 2nd Light Dragoons, the 1st and 2nd Light Battalions, the 3rd, 4th, 5th, 6th, 7th and 8th Line Battalions with the Garrison battalion and the depot companies, plus artillery. The 3rd Light Dragoons and the 1st and 2nd Line Battalions arrived in Denmark with Gambier's fleet.

on Russia, just as Napoleon had predicted. Events had, however, moved on at a pace and suddenly the window of opportunity had closed, but this meant that there was a sizeable force which was readily available to sail to Denmark at very short notice.

Castlereagh therefore proposed adding two further recommendations to the original: the admiral should prevent the passage of Danish troops from Jutland onto Zealand and that the disposable force at home should be prepared for service without delay. This was a very significant escalation in the scope of the expedition, but it was approved of by the King. Gambier was informed of the changes to his instructions and was also ordered to prevent, by force if necessary, any Danish ships of the line trying to sail out of Copenhagen dockyard. With this move, Castlereagh took effective control of the day-to-day running of the expedition from Canning and Mulgrave, it was now his operation.

Chapter 13

The Fleet Forms

On the same day that Admiral Gambier was sent his detailed instructions, Castlereagh also wrote to General Cathcart at Rugen, explaining the situation. Castlereagh ordered his troops to withdraw from Pomerania and to join up with the expedition whilst Cathcart was to take overall command of all the land forces; this was received on 3 August. Only now did Castlereagh spell out British demands fully; Denmark was to join Britain as an ally or remain truly neutral, but whatever their relationship, the minimum acceptable security was that the Danes must grant the British control of their fleet: this demand was non-negotiable. Once in British hands, the Danish fleet could not be used to close the Sound, nor could it be used to carry an invasion force to Ireland – without a navy Denmark would be neutered and the gates to the Baltic left wide open.

Before military operations began, however, an opportunity for the Danes to simply hand their fleet over without a struggle had to be at least attempted. Brook Taylor was deemed too junior for such a vital role and Francis Jackson, a very experienced but temporarily unemployed diplomat was selected. Jackson was briefed and was prepared to sail immediately with Taylor, but he was detained by an unexpected delay. The King was starting to have grave misgivings over the entire business and was no longer happy to give his unqualified approval. This caused a minor crisis for the Cabinet, but the Prime Minister William Bentinck, the Duke of Portland, attended on the King to explain all of the reasons underlying the Cabinet's decision and he was eventually able to gain at least a grudging acquiescence, although the King made no bones about making it clear that such an assault on Denmark would in his view, be 'immoral'. However, his approval had been given and orders flowed out of the Admiralty and Horse Guards on 21 July. War preparations began apace, but Canning, publicly at least, claimed that the Danes would surrender their fleet without a fight once they saw the futility of opposing such a large expedition. Privately no one believed that the Danes would hand over their fleet without a fight, indeed Jackson later claimed that his mission had been hopeless from the start, as 'there was not from the first to the last a single one in which there appeared the slightest glimmering of hope that it would succeed'.[1]

Up to this point, rather surprisingly, given their close ties for many years, little concern had been raised regarding Russia's reaction to the planned attack on Denmark. This was, however a major concern of the King's and part of the reason for his very reluctant approval to the whole thing. The government's view seems to have been, that Russia had been forced reluctantly into a peace treaty with France for the moment, but that did not necessarily mean that the friendly relationship between Britain and Russia had to end. Indeed, the peace treaty with Napoleon was viewed by the British government as perhaps a necessary short-term evil, which would give Russia the time to rebuild her forces, before she renewed the fight against Napoleon. However, this presumption was about to take a serious knock.

During the early hours of 22 July, Canning received a letter from a French émigré, Louis de Launay, the Count d'Antraigues, who resided at Barnes. He had spent his years in exile in Britain producing anti-Republican pamphlets, whilst regularly supplying the government with reports from the Continent, many of them, it has to be said, of questionable validity whilst also supplying reports on the political situation in Britain to the Tsar. The letter claimed that he had intelligence from a Russian general[2] who had been present at the meetings between Napoleon and Alexander at Tilsit – and one passage stood out above all others. It claimed that Napoleon had proposed a maritime league combining the fleets of France and Russia with those of Sweden, Denmark, Portugal and Spain, all to be employed against Britain. It was reported that Alexander had not replied to the proposition, but that the correspondent believed that he would eventually be persuaded to accept it. The evidence would indicate that d'Antraigues had received correspondence from Tilsit and that some parts of his report were true and had to come from someone who was there; however, the central claim regarding a league of Europe's navies does not correspond with any of the correspondence or memoirs emanating from these talks and does not appear to have any basis in truth. Although certainly false, it dovetailed perfectly with the British government's greatest fear, that Napoleon would combine the navies of continental Europe to challenge directly the superiority of Britain at sea. This simply hardened

---

1 Munch-Petersen, p. 112.

2 Munch-Petersen has produced compelling evidence that the correspondent was Prince Vassili Troubetskoi, one of Alexander's aides de camp and well placed to report on the meeting of the Emperors at Tilsit.

the Cabinet's view on the attack on Denmark; the need to remove the Danish fleet had now become even more urgent and vital.

It did, however, force the British government to actually consider the Russians in their plans. Prussia had closed its ports to British ships after Tilsit and it was confidently expected that Russia would soon follow suit, although no such stipulation had been published in the public treaty. There was now a real possibility that the fourteen or so Russian ships of the line at the ports of Cronstadt and Reval, fit for sea, could interfere in the operations against Denmark or more worryingly, even combine with the Danish fleet. Canning instantly sent Sir Stephen Shairp, consul-general at St Petersburg, back to his post (he had been home on leave), and ordered him to expedite the departure of all British shipping in Russian ports with their cargoes of invaluable naval stores and then to communicate the state of the Russian navy to Admiral Gambier who would by then be in the Sound at the entrance to the Baltic.

Meanwhile, Russia formally advised the British government of the peace treaty and offered officially to act as go-between in any talks between Britain and France. Canning prevaricated, advising his diplomats to stall and to avoid entering into any form of talks; but more disconcerting were the rumours that there was indeed a second 'secret' Tilsit treaty.

Jackson sailed for Denmark with two treaties in his portmanteau, one to conclude an alliance and the other to guarantee the continuance of Denmark's neutrality. But, whatever the outcome of his talks, Britain must be granted possession of the Danish fleet in 'safe-keeping'. Jackson could confirm that the fleet would be restored at the end of the war and could also promise that Britain would pay £100,000 per annum for the use of the Danish fleet; and if necessary Britain would make the surrender of the fleet appear to be 'by force' to avoid a reaction from Napoleon, or Denmark could sell the fleet to Britain at a value agreed with Admiral Gambier. However, there was the possibility that the Danes would initially reject the British ultimatum, but agree once British troops had landed on Zealand, in this case the same terms could be agreed, the British allowing the Danes to keep their frigates and smaller ships, for their own defence and that a number of foreign territories could be granted to Denmark as a sweetener. Clearly, Britain sought every which way to avoid having to attack Denmark, but ultimately the Danish fleet must be taken away from Napoleon's grasp at all costs.

Simultaneously, misinformation was released in the press, claiming that the Danes were blocking the Sound and seizing British ships and goods, all of which had absolutely no basis in truth. This did cause some popular clamour for the British government to deal with this upstart Denmark, but in reality, few people in Britain felt any great animosity towards the Danes.

Canning was also keen to ensure that the Danes did not have too long a warning of the British fleet, so as to prevent them from further strengthening their defences. Jackson was therefore given a specific timetable, requiring the Crown Prince to agree to the British demands within twelve days: this included the time required for him to arrive in Kiel from London, giving the Danish government no more than a week to decide in real terms. Simultaneous letters from Canning to Taylor at Copenhagen, informing him of Jackson's mission, also gave him permission to inform Joachim Bernstorff of proceedings, but he was also instructed to emphasize that any new preparations made to defend the city would cause the immediate landing of British troops and the commencement of operations to seize the Danish fleet. A letter to Cathcart also informed him of the mission and ordered that if he had not received news from Jackson within eight days of the receipt of the letter, he was to disembark his forces and if he had not heard within twelve days, then he was to commence operations to gain control of the Danish fleet. This covered the eventuality that Jackson was detained by the Danes and prevented from communicating his situation, it did not unfortunately cover the fact that Cathcart, nor his troops, were anywhere near Copenhagen at the time. One clear directive was added, that no delay was to be brooked and under no situation were the envoys or the military to delay operations whilst awaiting any requested clarification from London – they were to trust their own judgement and act on it with vigour.

Naval preparations had been finalized rapidly, as a large number of ships had already been at Yarmouth for some time waiting for the orders to sail. Only five days after the first orders had been promulgated, Admiral Gambier had already sailed for the Kattegat with a purely naval force of seventeen ships of the line, and twenty-one smaller vessels.[1] At the same time, the troops were rapidly assembling at the four embarkation ports of Hull, Harwich, Chatham and Portsmouth and by 30 July, the first fleet of fully-laden troop transports had sailed.

The government put in force a complete embargo of the British coast for four days either side of the date of sailing of the fleet, to avoid news of the expedition reaching Paris too early, but this was only partially successful, with reports that members of the Danish Ministry of Trade as well as merchants at Copenhagen, were convinced that the intentions of the British were hostile.[2] The Danish government still could not bring themselves to believe that the British could be guilty of such a crime. Bernstorff even brushed aside a warning from the Danish consul in Portsmouth in very similar vain.

---

1 A large number of reinforcements were sent later; see Appendix 10 for details.
2 Glenthoj and Ottesen, p. 29.

Chapter 14

The Fleet Arrives in the Sound

Gambier's fleet entered the Kattegat, after a relatively uneventful passage, on 2 August, when he immediately detached a squadron[1] under Commodore Keats to ensure that all communication between the island of Zealand and the Danish mainland was prevented. Keats was the perfect man for such an independent role, constantly patrolling difficult and dangerous waters with numerous shoals. He sent the *Mosquito* sloop in advance to sound the passage through the Great Belt, marking the banks and shoals as she went. Much of the work in these difficult waters would be undertaken by the much more manoeuvrable and shallower-draughted frigates and lesser warships: the ships of the line were there to protect these smaller ships from any Danish battleships sailing from Copenhagen into the Great Belt, a very possible scenario.

The following day Gambier's remaining ships entered the Sound and exchanged a polite gun salute with Cronborg Castle as the fleet sailed southward and anchored off Elsinore. The Danes had treated the British squadron with courtesy, assuming that it was intending to pass into the Baltic and having no suspicion of its true destination. Canning's letter had yet to arrive in Copenhagen and this had allowed the British fleet to pass its first hurdle – Cronborg Castle – without any problems, although Parker's fleet had already proven that it was no real threat in 1801.

Having anchored at Elsinore, the British fleet remained here for a fortnight, showing no hostile intentions, merely watching to ensure the Danish fleet did not emerge. In fact, the Danes had only one frigate at sea – as usual – guarding the mouth of Copenhagen harbour, the 32-gun frigate *Frederiksvaern*, which

---

1 The ships allocated to Keats were *Ganges* 74, *Vanguard* 74, *Orion* 74, *Nassau* 64, *Sibylle* 38, *Franchise* 36, *Nymphe* 36 and the ten brigs *Cossack, Leveret, Alert, Mosquito, Goshawk, Alacrity, Acute, Tigress, Urgent* and *Desperate*. Later the ships *Superb* 74, *Dictator, Leda, Banterer, Combatant, Halcyon, Procris, Sappho, Fearless, Turbulent, Flamer, Mariner* and *Intelligent* were added.

The British fleet passes Cronborg Castle.

continued to lie peacefully at anchor at Elsinore, within cannon-shot of the British fleet, seemingly unaware of the veiled threat that they posed.

Admiral Gambier was a cautious and very religious man, a dangerous mix in the eyes of most sailors, therefore he was not short of critics within the fleet. He was known variously as 'Jemmy the Good', 'Dismal Jimmie' or 'Jimmy the Miserable' by his sailors. He had initially to wait for the army to arrive, as the option of his ships attacking the heavily-defended harbour alone was never a realistic one, despite the fact that the Danes had virtually no ships ready to defend the city unlike six years previously. The force of 18,000 troops had sailed by the time he had arrived at Elsinore and the great bulk of these troops had arrived in two huge convoys on 7 and 8 August, allowing him to consider launching land operations as and when required.

The secret as to their eventual destination was so well kept in the fleet that it wasn't until 7 August that Surgeon Chambers[1] of *Prometheus* recorded in his daily diary that he finally knew for certain that the fleet was going to Copenhagen, despite the fact that General Arthur Wellesley and his two aides de camp, Captain Sir Colin Campbell and Captain Fitzroy Stanhope, had sailed from the Downs to the Baltic aboard his ship. The KGL troops at Rugen had not been informed of their new destination until the letter finally arrived with Cathcart on 3 August, but preparations were put under

---

1 'The Journal of Surgeon Charles Chambers of H.M. Fire ship *Prometheus*, the Bombardment of Copenhagen 1807', *The Naval Miscellany*, Vol. III, London, 1928.

way immediately. He was delighted with the news, his whole force's position in Pomerania being very awkward indeed. On 2 July, King Gustavus of Sweden had ended the armistice which had been in force since the end of April. His reasoning for this decision is unfathomable, but likely to have been linked to the imminent arrival of Cathcart's force and a belief that with these reinforcements Pomerania could be retained – how wrong he was.

The British troops had arrived six days later, but because of the shallow waters it took them over a week to fully disembark. Cathcart had not arrived himself until a week later, when he had found a complete mess. The French troops had renewed hostilities on 13 July and the fortress of Stralsund was already under siege when he arrived and it was very doubtful whether it could hold out for very long. Reporting his difficult situation to London, Cathcart was undoubtedly delighted to receive orders from Castlereagh to remain with his troops in the relative safety of the island of Rugen and soon after receiving further orders to sail with his force to Copenhagen. The reaction of Gustavus was a concern to him, but on this occasion the King took the news well, only insisting that Cathcart had to request his permission to withdraw his troops: he did so and received a gracious reply, approving it. His relief was so palpable, that he sailed almost immediately with his Staff officers for Denmark, joining Gambier on 12 August, whilst leaving his second-in-command, Lieutenant General Lord Rosslyn, to organize the re-embarkation, the German troops leaving Rugen on 13 August. Stralsund surrendered to the French forces on 20 August, the Swedish troops remaining on Rugen until 7 September when they were then fully withdrawn to Sweden.

Garlike was devastated when Taylor arrived and informed him of his immediate transfer to Memel. It was only now that he sent the reports of Hanchett and Beauman proving that the Danes had made absolutely no efforts to prepare their great fleet for sea, but it was a case of closing the stable door after the horse had bolted. Taylor took possession of the seals of office on 2 August, but Garlike was forced to delay his departure – not unhappily – after Prussia closed all of its ports to British ships. Meeting Joachim Bernstorff that day, Taylor immediately took the opportunity to inform the Danish minister of the Tilsit peace treaty and its secret clauses whilst seeking clarification as to whether Denmark had been approached to join a naval league. Bernstorff adamantly denied that any such approach had been made and the meeting broke up abruptly, denying Taylor the opportunity he needed to complete his mission by explaining the reason for the arrival of a British fleet in the Sound. The two men did not meet again until 11 August when the great scenes at Kiel had superseded all. Taylor's mission had not gone well. Garlike had, however, sent a copy of Beauman's report to Gambier, thereby relieving the admiral's main concern regarding the possibility of the Danish fleet emerging to fight.

A fair wind allowed Jackson to reach Tonningen on 5 August and he immediately dispatched his secretary overland with letters apprising Gambier and Cathcart of his arrival, his mission and their orders, giving himself eight days for negotiations from 6 August. He then set off the same evening for Kiel, arriving there twenty-four hours later, informing Christian Bernstorff by note of his arrival with an urgent commission, and requesting an early audience with the Crown Prince Frederick; they met at 11.30 a.m. on 7 August.

The reaction of both the Prince and Bernstorff to Jackson's mission was complex, as always. They denied the threat of a French invasion of Schleswig and Holstein, although knowing full well that it was strongly rumoured and that the evidence was that it was becoming very likely. They claimed any such attack would not succeed in its aims, as it would throw the rest of Denmark and Norway, its fleet and its army into British hands as her allies. Their real hope, however, was that Russian influence would persuade Napoleon not to carry out the threatened invasion, or that by maintaining a strict neutrality, they could spin things out long enough for the hoped-for pan-European peace treaty to be signed before any such invasion could occur.

With regard to Britain, the Danish government had maintained pretty good relations since 1801 and it is clear that they had no real suspicion at all of what was about to occur. The Danish envoy in London, Rist, did not help this perception. He had been reporting for months on the naval build up and the plan to send an expedition abroad, but despite widespread rumours that it was destined for Denmark, Rist continued to resist this explanation and talked of descents on Holland or Germany. Even the Crown Prince failed to pick up the signals, writing on 7 August to General Peymann, commander of Copenhagen, ordering him to strengthen Cronborg Castle and the defences of Copenhagen, but ended with the statement that 'we are not at war with England and do not expect to be'.[1]

As always, the Danes simply hoped to put things off in the faint hope that circumstances might change in the meantime; and with luck, avoiding any of the multifaceted threats materializing into fact. The Danish populace simultaneously feared that the French would invade Jutland, and that the British navy would blockade Norway, which would allow the arch-enemy Sweden to take it over. Even the Crown Prince and Bernstorff were openly critical of Napoleon, referring to France as 'a tyrannical power that was keeping all of Europe in a state of dishonour and slavery'.[2]

Jackson had a long, difficult and heated meeting with Christian Bernstorff, in which Jackson had repeated all of the reasons why the British government

---

1 Munch-Petersen, p. 152.
2 Munch-Petersen, p. 107

were unhappy with Denmark's seeming preference for France. Bernstorff clearly countered these and refuted the overall conclusion as simply wrong. However, Jackson continued by saying that Napoleon wished to close Danish ports to British merchants and to use her fleet in a projected attack designed to weaken British strength. The British government required a significant 'pledge' that Denmark would not turn against her, but seemingly stopped short of actually clarifying that the 'pledge' was the entire Danish navy; that could wait for his meeting with the Prince.

Whilst waiting for this interview, Jackson began to waver in his purpose. Numerous reports and conversations with trusted individuals convinced him that the rumours of defences being strengthened on Zealand and the Danish fleet actively fitting out for sea were fictitious. He could also plainly see for himself that the Danish troops were in their cantonments with no hint of marching anywhere: everything convinced him that the premise of the government's case regarding Danish preparations were simply wrong and he had found them all too easily disproven by Bernstorff during their long discussion. The only safe ground on which he could continue, was the threat of Napoleon's invasion and the seizure of the Danish fleet for his own ends, but he did actually contemplate simply abandoning his efforts. A letter from Canning which he had just received, incorrectly abusing him for purposely delaying his sailing from Yarmouth, steeled him again, making it plain that if he did not follow the government's plan to the letter, then his diplomatic career was at an end.

Jackson got his audience with the Crown Prince on the afternoon of 8 August, when the prince used the same arguments as Bernstorff had to counter all of the British claims. Playing for time, the Prince then suggested that Jackson should write to London with the correct information and to request revised instructions. The discussion they held would appear to have ended abruptly when Frederick seemed to believe that Jackson had basically offered him a stark 'peace or war' in a menacing tone. It is reported that the Prince replied 'I shall consider any power as my enemy, which shall endeavour to make me depart from my neutrality'.[1] Whether this is exactly what happened we will never know, but it would appear that it was still not clearly understood that the 'pledge' required meant handing over the Danish fleet.

No matter what was actually said, the outcome is all that matters. Frederick took a carriage that very night for Copenhagen to organize the city's defences. Jackson was only informed of his departure the following morning by Bernstorff, who attempted to maintain the negotiations with Jackson. When they met for a last time on 9 August, Jackson claimed that he saw in

---

1 Report in the *Naval Chronicle*, Vol. IV, p. 42.

Bernstorff's demeanour the look of a man resigned to a war they could not win, that would ultimately lead to their destruction, but determined to do so no matter what. This was clearly described with a very unhealthy dose of hindsight added in. Bernstorff tried to delay Jackson's departure, offering to treat, although admitting that no agreement could be reached without the complete backing of the Crown Prince. Jackson simply confirmed that he was leaving and that military operations would begin on 14 August and could not end with 'less than the delivery of our fleet'.[1]

---

1 Munch–Petersen, p. 158.

Chapter 15

Danish Preparations

Crown Prince Frederick reached Copenhagen at lunchtime on 11 August and immediately summoned together the senior military commanders and civilian officials of Copenhagen. He issued a stream of orders for the defence of Zealand and of Copenhagen in particular, and then left again in less than twenty-four hours, escorting his aged and infirm father whom he deposited at Kolding, before returning to Kiel on 15 August. On leaving Copenhagen, the Crown Prince issued a pretty meaningless proclamation, given the criticism that his departure was sure to garner.

> 12 August 1807
>
> Fellow Citizens!
> After having made all the arrangement which the present circumstances require, I hasten to the army, to operate with it as soon as possible for the welfare of my dear countrymen, unless circumstances should speedily arise, which may render it possible to settle everything according to my wish, in a peaceful and honourable manner.

The Danish crown jewels were removed for safety but the risk of trying to get them across the Belt was too great and they were concealed in a coffin at Soro Abbey, where they remained until recovered after the British had left. Frederick and his father had a narrow escape, it would appear, when a British ship boarded their vessel whilst they were crossing the Belt; the Prince hid in the hold and the King was passed off as a senile old gentleman, which was not that far from the truth. They were allowed to continue their journey, having aroused no suspicions; however, the British government had already briefed their naval captains that the Royal Family were not to be arrested or impeded in their travel if they had been discovered, as war had not been formally declared yet.

The King was not alone at Kolding; the Council of State, the entire diplomatic corps and all of the senior ministers of state and many of their clerks had soon decamped from Copenhagen. In effect, the entire government had fled and the Royal Family were leaving as quickly as possible, causing deep unrest amongst the populace, who were being urged to prepare to defend the city to the last whilst the great and the good ran away. Where, they might have asked, was the spirit of 1801?

The only senior figure to remain was Joachim Bernstorff, who now had a second interview with Taylor, who followed his instructions to advise that no preparations for a defence of the city would be allowed whilst talks continued. A further meeting was held on 10 August when Taylor demanded the cessation of defensive preparations which had clearly started in earnest, which Joachim refused bluntly, whilst castigating Taylor regarding the 'extraordinary and most insulting'[1] demand to hand over the Danish fleet. On the following morning, Taylor and his entire staff went on board the *Cambrian*, his mission over; it had never really stood a chance of success and Canning later praised him profusely, on behalf of the King, for his conduct during these discussions.

The British government's orders were to land the troops as soon as negotiations had failed – as they surely would. However, Taylor actually arrived aboard the *Cambrian* before the troops were in any way ready to land with Cathcart not even arriving himself until the following day, the 12th. As regards Jackson, he had set off after the Crown Prince to Copenhagen, but the Prince had gained a head start, so he boarded the *Fearless* brig in the hope that this would allow him to catch up. Wind and current were against them however and Jackson was finally forced to land at Kiel again and proceed overland. He arrived at Copenhagen on 13 August to find that the Crown Prince had already been and gone again. Jackson was also shocked to find that Taylor and his staff had already left, the innkeeper where he had been lodging stating that he had left all of his clothes and other effects in his room and had just vanished.

Jackson collected himself and requested an audience with Joachim Bernstorff, who saw him that evening at 8 o'clock, but no one had any hopes of a last-minute reprieve. Joachim informed him that Frederick had offered to keep Danish ports open to British ships and to refrain from any defensive preparations if, and only if, Britain would refrain from an attack whilst the Russians sought to broker a diplomatic agreement. Jackson angrily countered that he had been led a merry dance by the Prince, but now he needed a final unequivocal answer to the British demand for the Danish fleet. Bernstorff refused and all was at an end; the diplomatic game had finished, it was now for the military to force a decision. Jackson demanded his passport and he boarded the *Cambrian* that night, his duties at an end.

---

1 Munch-Petersen, p. 160.

When Napoleon had left Tilsit and returned to Paris, he had with him a copy of the second 'Secret' treaty signed with the Tsar. This had given Russia until 1 December 1807 to mediate between Britain and France in the hope of gaining a peace throughout Europe. However, if mediation failed by this date – something Napoleon confidently expected would happen – then it was agreed that France and Russia would simultaneously demand that Sweden, Denmark and Portugal must immediately close their ports to British shipping and declare war on Britain.[1] Sweden was of course an ally of Britain and therefore an enemy of France, so that situation would take longer to fix; however, the two 'neutral' states would have to choose sides immediately or face the consequences. In fact, Napoleon had no intention of waiting until the 1 December deadline and on 19 July, he was already sending orders for an ultimatum to be sent to Portugal, insisting that her ports be shut to Britain by 1 September: if not she would be invaded by French and Spanish troops. Just over a week later he ordered the formation of an army at Bayonne under the command of General Junot, openly designated 'The Army of Portugal'. The Portuguese ambassador at Paris was summoned and told in no uncertain terms, that not only were her ports to be shut, but British goods were to be seized and all British citizens arrested, and most significantly, Portugal was to 'unite her squadrons with those of the continent'. This was exactly what Britain had predicted and was so afraid of.

As regards Denmark, Napoleon moved a little more slowly, only issuing instructions regarding her position on 31 July. The Danes were to be warned of Napoleon's severe displeasure that British goods and correspondence was still flowing through Tonningen and Husum and of their failure to prevent British shipping entering the Baltic, despite the fact that as a neutral all of these were perfectly legitimate proceedings. The French Foreign Minister Talleyrand was, however, deputed to deliver the core message in a meeting with the Danish envoy at Paris. At this meeting, held on 6 August, they were still oblivious of British intentions, although the fact that a British fleet was sailing into the Baltic was known. Talleyrand was to raise the possibility that a peace treaty might not be possible with Britain; in which case he was to explain that Europe would have to declare war on her and that all European ports would be shut to her ships. If this happened, Denmark would simply face a stark choice – war with Britain or war with France.

In fact, Talleyrand sugar-coated it and never actually mentioned war nor the Danish fleet, apparently. He did, however, emphasize that Denmark had to realize that in such a situation, the threat of British reprisals were purely hypothetical, whereas the reaction of Europe (he meant France), if Denmark

---

1 Munch-Petersen, p. 162.

Lynetten Battery looking out towards Trekroner Battery, 1809, Print by Eckenberg.

refused to adhere to the rules, was real and very apparent. However, a few days later he confused the issue further by saying that Denmark should respond with their 'usual wisdom and moderation'[1] whilst rejecting his demands! Why Talleyrand failed to impart his Emperor's demands emphatically can only be known by him, but he did choose to leave office a few days later. Whatever the reason, the Danish envoy was left believing that there was nothing to worry about.

Nothing came of these discussions, because events overtook them, but it is interesting that Napoleon mentioned the British fleet on 16 August and stated that he could see no other reason for it, other than to capture Copenhagen, to capture the Danish fleet and hold the island of Zealand. It turned out to be a very accurate assessment, almost certainly based on what Napoleon would have done had he found himself in the same situation as the British, although he was not going to admit that to the Danes. The Emperor did, however, put his own forces on alert, particularly Marshal Bernadotte's corps consisting of 15,000 Spanish and almost as many Dutch troops centred around Hamburg and Emden. This corps was not there to invade Holstein unless the Russian

---

1 Munch-Petersen, p. 164.

mediation failed but Bernadotte could expect to receive further significant numbers of French troops, up to 20,000, once the Swedes were cleared out of Pomerania. The British move had surprised Napoleon and had put him on the back foot, but he was in no position to influence the outcome; his plan was therefore to wait it out and to gain the moral high ground by letting Britain appear as the aggressor.

General Heinrich Peymann, a 70-year-old Hanoverian engineer officer and commander of the Copenhagen garrison, had no more than 5,500 regular troops and 2,500 Landvaern[1] in six battalions,[2] with which to defend Copenhagen. The civilian population was also keen to defend the city and at least another 5,000 joined the ranks of the city militia and the numerous patriotic corps to help in the defences, whilst up to 30,000 of the city's 100,000 inhabitants were liable to be called into local militia units. There were at least 13,000 defenders, but their actual worth was limited, having very little time for training and they were dreadfully short of experienced officers and modern weapons. Many of the country militia had no uniform and fought in their traditional wooden clogs, armed only with pitchforks, swords or spears hastily made from farm implements tied to wooden poles. The Danish sea defence was commanded by an old friend, however, Commander Steen Bille, who had been so involved in the battle of 1801.

The defences of the harbour were now extremely strong, the Trekroner Battery having been strengthened since 1801 and now mounting sixty-eight guns, the Arsenal batteries mounting fifty guns and twelve mortars whilst the citadel had seventy-eight guns and thirty-five mortars.[3] The ramparts of Copenhagen were armed and new fortifications had also been constructed, especially the *Provestenen* hulk which had been sunk as a platform for a gun battery at the southern end of the King's Channel in 1802 and was now flanked by two of the floating batteries, making a battery of 89 guns crewed by over 900 men, while another battery on piles had been built just off the citadel carrying no less than 36 cannon and 9 mortars. Beyond these static defences the 64-gun *Mars*, the *St Thomas* of 20 guns and the *Elven*, *Eyderen* and *Gluckstadt* prames of 16 guns each, were anchored in the channel into the

---

1 These troops were not militia, but Landvaern, troops who had seen out their service in the army and had retired, but were liable to be recalled to the colours in times of national emergency. They were required to turn out for five days of company training and one day of battalion training every two years.

2 These consisted of 1st, 2nd, 3rd, 4th, 8th and 9th North Zealand Landvaern Battalions. Each battalion consisted of four companies of 150 men.

3 Forty-five guns and thirteen mortars faced towards the sea and harbour, and thirty-three guns and twenty-two mortars faced to landward.

harbour and thirty Danish gunboats, each carrying two long 24-pounders, were also available to aid the defence of the city.

The earthen ramparts of the city mounted no less than 321 guns and 82 mortars. The eastern land defences on the island of Amager were extremely strong, the earth ramparts and bastions of Christianshavn being armed with thirty-four heavy guns and protected by a wide water-filled ditch between 40 and 60 yards wide and at least 6ft deep. Facing to the west on the Zealand side, the defences were also strong and just as complete, with a wet ditch, albeit much narrower than on the eastern side. The ramparts on this side held no less than 119 guns and 27 mortars. In the central part of this flank it was further protected by large expanses of water, which formed the reservoirs for the city. These waters stood 1,000 yards away from the bastions at maximum effective cannon range and were divided into three separate lakes, divided by the wide roadways leading to the three gates in this flank giving access to the city. These bodies of water in theory gave further protection to this flank, although they did not extend far enough to cover the approaches to the city at both the northern and southern extremities. They were also a serious source of weakness, it being possible to cut the pipes leading from them into the city with relative ease and thereby causing severe water shortages, whilst the area in between had been allowed to develop, with the large number of buildings which had sprung up offering protection for the besiegers. The ramparts were completed and heavily protected at their northern end by the large guns of the formidable citadel, which also dominated the approaches to the harbour. At the very southern end, there was no outer lake, but this had been partly replaced by the cutting of an outer defensive water course with bastions which ran from the lakes to the sea. The defences of the city were therefore pretty formidable and would require a very protracted formal siege to breach them, but the city's Achilles' heel, was that with the invention of longer-range artillery, shells could be lobbed from long range, over the walls into its soft underbelly with relative impunity.

The defence of the fleet, which remained mothballed in the harbour, was to be paramount and the Crown Prince was clear that under no circumstances would the fleet be handed over to the British; but for some strange reason, he never gave full instructions on what must be done to the man in overall charge, General Peymann. The Prince left the city on 12 August having had a long meeting with Peymann, but it appears that at no time did the Prince indicate to him that the fleet must not be handed over under any circumstances, but that it must be destroyed instead. He did, however, apparently tell Admiral Lutken this in a conversation before he left and he told Steen Bille who was in charge of the naval forces, but neither of them ever told Peymann. On 18 August Frederick finally wrote to Peymann sending him the orders to destroy the fleet before he had to capitulate, but he never received them. Lieutenant Peter Steffens was entrusted with the dispatch and managed to get across the Great Belt without being detected, but was then captured by British troops outside Copenhagen. Steffens was allowed to write to his brother in the city informing him of his capture and mentioned that he had been carrying dispatches, but could give no hint of their content. Peymann was therefore left completely in the dark.

On 21 August Bille ordered Commander Ole Kierulff, who commanded the dockyard, to draw up a plan for the destruction of the fleet and to make the necessary preparations. Burning such a sizeable fleet within the city would be far too dangerous, therefore everything was prepared to scuttle the ships and to cut up the masts. Because the waters were so shallow this would not permanently destroy them, but it would cause great inconvenience and delay to the British. Steen Bille had even written up the orders by 2 September and signed them, but did not date it, as he awaited the outcome of the threatened bombardment. He estimated that it would take up to six hours in total to carry out this plan.

Chapter 16

British Troops Land

The British fleet had remained quietly at anchor whilst the negotiations continued and parties of officers were allowed ashore to make small purchases and to take the air without any molestation at all, neither side really suspecting what was about to happen. Surgeon Chambers records that he went ashore at Elsinore on 8 August and purchased a Danish brooch for the princely sum of 10 shillings and 6 pence,[1] whilst Captain Jonathan Leach of the 95th Rifles was happy that they were abundantly supplied with excellent fish from the Danish fishing-boats and at an inconceivably moderate price.[2] Ensign Robert Blakeney of the 28th Foot however, felt sorry for the unsuspecting Danes:

> For some days the most friendly intercourse was maintained between the inhabitants and the British officers. Parties from the fleet landed daily, were hospitably received, and both liberally and cheerfully provided with all such articles as could contribute to their comfort; no suspicion of our hostile intentions was even conjectured by the deluded Danes.[3]

Excursions were even made across the sound to Sweden, Captain Thomas Browne of the 23rd Foot recording that he

> . . . went with a brother officer to Helsinborg on the Swedish side of the Straits. This place is the Brighton of Sweden, and the summer resort of the king. . . . My brother officer and myself were dressed in our English uniforms, and were treated with the greatest kindness and civility.[4]

As time went on the Danes became more suspicious and noticeably less welcoming and on 9 April the Danes arrested four British officers walking

---

1 About £25 today.
2 Leach, p. 28
3 Blakeney, p. 7.
4 Buckley, p. 48.

ashore disguised as simple sailors.[1] Captain Leach saw at first hand the increasing tensions:

> I went ashore with a party of our officers at Elsinore. Of Cronborg Castle, we were, of course, not permitted to see more than the exterior, which appeared extremely formidable. . . . on returning to the boat, about sunset, to go on board our transport, a large concourse of Danish sailors, and of the lower orders of inhabitants of Elsinore, assembled in a tumultuous manner on the pier, and were by no means nice or scrupulous as to the manner with which they conducted themselves towards any Englishman then ashore. A captain of our navy and his boat's crew were maltreated, and some of them thrown into the water. Our party did not escape without being hustled and jostled and pushed into our boat.[2]

By 11 August rumours were rife in the fleet, especially after two artillery officers went along the coastline in the *Safeguard* brig to reconnoitre a spot for the landing of troops.[3]

Jackson held his first meeting with Admiral Gambier and General Cathcart on board the *Prince of Wales* on the morning of 14 August, when he confirmed that his diplomatic efforts had failed. Lieutenant Colonel George Murray, as Deputy Quarter Master General of the expedition, presented a huge report to Cathcart detailing the options for an attack on Copenhagen. Murray began with a comprehensive dismissal of the option of a hazardous surprise attack on the Trekroner Battery and then using it as a base from which to bombard the Danish navy, which had been put forward by Captain Paget of the *Cambrian*. He also ripped apart another suggestion of landing the entire army on the island of Amager and carrying out operations against the eastern defences of Copenhagen. His preferred option was to land troops on both Amager and Zealand and to invest the city from both sides at once. It was planned to land on Zealand first and to put troops on Amager at a later stage.

It was immediately agreed that the army would disembark on Zealand at the earliest opportunity, the landing would take place near the sleepy fishing village of Vedbaek, some twelve miles north of Copenhagen. The idea of landing troops on Amager was eventually quietly dropped, almost certainly because Cathcart wanted to ensure that all of his army was in a position to concentrate quickly in case of a Danish army landing in his rear on Zealand at any time.

---

1 Navy Records Society, *The Journal of Surgeon Charles Chambers* – 9 August 1807.

2 Leach, p. 29.

3 Navy Records Society, *The Journal of Surgeon Charles Chambers* – 11 August 1807.

It would clearly be an army operation, which was not to the liking of many in the navy. Captain Bowles spoke for most of them in a letter to his father on 25 August, stating that 'I think we ought not to be idle, and see the army take the town by themselves'. There would be a delay, however, as the wind was contrary for the movement of the fleet from Elsinore Roads. This did, however, have the advantage of bringing in the first wave of troops, including the KGL cavalry regiments, from Stralsund, who joined the fleet before the disembarkation began. The fleet now numbered an incredible 25 ships of the line, with some 71 smaller naval vessels[1] and these were accompanied by some 377 transports or 78,000 tons of shipping carrying just short of 30,000 troops.

It did give them time to write an appeal, which was printed in Sweden, for distribution amongst the Danish people as they landed, giving the reasons for the actions of the British government. It explained that France's increased influence on mainland Europe now meant that Denmark's ancient policy of neutrality could no longer be maintained. Therefore, the British were determined to remove the Danish fleet to a place of safety, well beyond the reach of Napoleon, and promised that the fleet would be returned in the same condition as soon as a general peace was agreed. As part of this operation British troops would land on Zealand, and they could be assured that the troops would respect Danish property and maintain strict discipline, whilst paying for all supplies received, as long as they were not attacked by the populace. The whole operation was not to be seen as an act of war, but an act of self-defence, whilst maintaining the dignity of Denmark at all times. It did not avoid the alternative scenario, however, issuing a stern warning to the Danes that if they turned away from this proffered hand of friendship and resisted the British forces, then innocent blood would be spilt and the horrors of Copenhagen being besieged and bombarded would be the inevitable result. The appeal was well intentioned, but at its heart, it was asking the Danes to welcome them ashore and to stand by and watch whilst they ran off with their entire fleet – their pride and joy. It was almost certain to be rejected.[2]

The first firing in anger occurred on 14 August at sea, when the *Frederiksvaern* frigate of 32 guns, which had co-existed peacefully alongside the British fleet for so long, was ordered to make her way into Copenhagen harbour or if unable to, to burn herself. Captain Henrik Gerner slipped his cable in the early hours of the 13th but as the wind was just as unfavourable for him as for the British fleet to proceed down the Sound, he made a break for Norway. When her departure was detected at first light, Admiral Gambier immediately sent the *Defence* 74 and the *Comus*, a 22-gun frigate, in pursuit,

---

1 See Appendix 10 for details.
2 The entire appeal can be seen in Appendix 12.

determined not to let her escape. Being the faster vessel, the *Comus* caught sight of the *Frederiksvaern* during the morning of the 14th off Marstrand, just north of Gothenburg in Sweden. The *Comus* eventually caught up with her at midnight and despite her smaller size, she launched an immediate attack. Having raked the Dane and largely dismasted her, she was boarded and carried without much further resistance. The *Frederiksvaern* had twelve men killed and twenty wounded, the *Comus* only having one man wounded. The surprising ease of the British victory against a much more heavily-armed ship and with a much larger crew does suggest that this time the Danes' hearts were not in it, not like in 1801. This action very quickly changed the attitudes of the Danes ashore, Ensign Robert Blakeney recalling that 'this hostile act put an end to all further intercourse on friendly terms. Some English boats which approached the shore next morning were fired at, and none were thenceforward allowed to land.'[1]

The wind finally became favourable on 15 August and the fleet escorted the transports with the 18,000 troops they had brought from Britain down the Sound, the majority anchoring off Vedbaek. Realizing that the battleships could not enter the shallow coastal waters and aware of the danger from the Danish gunboats, Admiral Gambier appointed Captain Peter Puget to command an 'Advanced' or 'Inshore' Squadron consisting of three sloops, seven brigs, five bomb vessels, three armed transports and ten ships' launches.[2] Major General Spencer's brigade proceeded on however, closer to the city, escorted by Admiral Essington to act as a diversion.

The first British troops began to land, unopposed, at Vedbaek shortly after dawn on 16 August. An officer of the KGL explained how they went ashore: 'In each boat were from twenty to thirty soldiers &c, they were severally towed by still smaller craft wherein sat the officers.'[3] Peymann had sent a force of just over 500 men, with as many as sixteen guns, out from the city to observe the British landing. The Prince had, however, ordered Peymann to avoid appearing as the aggressor or the instigator in any situation they found and because of this Peymann had ordered that under no circumstance were his troops to fire the first shot. They therefore merely observed the landing and then returned to Copenhagen to report the same in person. Captain Browne recalled how

> Preparations were made for landing, it was a beautiful morning. The boats filled with troops, assembled alongside the respective ships, and on a gun being fired from the Admiral and a flag hoisted at the main, the

---

1 Blakeney, p. 7.
2 See Appendix 17 for full details.
3 Anon, *Journal of an Officer of the King's German Legion*, p. 82.

The British army lands.

whole pushed off at once for the shore. They kept in line as they rowed, in every tenth or twelfth boat, the colours of a regiment uncased and blowing open with the breeze. In different parts of the line were boats having field pieces in their bows. The men were ordered to sit down and keep silence. There was some surf on the beach, but not sufficient to obstruct the landing seriously, and few accidents happened. When the boats touched the shore the men leaped out and immediately formed themselves into companies, and regiments, loaded their firelocks and fixed bayonets. They then moved forwards, and occupied strong ground, on the right and left of the landing place. Two Danish cavalry videttes were seen, observing our landing, but not a shot was fired to oppose it.[1]

Without meeting any real resistance, the main body of the British forces was soon landed by that evening and immediately began to prepare to commence operations in the morning. That same day, the Crown Prince formally declared war on Britain, calling for the sequestration of all British goods[2] and calling all Danes to take up arms in the defence of the city.

---

1 Buckley, p. 49: Browne incorrectly records it as occurring on the 17th.
2 In a letter sent to the *Naval Chronicle* in 1813, by F.Y., he reports that the value of goods seized by the Danes was initially estimated at £500,000, but because many Danish merchants had paid their dues despite orders to the contrary by the King, only £280,000 was lost (about £12 million today), whereas Britain had captured merchant vessels valued at no less than £1.6 million (some £60 million today), around 320 ships in all. *Naval Chronicle* IV, p. 92.

General Peymann wrote to Cathcart on 16 September requesting passports for the two Princesses of Denmark, the King's nieces, to go from Copenhagen to Colding. This was granted immediately and the Guards presented arms as their carriage passed through the lines near the Palace of Frederiksberg, the following morning.

At dawn on the 17th, the troops marched in three columns towards Copenhagen and by late morning all communication by land between the city and the rest of Zealand was cut. Ludlow's Division occupied the British right covering a wide front of about four miles, from the southern shoreline, through Fredericksberg and Vanlose to Gladsaxe. Wellesley's Reserve Division covered the centre of the British line, stretching about three miles from Gladsaxe to Emdrup, whilst Baird's Division covered the two miles from Emdrup to Tuborg on the coast north of the city. The 1st Brigade KGL had also landed and acted as a rearguard and to defend the landing area. The British forces were initially therefore spread in a relatively thin cordon stretching over some nine miles in total. The troops were spread along this arc, with little resistance being offered by the Danes, comfortable in the summer temperatures, with plenty of corn to cut as bedding and to build themselves shelter, as they were not furnished with tents. Pickets were however, sent out both to the front, but also to the rear, to prevent any possibility of attacks from the local population, although many appeared to have cleared out of the area. Arthur Wellesley wrote to Lord Hawkesbury on 21 August regarding the difficulties of obtaining supplies: 'We are very unpopular in the country, and derive but little resources or assistance from it, and that little is procured with difficulty. The inhabitants have fled from their villages in many places; and in none have we yet succeeded in prevailing upon them to cut or bring in their harvest.'[1]

To try to avoid the British army making depredations on the villages, Count Schulin of Frederiksdal and the Reverend Ronne at Lyngby volunteered to act as commissaries to supply the troops with their needs. They did this in the hope of avoiding unbridled theft, perhaps with menaces, against the local populace, but unfortunately the Crown Prince did not see it this way after the siege and they were both arrested and tried. It cannot, however, be assumed that these efforts stopped all pillaging from the villages. The Assistant Quarter Master General, Major John Pine Coffin reported that:

> At least you would imagine that the discipline of the army was preserved. No such thing. The villages around our lines give damning evidence to the contrary, and the outrages committed by our troops were worthy of a band of Cossacks. What were the steps taken to repress this spirit of

---

1 *Supplementary Despatches of the Duke of Wellington*, Vol. VI, p. 5.

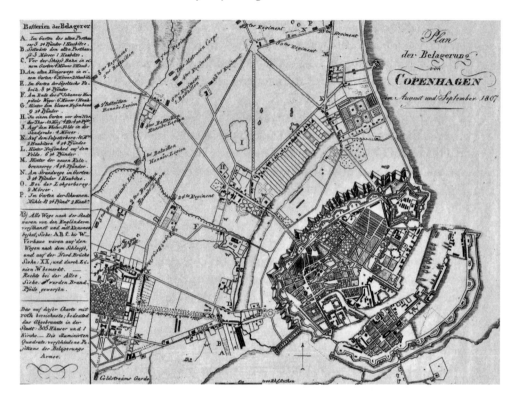

indiscipline? Court-martials were assembled, and instead of the culprits being executed in front of the Army as an example to the rest, the tender feelings of his lordship [Cathcart] would not permit him to approve a court-martial but they were all sent home to England, and there are now under the care of the Provost Marshal, two men for the rope, one for striking Lieut. General Lord Rosslyn in the attempt to secure him, when in the act of plunder, and eleven artillerymen for robbing a house of near £10,000. In short, what will you think of an Army of 25,000 men, which for above a week after its landing had no Provost Marshal appointed, or rather, what you will you think of the man who commanded it.[1]

Spencer's brigade, which had been sent as a diversion, returned and landed during the afternoon at Skovshoved, five miles south of Vedbaek and joined Baird's troops near there. Cathcart set up his headquarters in the country mansion of Mr Ericksen at Hellerup, just north of Tuborg whilst the cavalry and artillery transports also moved to Skovshoved and began the difficult work of landing the horses and guns, covered by two battalions of the KGL at Charlottenlund.

---

1 Letter from John Pine Coffin to Lieutenant Colonel John Le Marchant dated 9 November 1807.

However, the first Danish reaction was not long in coming, when on the 17th Peymann launched a sortie of about 700 men under the command of Major Holstein with four guns against the British troops as soon as the investment of Copenhagen was complete. The Danes supported this attack with the fire of three gunboats under the command of First Lieutenant Suenson hugging the coastline, whilst eight others sought to attack the transports and indeed they successfully boarded two merchant ships, releasing one as an American but setting the British one on fire.[1] The British gunboats were rather ineffectual this day, firing only at very long range and failing to drive the Danes away, but killing nine and wounding twelve Danish sailors, whilst the Danish infantry finally retired having lost only one dead and thirteen wounded. The Danes were reportedly shocked when they noticed that their gunpowder was so inferior to that of the British that when firing they saw that their shot fell short, whereas the British balls flew far past them.

The following day, the Danish gunboats looked to follow up their success of the previous day, but a recently-landed artillery battery was hastily sited on the shore near Swan Mill and was able to successfully drive the gunboats away, the Danes losing two men killed and one wounded, while three gunboats had to retire for repairs. The Danish attack may have succeeded had an infantry sortie been launched at the same time, which would have threatened the battery at Swan Mill. Separately, the navy sent two bomb vessels to shell the Provestenen and Quintus Batteries, which returned fire, but with little effect on either side.

The three regiments of KGL cavalry were successfully landed on the 18th and stationed at Charlottenlund, nearby Jaegersborg and the third at Vanlose near Frederiksberg where it could cover the Roskilde road. These cavalry units greatly enhanced the security of the troops, by sending out regular patrols into the hinterland to detect and intercept any attempts to attack the British cordon by the populace or troops who had potentially managed to land on Zealand from the mainland by avoiding the British navy patrols. To further these defences in their rear, one battalion of the King's German Legion was posted at Sorgenfri and Kollekolle, covering the two main roads from Hillerod and the north of Zealand. The discipline of the British troops was generally good, although inevitably there was some looting which was punished severely if caught. The reaction of the Danish country people was restrained, forced to endure enemy soldiers on their land, but perhaps wisely refraining from outright opposition, it was to the advantage of neither side to damage this tense but peaceable interaction. Both Admiral Gambier and General Cathcart

---

1 Postscript to letter of Captain Bowles RN of the *Zebra* bomb vessel to his father dated 17 August. Published in Malmesbury, Vol. 2.

wrote appeals to Peymann summoning him to surrender, but they received a firm refusal.

The city was still in need of as much gunpowder as possible to help it endure a long siege. The gunpowder factory was at Frederiksvaerk at the northern end of the Roskilde Fjord, well away from major centres of population for good reason. The works also included a cannon foundry, with a number of guns ready to be sent to the city. At these works two huge wagon trains, each of 250 vehicles, were maintained for the transportation of the gunpowder and Major Tscherning[1] hurriedly tried to pass two such convoys into the city before the British completed their encirclement. They set out early on the 17th, protected by escorts of the Prince's volunteer unit, the one convoy passing through Gorlose and Farum in an attempt to enter via the north and the other passing through Slangerup and Malov, thus arriving from the west. Arriving at Farum late on the 18th, the former convoy was detected by General Frederick von Decken and a squadron of the 1st KGL Hussars commanded by Captain Krauchenberg,[2] which forced Major Tscherning to order this convoy to retire towards Frederiksborg, which it reached in safety, although the Germans did capture twenty-one of the cartloads of gunpowder.

On the following day, Von Decken and Krauchenberg, with his squadron, learned of the second convoy in the direction of Roskilde, which it appears was also returning to Frederiksvaerk having failed to get to the city. A corps of 800 Danish militia were protecting the convoys and the cannon foundry at Frederiksvaerk some twelve miles to the north of the British lines. Showing a very determined front, Kraunchenberg's squadron arrived at the works and successfully broke the morale of the Danish militiamen with a fearsome display of drawing their sabres, ready for a charge. The Danes promptly surrendered en mass with scarce a shot fired. The weapons of the troops were taken and the 80 tonnes of gunpowder and numerous guns discovered there were claimed for the British Crown, but being unable to protect it themselves, the Danish troops were left to protect the gunpowder on their honour of parole and were not to issue any material to the Danish army. A huge number of firearms were also captured, which had been destined to arm the local militias, helping to prevent armed groups springing up in the army's rear. With this agreement, the Germans left on the morning of the 19th with only four of the guns in tow, never to return again. The Danes kept scrupulously to the agreement until released from its restrictions by the eventual departure of the British

---

1 Major Eilert Peter Tscherning (1767–1832).

2 He had with him eighty-two men of the 1st KGL Light Dragoons and a detachment of eighteen men of the 3rd KGL Light Dragoons. See the report of this action in Appendix 14.

army from the island. On leaving, Von Decken reported that the squadron was attacked by groups of local inhabitants forming small bands against the British, armed apparently only with pitchforks, but in this case a charge led to the capture of fifty of them and five horses. They were warned that there were many such groups in the woods and towns around, but in fact there were very few reports of organized resistance such as this. That day, another Danish gunboat attack, without infantry support, was made by five vessels, with very little effect and a convoy of wagons carrying the King's furniture, belongings etc, was allowed to pass through the British lines to Colding.

On the 20th a sortie by 2,000 men was made out of the East Gate under the command of Lieutenant Colonel Voigt, in an attempt to destroy the Swan Mill battery, which had caused so many problems for the Danish gunboats. The attack was made in two columns[1] supported by nine gunboats, but failed to achieve its objective before they had to retire, having lost five men killed and Lieutenant Holstein and three men wounded, with one gunboat having to retire for repairs. The Danes also attempted to shell the transports with the German troops on board in Kioge Bay, but gave up after two hours, having achieved little.

On the 21st a squadron of KGL light dragoons under Colonel Reden went looking for a force of Danish cavalry and infantry reported to be near Roskilde. Discovering the cavalry and immediately charging, the Germans captured three men and twenty-nine horses, the Danes losing around eighteen killed. Moving on, the light dragoons also found the infantry, but they were too strong to attack. These early easy victories heartened the British troops and led them to believe that the capture of Copenhagen would equally simple. It was on this day, however, that Cathcart was finally able to safely reconnoitre the entire landward defences of the city, and he now realized their immense strength, concluding that Copenhagen would only fall to a protracted formal siege. He informed the admiral of his judgement in a letter, which betrayed little belief in the ability of his forces to successfully carry out such an operation and he particularly lamented his inadequate number, if not complete lack, of siege guns and equipment. Gambier's reply was perhaps not what he expected, as on reading the letter, he immediately wrote a reply which offered that the navy would take over the entire operation and he was sure that they would soon succeed. Such a challenge from Gambier struck home and

---

1 The right column consisted of one battalion each of the Danish and Norwegian Life Guard, the Life Jaeger Corps, Herregaardsskyrtten, Life Regiment and Garden Chasseurs supported by the Royal Horse Guards and 100 men of the Zealand Cavalry Regiment totalling about 1,800 men. The left column also numbering around 1,800 men, consisting of four Landvaern battalions, Hussars and six amusetter (1-pounder guns).

forced a rapid rethink by Cathcart, who genuinely seems to have struggled with the morals of having to besiege and quite possibly bombard the Danes. The entire operation does not seem to have been to his personal liking and it seems to have severely depressed his spirits, making him look for reasons why he should fail. However, inter-service rivalry seems to have forced him to re-think his negative views. Suddenly, the army could achieve it all without any naval support!

On 21 August, the remainder of the KGL force from Stralsund arrived under General Rosslyn and promptly landed in Kioge Bay just to the south of Copenhagen, the disembarkation being covered by five companies of the 28th Foot and a detachment of cavalry. A force of 4,000 Danish troops at Kioge town, only three miles from the landing place, did nothing to disturb the disembarkation and on the 23rd this force marched to form a second, reserve line in front of the city. Cathcart now had a total force of close on 30,000 men with which to prosecute the siege.

The following morning General Macfarlane's brigade finally arrived from England and promptly disembarked at Skovshoved. A meeting between Cathcart, Gambier, Jackson and Home Popham[1] on 22 August, led to the others urging the general to increase the pace of operations and with the arrival of the last of the KGL troops and Macfarlane's men, he began to show a great deal more urgency and confidence.

On the 23rd the opposing squadrons of gunboats fired on each other for some eight hours with minimal effect on either side although the British squadron did eventually retire, the British losing four killed and thirteen wounded and the Danes losing seven killed and eleven wounded.

At dawn on the 24th Cathcart had the right and centre of the British cordon drive the Danish skirmish line back and soon the Danes retired beyond the line of the outer lakes or reservoirs, the Guards advancing to occupy the suburbs and capturing thirteen small field guns abandoned by the Danes as they retired. The Danish resistance was negligible, one witness describing how 'they were very soon driven under the walls by our riflemen only, who maintained themselves in a wood, within musket shot of the citadel, as long as we could see them'.[2]

A major sortie was launched by the Danes from all three gates simultaneously to force the British back, but it failed with little achieved and the British

---

1 Home Popham had been sent again as Captain of the Fleet, because of his expert knowledge of the Baltic, but Admiral Hood, Keats and Captain Stopford put in formal complaints, which were not upheld. Hood and Keats were, however, granted the rank of Rear Admiral as a sweetener.

2 Captain Bowles' letter dated 25 August 1807.

skirmish line occupied the suburbs throughout. The British cordon was now established at no more than 800 yards and in some places as close as 400 yards from the city's earthen ramparts, the buildings in these suburbs carelessly left standing by the Danes and therefore offering excellent cover from the direct fire of their heavy guns. The Danes maintained a slow, steady fire from their batteries on the walls, but generally they had little to fire at, so it was all rather pointless. During this advance Sir David Baird's troops captured a redoubt which the Danes had been constructing outside the East Gate for some days and its construction was continued by the British troops.

The British now began to construct a number of batteries for the heavy guns to allow them to begin siege operations. Six hundred men were employed continuously in digging trenches and siege batteries, each group being relieved after four hour's work. The navy was employed bringing the heavy guns and stores ashore and then helping to move these up to the front line. These siege works were largely concealed from the view of the defenders by the buildings and trees left standing in the suburbs. The fire from the regular gunboat attacks, particularly against the Guards in the south-western suburbs, were little more than a distraction with little serious damage done.

The Danes sent out a request to allow a passport for His Highness the Prince Ferdinand and his tutor to pass through the British lines and leave the city. He was granted a passport, but Cathcart also made it clear that this was the last one he would authorize. How ordinary Danes felt about the Danish Royal Family vacating the city before any threatened bombardment occurred is not recorded, but it is most likely that the news was not received well and that it further depressed morale amongst the populace.

Cathcart had come to the conclusion early on that the only way that Copenhagen could be taken was by a protracted formal siege, but he was well aware that he could not rely on having a long period to carry out the operations before Danish regular troops or even French forces began to appear in his rear. It was also already late in the season and the navy would have to leave the Great Belt in November at the latest. He was therefore forced to consider how these operations could be speeded up and it was clear that Murray's suggested bombardment of the Danish fleet would be very difficult to achieve with any accuracy. Murray had gone further however, noting that:

> If it is found by experience that the destruction of the fleet is actually not within the power of our mortar batteries, we must then on necessity resort to the harsh measure of forcing the town into our terms, by the sufferings of the inhabitants themselves.[1]

---

1 Murray Papers Adv. Ms 46.1.12 *Plan of Attack on Copenhagen submitted by Lieutenant-Colonel Murray to Lord Cathcart, 14 August 1807.*

The only realistic option for achieving a rapid victory, therefore, was a heavy, indiscriminate bombardment of the city, in the hope of turning the civilian population against the governor and forcing him to capitulate quickly. Cathcart saw the sense of this and he quickly abandoned the plan of attempting to bombard the Danish fleet at all, the bombardment was to be indiscriminately against the city from the start. This all-out bombardment may have been hinted at by Murray, but it was Cathcart's decision to forego all other options and was therefore his and only his decision alone, it was never ordered or even contemplated by the British government. This is not to say that Cathcart was happy with the idea of a general bombardment; indeed Jackson mocked the general in his private journal for worrying over the 'horror of knocking down the houses and of the chance of a shell falling upon a girl's boarding school'.[1] Jackson missed the point, however. Cathcart may not have liked the idea of a bombardment, but as a professional soldier he saw it as the only way of guaranteeing a swift successful outcome and he had therefore determined to carry it out, if the Danes would not listen to his summons. Cathcart hoped above all that Peymann could be convinced of the futility of resistance and that he could be persuaded to surrender before a bombardment began, but if he would not capitulate, then the bombardment would happen and would be carried out with full vigour.

One opponent of this method of attack, rather surprisingly, was Arthur Wellesley, who on humanitarian grounds wrote 'I think it behoves us to do as little mischief to the town as possible, and to adopt any mode of reducing it, rather than bombardment.'[2] Wellesley had advanced the plan to land on both Amager and Zealand, explaining that no city could last long if cut off from all supplies. Whether starving the inhabitants to death was a better option to bombardment is a moot point, but Cathcart ignored the suggestion as it would take too long.

Therefore, as soon as a tight cordon had been set up at less than a thousand yards from the city defences, plans were immediately set in motion to prepare batteries for the bombardment of the city. Cathcart did go one step further, in that he had considered what he would do if the Danes withstood the bombardment and still stubbornly refused to capitulate. He had decided that in this case, he would launch a full-scale assault on the city by storming parties, which he knew would be risky and could possibly lead to heavy British losses. Even in the event of a successful storming, there would then be the

---

1 FO 353/56 '*A Review of the last two months of my Life written at Broadstairs in October 1807.*'

2 Letter of Arthur Wellesley to Lord Hawkesbury dated 28 August 1807. *Supplementary Despatches of the Duke of Wellington* Vol. VI, p. 9.

inevitable horrific consequences of the city being sacked by the soldiers to be contemplated. No matter how much the thought revolted him, he made plans for just such an assault, to be launched within a few days of the failure of the bombardment to achieve its goal.

The Danes attempted a major sortie at 2 p.m. on 25 August, when a force of about 600 men, consisting of the Life Jaeger Corps, the Herregaardsskytterne (mounted sharpshooters) and the Jaeger companies of the two Life Regiments, the Garden volunteer corps and eight guns under the overall command of Major Holstein, attacked the British lines in the area of Blaagaard. They clashed here with Lord Rosslyn's troops who had recently relieved Wellesley's division in the centre. Major Baring's 1st Light Battalion KGL and Colonel Reinbold's 5th Line Battalion were driven back initially, but taking a position behind a wooden fence, they halted the Dane's advance with a heavy and accurate fire. With reinforcements arriving the KGL troops soon pushed the Danes back to the city, the Danes having lost twenty-one dead and fifty-five wounded, with the KGL suffering about sixty casualties.

On 26 August, a major attack by the Danish gunboats on the Swan Mill battery was eventually beaten off, the Danes having the better of the exchanges between the boats, being much more heavily armed, but the Danes suffered from the accurate and heavy fire from the shore batteries erected by the British. During this action, the Danish gunboat *Stubbekjobing* received a direct hit from a British mortar and exploded, with thirty-one killed, twelve wounded and seventeen rescued unharmed. Other British and Danish losses this day were light. Rightly worried about the possibility of the British cutting the water pipes from the lakes, the governor ordered a full survey of the city to establish how many wells there were, the Danish police identified no less than 411 wells within the walls, relieving any immediate anxiety over their continued water supply. On the following day, three Danish gunboats operating to the south of the city took severe damage from a shore battery and the *Naskov* gunboat was run aground and abandoned, with many of the crew being casualties. The boat was eventually recovered and towed in for repairs.

It became clear that St Hann's Hospital for mental patients, which lay in the suburbs, was in danger of being hit unintentionally by the fire of both besiegers and defenders and a cessation of operations for thirty-six hours was requested by Peymann to evacuate the patients. Cathcart allowed four hours for the evacuation of the patients and staff into the city, which was not taken up and a number of shot did crash through the buildings – almost certainly fired by the Danes. Another gunboat attack to the north of the city was made by the Danes, but retired having been heavily damaged by the shore batteries, the Danes losing seven dead and five wounded. A party of firemen

The attack on Mr Classen's property.

also sortied from the west gate this day and set fire to a number of structures in the suburbs which were restricting the defender's field of view.

On the 29th the patients of St Hann's were finally safely removed to the chapel at Frederiksberg by the British, General Peymann ordering that the Danish guns were not to fire on them and declaring that the hospital had not been fired on by his orders. They were eventually moved to the safety of Frederiksvaerk.

On 31 August two Danish mortar vessels fired on the British ships in Varto Bay and the British armed transport *Charles of Kircaldy* exploded with eleven men killed and twenty-one wounded whilst several other ships had close calls as the Danish gunboats launched another attack, the Danes only losing four wounded this day. One eyewitness complained that 'these confounded boats are so small that we may fire all day without being able to touch them, while they hit us every time'.[1]

The Danes also launched a large-scale sortie at dawn into an area of the suburbs around Mr Classen's country house, which they suspected was hiding British preparations for a sizeable battery. It consisted of two battalions of the Danish Life Regiment and one of the Norwegian Life Regiment the light troops of the King's Life Guard and of a number of other regiments, a number

---

1 Letter of George Bowles RN, dated 1 September 1807.

of the rifle corps with eight guns, totalling 2,500 men. The Danes found to their consternation that there were no works under construction, but fifty firemen and fifty carpenters who accompanied the troops set fire to a number of houses and cut down a number of trees to clear the area, to prevent its use by the British.

The British 95th Rifles and 50th Foot counter-attacked and were supported by troops sent by Sir David Baird, driving the Danes back into the city with the loss of twenty-four killed and ninety-eight wounded. Amongst the casualties was General Peymann who received a musket ball which went clean through his left leg, luckily missing the bone, but this injury did lay him up in bed for the rest of the bombardment, although he did not give up any of his duties. Baird also received a wound in the chest and lost a finger during the fighting this day. This attack was supported by the fire of three Danish gunboats which lost one dead and two wounded.

Captain Thomas Browne was a witness to the fighting and of the novel way used to dispose of the Danish bodies.

> Our picquets were surprised this morning in a wood behind the house of a Mr Tutin [*sic*] . . . a sharp skirmish took place, which ended with the repulse of the enemy. General Peymann was shot through the left thigh & when our picquets reoccupied the post from which they had been driven, they found on the ground about 80 of the Danes, who had fallen. Amongst the dead, there was a considerable proportion of the young Danish students, some of whom did not appear to be more than sixteen years old, and our sun-burnt soldiers really grieved, to see the fair faces and curling locks of their gallant young opponents, as they lay extended on the ground. They must have resisted gallantly, as some had fallen from bayonet wounds given by our troops. There were in these woods, which were enclosed as part of the ornamental grounds of Mr Tutin, several square holes, about 15 feet deep, with water in them. They were full of fish, which were no doubt kept there for the use of the kitchen; each hole had a wooden cover, pierced here and there, to let in air and hung on hinges. To save the trouble of digging graves, as the most ready way of disposing of the dead Danes, our soldiers carried them to these holes, and when they were thus filled, dropped down the covers. We lost an officer and about 20 men on this occasion.[1]

---

1 Buckley, p. 52. Browne again mistakes the date of this sortie as 23 August. He seriously over-estimates the number of dead.

Chapter 17

The Battle of Kioge

Cathcart feared an attack on his rear by elements of the main Danish army successfully avoiding detection by the British ships patrolling the Great Belt under Keats and crossing from the mainland. This remained a worry, but in fact the attack on Copenhagen had left the Crown Prince unsure what to do, knowing that the chances of seeing off the British without his main army were minimal, but also knowing that the chances of getting his army safely onto Zealand past the Royal Navy were slim, whilst also suspecting that the second his army marched from Kiel and passed over to Zealand, Napoleon would march his troops into Holstein and even Jutland, whilst claiming that he was merely supporting the Danish effort in resisting the British. Unsure what to do, he effectively did nothing and hoped that the city could hold out until the winter, when the British ships would have to leave the Baltic. However, he did make an appeal to the militia units on the islands of Lolland, Falster and Moen which lay very close to Zealand.

> The Crown Prince to the inhabitants of Moen, Falster and Lolland
>
> 20 August
> Countrymen! I call upon you to take up arms against an enemy who has not only taken you by surprise, but has approached your coast under the mask of friendship. Remember the ancestors from whom you are descended, and that they, through their courage and unanimity, acquired immortal fame. Your King! Your Country! And your Home! Let these be your watchwords, and nothing will be impossible to you. Advance then to arms! Assemble under the banners of a Danish Prince: drive back the enemy; for, nothing can withstand you: I only regret that the circumstances of the present moment do not permit me to put myself at your head.

These troops – four battalions in total – could pass over with great ease and they were ordered to do so as soon as they could. They were then to join

Passing Cronborg Castle, by Robert Kittoe.

Toast on the Eve of the Battle of Copenhagen, by Thomas Davidson.

Sub–Lieutenant Peter Willemoes fights Gerner Radeau *at Copenhagen 1801, by Christian Molsted.*

A moment at the Battle of Copenhagen 1801.

Danish floating battery under fire, Copenhagen 1801.

Battle of Copenhagen 1801, by Nicholas Pocock.

Forestilling af Slaget d. 2den April 1801 om Eftermiddagen Klokken 3, da Admiral Lord Nelson sendte Parlementer Baaden i Lan
Krigskibet 3. Kroner. 2. Krigskibet Dannemark. 3. Fregatten Iris. 4 Blokskibet Dannebrog. seyler fra Battallien da Ilden var udbrudt, og kort efter spr...
...time Lord Nelsons Skib. 6. Admiral Parker's Skib. 7. det store Batterie. 8. det ladet Batterie. 9. Parlementer Baaden, med tvende Engelske Officerer.

A contemporary Danish print of the 1801 battle.

Trekroner Battery.

Another contemporary Danish print of the 1801 battle.

Battle of Copenhagen 1801, by C.A. Lorentzen.

The Battle of Copenhagen 1801 – Danish painting.

Nelson's note to the Crown Prince is delivered, by C.A. Lorentzen.

British Naval General Service Medal for Copenhagen 1801.

Danish Defence Medal 1801.

The mass grave for the Danish dead of 1801, in Holmens Cemetery.

Two Danish Ships Arrive at Portsmouth, by J.W.M. Turner.

Danish artillery in action with British gunboats, 1807.

British soldiers observe the bombardment of Copenhagen, 1807.

Danish Families Flee to Amager – contemporary print.

The Bombardment of Copenhagen 1807, by Johann Jurgenass – contemporary print.

British Highlanders, Copenhagen 1807 – contemporary print.

The ruins of Copenhagen 1807 – contemporary print.

British brig boarded by Danish gunboats.

Danish gunboat – contemporary image.

General Castenschiold with his eleven battalions[1] of Zealand Landvaern which were forming up near Bjaeverskov and to attempt together to break the siege.

Cathcart had become aware of a large force of Danish troops arriving in the area of Kioge on 23 August, but was unsure as to its real strength. He therefore ordered a plan of attack to be prepared by Sir Arthur Wellesley and his reserve troops, which exchanged positions with Earl Rosslyn's Germans on 25 August, who now formed the centre section of the besieging force. Cathcart then sent him on 26 August, with his entire reserve corps, with the addition of one British and one KGL horse artillery battery and eight squadrons of KGL dragoons, to deal with this unwelcome threat once and for all.

Wellesley divided his force into two columns, with one under the command of General von Linsingen[2] intended to march in a wide arc around Roskilde to threaten the Danish rear and escape route, whilst Wellesley's column[3] would attack frontally. The troops were force marched, but on their approach the Danes rapidly retired on Kioge. An officer in the KGL records that 'We marched during extremely hot weather and oppressed by many privations, until very late in the night. After passing three days on this disagreeable march, we reached Roskilde.'[4] One squadron of the 3rd Light Dragoons KGL did surprise the Danish outposts and killed sixteen Danes, and captured three men and forty-five horses, for the loss of four men wounded.

The four battalions of Landvaern from the islands eventually arrived at Kioge on 28 August with Colonel Oxholm[5] becoming second-in-command of the combined force. Oxholm initially had a great deal of trouble persuading the troops to leave their own islands while the harvest was ready to be brought in, but he eventually persuaded them to move into Zealand by appealing to their patriotism.

---

1 The force consisted of the 5th, 6th and 7th North Zealand Landvaern and the 1st, 2nd, 4th, 5th, 7th, 8th, 9th, and 10th South Zealand Landvaern, seventy men of the Zealand Cavalry Regiment and eighty of the Zealand Landvaern Cavalry.

2 Linsingen's column consisted of six squadrons of KGL dragoons, three guns of Sympher's KGL horse artillery battery, a detachment of five companies of the 43rd Foot, five companies of the 2/95th and the 6th KGL Line Battalion, a total of about 3,000 men.

3 Wellesley's column consisted of two squadrons of KGL dragoons, one British Royal Horse Artillery battery commanded by Captain Newhouse and three guns of Sympher's KGL horse artillery, a detachment of five companies of the 43rd, the 2/52nd, 1/92nd and five companies of the 1/95th, a force of about 3,500 in total.

4 Anon, *Journal of an Officer of the King's German Legion*, p. 85.

5 Often mistakenly called Oxenholm, this was Colonel Peter Lotharius Oxholm (1753–1827).

Marching towards Kioge on 29 August, Wellesley's German dragoons detected Danish troops just to the north of the town who were lining the bank of the Kioge stream. The force was sizeable, three or four battalions being visible in line, with cavalry positioned on either flank and a few guns placed along their front. There were also clear indications that further troops were concealed behind them in reserve – indeed the Danes numbered around 7,000 troops. Sergeant Duncan Robertson of the 92nd described the Danish position: 'We had not gone far before we perceived the Danes drawn up in line ready to receive us, having their artillery, amounting to six or eight pieces, placed on a rising ground, with a windmill in front, and the cavalry in the same line, protected by a garden hedge.'[1]

Wellesley halted to await the pre-arranged time for Linsingen to launch his flanking attack, but the hour passed with no sign of the flanking column, which had become delayed on its route, finding the bridges broken. The Danes did not make a great impression on the British regulars, one British officer recalling 'They appeared poor raw troops, and we could not help smiling at the indifferent figure they cut.'[2] With no sign of Linsingen and no message to indicate where he was, Wellesley chose to launch his attack before he lost contact with the Danish force in the night.

Wellesley had his artillery open fire on the Danish infantry whilst the 95th Rifles advanced to skirmish with them. With minimal delay, he then ordered his troops to advance in line, in echelon from the left. This meant that the 92nd Foot, whose left touched the sea, marched forward first. Sergeant Robertson described the moment:

> The Danes now opened a cannonade upon us; but so ill were their guns served, that only one shot took effect, by which a file of the 1st company of the 92nd was killed. Their line then fired a few rounds which wounded a good many of us, but few dangerously. At this time the 92nd light company, being on the left of the rifles, came in contact with the Danish cavalry, and had got up a 6-pounder, from which we had only discharged one round when they wheeled about and galloped off. The line now advanced, the rifles still skirmishing; and as the Danes did not seem inclined to leave their position some of the riflemen called out to charge, which word soon ran from one end to the other. The charge was successful; but it might have proved otherwise, had the Danes taken advantage of their ground. Instant retreat on the part of the enemy was the result.[3]

---

1 Robertson, p. 40.
2 Buckley, p. 53.
3 Robertson, p. 40.

The Danes were unable to withstand such fire without becoming nervous and the sight of the line of British infantry advancing with determination caused the Landvaern to turn and run.

The Danes attempted to hold a second position with their cavalry poised to attack the 92nd in flank, but Wellesley observed this and countered it by bringing his own cavalry on to that wing and forming the 43rd Foot in a second line in case of a concerted attack. The 92nd continued their advance and the Danes turned and ran, closely followed by the German dragoons and the 95th. Sergeant Duncan Robertson described the confusion:

> . . . the streets were full of Danish troops, retiring, or rather running away, some of whom were discharging their muskets in Parthian fashion while making their escape. We fired down the street amongst them, while in a very crowded state in the small space, and killed a great many both of the inhabitants and military. There was a bridge at the end of the street, on which the Danes had placed a cannon, but before the gunner had applied the match to it one of the advanced guard under my command brought him down. The gun was immediately turned upon the fugitives, who now began to throw away their arms and accoutrements, and to run off in all directions.[1]

At this point Linsingen's column, which had been delayed by broken bridges,[2] appeared and joined in the pursuit, they having arrived too late to cut off the Danes' retreat as originally planned.

At Herfolge the four Danish battalions under Colonel Oxholm attempted to make a stand, one battalion defending the walled churchyard to cover the retreat of the main body, but it was soon virtually surrounded and overpowered – Count Wedel Jarlsberg and 400 men being compelled to surrender – and the rest broke, the pursuit continuing in earnest. Private William Green of the 95th recalled that:

> The Rifles pushed on in extended order, as is always the case in action. The 79th and 92nd Highlanders made a brilliant charge with the bayonet, and they soon dispersed; our cannon played through the town, and we overtook them; they were shod with wooden shoes, except the officers, so that it was impossible for them to run fast. I believe they were all taken prisoners![3]

---

1 Robertson, p. 41.

2 The planks had been removed, but the cavalry crossed the stream and wood was found to let the men cross in single file to continue the advance.

3 Teague, p. 10.

It was a particular feature of this action that when the Landvaern turned to flee,[1] they discarded their wooden clogs, with which they were issued, so as to run faster. The streets of Kioge were apparently carpeted with wooden clogs and the Danes often refer to the battle, if one can call it that, as the 'Battle of the Clogs'. Unsurprisingly, Private Richard Howarth of the 95th believed that his battalion had won the battle singlehandedly. He recalled:

> When we came within 50 yards of the enemy, our five companies, that were in front, were ordered to the rear of the other regiments to let them charge, but they would not go, so we gave three cheers and charged them ourselves, with three companies of the 92nd and two troops of light horse we drove them all out of the town with great loss on the enemy's side. We pursued them for two or three miles into the country.[2]

The British pursuit was ruthless, but not inhuman, those being caught generally being allowed to surrender without receiving a cut, although almost certainly deprived of their valuables. Some 1,500 militiamen were made prisoners, including Colonel Oxholm and a number of senior officers. General Castenschiold was able to pass onto Moen and Falster islands with the remnants of his force, where he was able to remain relatively safe. Linsingen's forces had chased them all the way to Vordingborg on the southern tip of Zealand, only to see the Danes sail away just in time, but Zealand was now clear of enemy forces.

Wellesley was critical of General Linsingen when he wrote to Lord Hawkesbury on 3 September: 'Not a man would have made his retreat if General Linsingen had carried into execution his part of the plan ...'

It is impossible to be exact about the British losses as they were not listed separately, but added into the total losses between 16 and 31 August inclusive. This total was only 29 officers and men killed and 122 officers and men wounded with 21 missing, but it can be deduced that no more than half of these losses were incurred at Kioge. Danish losses were 152 officers and men killed, 204 wounded and some 1,500 prisoners taken.

The Danish view of some of their own troops was also poor, the Lolland and Falster Militia actually being deemed cowardly and mocked by their own countrymen.[3] Thirteen 3-pounder guns and eighteen supply wagons were also captured. Oxholm and around sixty officers were released on their parole soon after, but the Danish troops were marched to the north and loaded aboard

---

1 The Danish reports of Kioge show that most of the men who fell were shot in the back as they ran.
2 Undated letter of Private Richard Howarth, quoted in Muir, p. 204.
3 Glenthoj and Ottesen, p. 39.

British warships as prisoners, in order to dissuade others from joining the Danish forces.

Francis Jackson saw the prisoners on board the British ships and was less than complimentary.

> The men are on board prison ships, and miserable wretches they are, fit for nothing but following the plough. They wear red and green striped woollen jackets and wooden sabots. Their long lank hair hangs over their shoulders, and gives to their ragged features a wild expression, the knowing ones say that after the first fire they threw away their arms, hoping, without them, to escape the pursuit of our troops. In fact, the battle was not a very glorious one, but this you will keep to yourself.[1]

Much has been made of this battle, as the first victory of Arthur Wellesley in Europe and hence removing the tarnish from his reputation as merely being 'a Sepoy General'. Kioge really cannot seriously be viewed as a significant battle and it was largely dismissed by the troops present as nothing more than a skirmish. Captain Leach of the 95th explained that 'Our loss in this affair was very trifling, as it was impossible that the Danes could offer any effectual resistance to disciplined troops'.[2] It did, however, remove all hope of relief for the garrison of Copenhagen: they were all alone and morale within the city crumbled with the news.

---

1 Francis Jackson to his wife dated HMS *Prince of Wales* 1 September 1807.
2 Leach, p. 34.

Chapter 18

The Bombardment

On 31 August, the batteries were complete and armed with a total of forty-four mortars, eight howitzers and thirty-six guns, along with a number of heavy Congreve rockets. Cathcart sent a final formal summons, making an impassioned appeal requesting that the governor would admit defeat and surrender before the barrage began and they rained terror on the city. The city authorities issued directions to its citizens on what to do in the case of a bombardment.

> Watch and Listen are powerful means of preventing harmful consequences from the effect of falling bombs. In case of a bombardment. Beware residents! Do not let your homes become cemeteries! From the first, we can accomplish much. Men, be particularly aware of the spot where a bomb falls! Fly from such a place as far as possible, from one room into the next, and as far as you have time, until the bomb explodes; when it has exploded, which you will hear, rush to it with a bucket of water, and you shall with some splashes thereof, prevent any outbreaks of fire, which would otherwise occur and once taken hold is only with great difficulty stopped! Only madmen expose themselves to death, no man should deliberately try to extinguish a bomb, whatever the conditions. Safety is preferred to increased parts! The man in an open space when a bomb falls nearby, stretch out on the floor and look to get away from it! Keep sea water on all floors and remember to beware!

The inhabitants of Copenhagen had been warned of the impending siege and large food stores had been filled before the British cut off all communication with the city. An indication of the plentiful supply of foodstuffs within the city is that prices did not rise significantly during the short siege. The patriotic appeals and the Prince's orders to arrest British citizens were not fully complied with as many had lived there for many years, but it did lead to an air of uncertainty and fears of treachery, with many being arrested on suspicion of spying. During the early days of the siege, when there was a minimal bombardment, was largely met with nonchalance, for they had seen in 1801 that it was not particularly terrible, the few shells either exploding too high or landing and their fuses spluttering on long enough for the nimble-fingered to pluck the fuse out before it exploded.

Cathcart received a clear and unequivocal refusal from Peymann, but he delayed opening fire until the following evening, in the hope that given a little more time to reflect he might alter his decision. He did not, and at 7.30 p.m. on the evening of 2 September all of the batteries opened fire simultaneously. The Danish populace were caught completely by surprise, people were enjoying the evening warmth and strolling in the King's Garden whilst the bands played and children frolicked in the streets. All of a sudden, shells and rockets streaked through the sky, causing instant horror and panic. The rockets made more noise than they did damage, but they certainly frightened the people, Peymann calling them an 'uncivilized' weapon. Ensign Blakeney watched the rockets streaking across the night sky and was not overly impressed: 'I saw the first Congreve rockets ever fired against an enemy. They seemed reluctant to add to the conflagration, many of them in the midst of their orbit turning back to whence they were sped.'[1] The fleet looked to manoeuvre its bomb vessels into range of the city, to add their destructive capability to the overall sum, but they were kept away by the fierce resistance put up by the Danish gunboats and the guns of Trekroner Battery. At the same time, the water pipes from the reservoirs to the city which had been previously discovered were cut, in an effort to deprive the city of its main water supply.

After firing all night at a slow and deliberate rate, using the high spires of the northern districts of the city as their targets, the guns finally fell silent at 7 a.m. after twelve hours of incessant barrage, allowing the gunners some well-earned rest. The Danes had fired back, but had few targets to aim at and they failed to destroy any of the besieging artillery. There had been a great deal of destruction in the area of northern Copenhagen, where the remaining crowded wooden medieval houses allowed the fires to spread rapidly. Numerous fires had broken out, one Danish historian stating that there were thirty-eight separate major fires that night, but they had generally been quickly extinguished by the excellent work of the city's large and efficient force of firemen. One cotton manufactory is recorded as having been entirely destroyed on this night. One of the tactics used by the British gunners was to shell the areas where fires had taken hold, specifically to hamper Danish attempts to extinguish the fires and caused the deaths and injuries of many of the Danish firefighters who were trying to prevent their spread.

George Jackson recorded the awful scene from his ship:

---

1 Blakeney, p. 10.

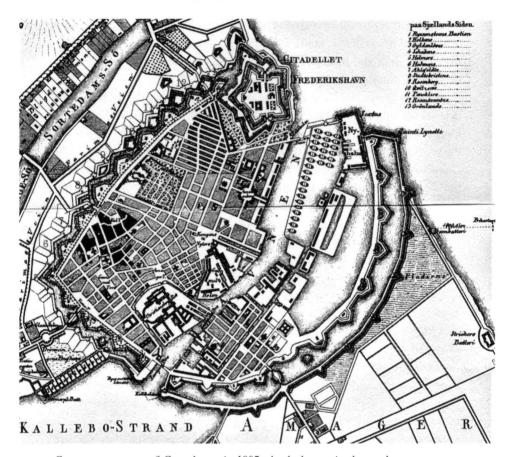

Contemporary map of Copenhagen in 1807, the dark area in the north-western corner representing the area destroyed by fire.

We found the Admiral and my brother in the stern gallery looking at the conflagration, for the city was on fire in three places. I never saw, nor can well conceive a more awful, yet magnificent spectacle. It was the beginning of the bombardment in forma. We saw and heard it going on until daylight, as we lay in our cots; and as the work of destruction proceeded. I cannot describe to you the appalling effect it had on me. Our cabin was illuminated by an intensely red glow, then suddenly wrapped in deep gloom, as the flames rose and fell, while the vessel quivered and every flank in her was shaken by the loud reverberations of the cannon. Alas, poor Danes! I could not but feel for them.[1]

With daylight, many Danish civilians quickly packed a few valuables and whatever food they could carry and made their way from these dangerous

---

1 George Jackson letter of 14 September 1807, quoted in Muir, p. 204.

areas, over the bridges into the relative safety of Christianshavn and onto the island of Amager itself.

Rumours abound in such situations, but one particularly strong one, mentioned by many, may well have been spread by the city authorities. It was stated that if the city could hold on until the winter, then troops would be able to come to their relief over the ice from Fynen: all they had to do was to hold on for three months!

At around 6 p.m. on the evening of 3 September the guns began to rain death once again but more slowly and deliberately, as there was a shortage of ammunition. It went on all night again, wearing down the inhabitants and igniting even more fires which the heavily depleted surviving firefighters now struggled hard to extinguish. At least twenty major fires were started this night, including the huge timber yard which went up a treat, but apart from the fire in the wood yard, they were all successfully extinguished by the valiant local firemen, although after two nights of constant firefighting they were now completely exhausted. The firing ceased around 8 a.m. apart from sporadic Shots and most of the surviving inhabitants, who had not already fled from the northern and western suburbs of the city, took the lull as an opportunity to evacuate their families to the safety of Amager, passing the numerous charred corpses of those who had been killed which still littered the streets.

The bombardment on the third night, which began at 7 p.m. on 4 September was truly dreadful. Having had their ammunition replenished, the bombardment was incredibly heavy and much more devastating, as few of the surviving firemen were able to continue and with little of their equipment still working, the flames took a serious hold. The old wooden houses of the medieval town took fire again and the conflagration raged through the narrow streets, easily passing from one to another and spreading with great rapidity, but this time there was virtually no-one left to put them out and the entire area was devastated. It was reported that some of the Danish militia abandoned their posts on the ramparts to save their families, morale and discipline were beginning to break down and with the lack of firefighters available the city was effectively abandoned to the flames. The most dramatic moment in the entire bombardment was when the tallest spire on the Copenhagen skyline, that of the Frue Kirke, or the Church of Our Lady, came crashing down amongst the flames just before dawn. Captain Thomas Browne watched the bombardment in awe:

> The fire from our batteries, and from the Danish ramparts, resembled a constant succession of flashes of lightning, and the very firmament shook with the unceasing explosions. A church steeple was set on fire by a shell lodging in the belfry, and, it fell a mass of flame, with a tremendous crash on the houses near it, and communicated flames to a whole street.[1]

---

1 Buckley, p. 59.

The *Glukstadt* frigate was also apparently set on fire by a shell, but it was extinguished.

Small numbers of Danish militia troops had assembled on the islands of Funen, Fehmarn and Langeland and during the bombardment attempts were made to pass these troops over to Zealand as opportunities arose. Three hundred and fifty men were passed over safely on 4 September without being discovered by Keats' patrol ships. Further small parties were passed over, none of which were discovered by the British squadron. However, the numbers successfully passing across never rose to anything like a significant level and they were unable to achieve anything of significance.

On 4 September, Gambier and Cathcart received letters from Castlereagh dated 27 August, which could potentially have disrupted the entire operation. The government needed troops urgently for 'a particular service' – almost certainly to rescue the Portuguese fleet in a similar operation to that at Copenhagen, following a French ultimatum on 12 August for Portugal to declare war on Britain and to allow its fleet to be used by France and her allies or she would be invaded. Castlereagh therefore requested the immediate return of at least 10,000 men, but preferably 15,000, including the Guards Brigade and Wellesley's reserve, and a large proportion of the artillery and engineers. The government were anxiously trying to rescue both fleets from Napoleon's clutches, but trying to do both with the same troops risked complete failure. Gambier replied on 5 September, taking advantage of the discretion given in Castlereagh's letter, declining to send any troops back at all, particularly at such a decisive phase in the proceedings: the government would have to look elsewhere for troops. It was a brave stance and one that Cathcart must have supported wholeheartedly.

Major General Stricker, the commandant of Cronborg, issued an extraordinary appeal to the Hanoverian troops to change their allegiance. It failed spectacularly as it was quite clear that Copenhagen was on the verge of surrendering or being stormed.

> You Hanoverians, we consider as innocent people, forced to accomplish the cruel commands of your government. But you will be the sacrifice; it is yet time to save your lives. Being Hanoverians, you are long since discharged from your duty and faith towards the treacherous government of England. Do not obey the commands of this inhuman and bloody ministry in order to subjugate an innocent nation. Let us associate ourselves together. The Danes will always receive you like friends. You will find the most secure refuge at Copenhagen or Cronborg. Hasten thither! The Danes, the faithful Danes, who will shew you kindness,

security, and support, promise you in the most solemn manner, at the conclusion of the war, to lead you in safety to your native land.

Hanoverians! Hearken to the voice of friendship and reason![1]

At around noon on the 5th, the British guns finally fell silent after a night of sheer terror and great devastation. The population was stunned after three sleepless nights of horror, when it was claimed that up to 2,000 people had been killed and wounded.[2] Just under 10 per cent of the city had been entirely destroyed and up to a quarter of the city had sustained damage. The flames in some parts around the Frue Kirke were apparently not fully extinguished until the end of September. One particularly potent symbol of the British bombardment was the first use of Congreve's rockets against a city. It is well known that Wellington was never a great fan of rockets, but it is also clear that the Royal Navy at Copenhagen had little faith in the weapon or its designer, William Congreve, who personally attended the batteries at Copenhagen to view their performance and was to be seen striding around in his distinctive white cloak and hat – which luckily for him did not attract a Danish rifle bullet from the many marksmen they employed. Charles Chambers of the *Prometheus* fire ship mockingly called him 'Commodore Squib' and thought the weapon was useless. This was not a view shared by the inhabitants of the city, who had found these hissing, fast-moving demons, with flames and smoke trailing behind them as they traversed the night sky had a hugely disproportionate effect on the civilian population, having a psychological effect much like that of the 'doodlebugs' on the inhabitants of London, who had coped so stoically with the years of bombing raids that preceded them. Indeed, it is calculated that only 300 rockets were fired out of a total bombardment counting over 6,000 projectiles over the three nights, less than 5 per cent of the total. However, their psychological effect was so great that the inhabitants of Copenhagen talk of them as if their numbers were nearer 90 per cent of the total. The apocryphal stories of the destructive power of the rockets, which were reputed to have broken through every floor and killed families sheltering in their own basements, had a terrible effect on morale. Surgeon Chambers of the *Polyphemus* described the awful but brilliant scene:

> The extensive brilliancy and velocity of the shells as they traverse the air is far greater than I could have imagined, and their altitude almost incredible, 'twas curious to see those fired by the opposite parties cross each other in the atmosphere, and we several times thought a collision

---

1 Quoted in Beamish, Vol. 1 p. 127.
2 The latest research seems to indicate that the actual Danish toll was 195 civilian deaths with 768 wounded: see Jelsdorf.

must have taken place between some of them as they passed extremely close together.[1]

The final parallel had been constructed, pontoons had been prepared to cross the lakes and the batteries were ready to make a breach. No specific plans or a date for such an assault have been discovered, but both the army and the navy clearly believed that such an assault was imminent if the Danes did not succumb to the bombardment. To support such an attack, it was planned that a number of warships would approach very close to the Trekroner Battery and engage it at point-blank range. Despite the innate weakness of wooden warships attacking stone batteries, the navy expected to succeed, having prepared large numbers of seamen and marines (about fifty men per ship) to attempt to escalade the fort from ship's boats, under the protection of the barrage from the gunboats. This intense fire, it was thought, would destroy the Danish guns and their crews as the batteries were not casemated, but merely 'en barbette' or firing over the parapets without having any overhead protection.

A battalion of seamen had been landed on 5 September from the British fleet under the command of Captain Watson of the *Inflexible*. They were to have aided the British troops passing over the wet ditch during the storming of the city, which would have occurred within the next few days, had the bombardment not brought about the capitulation.

Peymann had come to realize that the city could take no more and he therefore requested an armistice of twenty-four hours in which to arrange a capitulation. Cathcart had initially smelt a rat and although he temporarily ordered the guns to fall silent, he suspected another Danish delaying tactic. He sent George Murray into Copenhagen with a letter requesting Peymann to specify the conditions of the capitulation and telling Murray not to listen to any proposal which fell short of the handing over of the entire Danish fleet.

Peymann felt unable to make such a decision alone, although he would bear ultimate responsibility. He therefore called a Council of War and promised to give Murray a definite answer by noon on the 6 September. The Council met at 10 a.m. on 6 September at Peymann's headquarters at the Raus Hotel[2] with the senior figures of the army, navy and city government all being present, twenty-three people in all. Peymann painted a bleak but honest picture; the city's defences could not withstand a serious assault, food supplies were dwindling – much having been destroyed by the flames – there was no hope of relief by the Danish army and the morale of the populace was

---

1 Navy Records Society, *The Journal of Surgeon Charles Chambers*, p. 406.
2 Today the five-star Hotel d'Angleterre on Kongens Nytorv

exceptionally low. When asked if they should continue the struggle or admit defeat and capitulate, the vote was unanimous for capitulation. Even now, however, the naval officers still did not mention the secret orders to destroy the fleet. Instead, Steen Bille called for a final sortie against the British and the carpenters and seamen marched on Peymann's hotel, demanding action, but the students of the King's Volunteers managed to keep the peace and things eventually calmed down.

A letter was sent to Cathcart proposing a convention of capitulation and Gambier and Cathcart spent a few hours deliberating on their list of demands. Cathcart had envisaged a formal capitulation including the garrison marching out and laying down their arms to become prisoners of war; however, Cathcart insisted that beyond removing the fleet, nothing further should be demanded which would humiliate the Danes, so the terms of the capitulation were eased, against Jackson's wishes, who had become aware of the British government's new considerations regarding the possibilities of holding Zealand.

Sir Home Popham was selected to represent the navy in the talks, Murray and Wellesley would represent the army. The three officers met their Danish counterparts at the East Gate at 8 p.m. on 6 September and the negotiations went on throughout the night at Peymann's headquarters. The articles were signed at 2 a.m. on 7 September, the British pledging to evacuate Copenhagen, indeed the whole of Zealand, within six weeks, taking the entire Danish fleet with them. All prisoners on both sides would be returned and Danish persons and private property were to be respected. An initial British demand for possession of Trekroner battery was dropped, but the Danish fleet was now taken without any promise to ever return it, or to pay for them: the ships and naval stores were now simply viewed as prizes of war. Murray describes a moment when a Danish admiral attempted to haggle over the naval stores, when Wellesley answered loudly 'Now Admiral, mind, every stick! Every stick!'

The Danish Council of War reconvened and a few mentioned the possibility of destroying the Danish ships, but it was dismissed, as it would be deemed a major breach of the capitulation and would undoubtedly lead to much tougher sanctions by the British. Peymann still remained ignorant of the Prince's orders; Steen Bille however, wrote to the Prince the day after the capitulation to absolve himself of any culpability for the loss of the fleet. It was all very odd, as though no one really wanted to go through with the destruction of the fleet – but Peymann got all the blame, even though he had never been told of the order – but the Crown Prince didn't bother with such niceties when looking for scapegoats for the disaster that had befallen them.

Chapter 19

The Aftermath

At 4 p. m. on 7 September, Colonel Cameron of the 79th Foot marched the flank companies of the regiments in his brigade into the city and took formal possession of the citadel. At the same time, the navy embarked Major General Spencer's brigade in boats and rowed them over to the dockyard to take possession of the Danish warships and the arsenal. At each vessel, the Danish sentries only retired as the British sentry actually took up his post in succession. Captain Thomas Browne was immensely impressed by the Danish organization:

> Nothing could be more complete, than the arrangement of this arsenal, which perfectly verified the inscription over the gate 'Quantitas, Qualitas, et Ordo'. Each ship lay alongside a store-house, in the lower room of which were her anchors, masts and spars. On the second floor, were her cables, ropes, and heavy rigging. On the third floor, were her top sails, colours and light rigging. There were cranes from each of these floors, from which to lower their contents into the ship. Guards were placed in each of these store houses and on board every vessel.[1]

The damage to the city was immense; the official Danish reports list some 305 dwellings and one church having been completely destroyed, with many thousands more receiving some damage. Rifleman William Green was shocked at the destruction:

> I was astonished to see the havoc our bombardment had made. Whole streets lay in ruins; churches burnt down; and we had hard work to get through the streets to the dock-yard, and to go on board, our road being blocked up with bricks, stones, tiles and timber.[2]

---

1 Buckley, p. 60.
2 Teague, p. 10.

Captain Leach was also appalled by the destruction caused and he reflected the horror that many of the British soldiers felt regarding the destruction they had caused:

> Callous and insensible must he have been who could have walked through the streets and witnessed the horrors occasioned by the bombardment, and the misery inflicted on thousands of the unoffending inhabitants, without bitterly regretting that our government should have considered it necessary to adopt such rigorous measures.[1]

Captain William Gomm was both astonished and ashamed at the level of devastation:

> The sight was dreadful, but it was truly magnificent; the church of Notre Dame, the cathedral and the church, which made the finest appearance in the town, fell to the ground at five in the morning, and nothing is standing but the bare foundation. Do us justice to believe that we felt the horrors of this scene in all its extent; and imagine us at the same time redoubling our exertions as the calamity increased, and throwing showers of shells towards the parts where the fire raged most to render ineffectual the means employed to extinguish it.[2]

Ensign Blakeney was shocked but equally impressed by the stoic reaction of the Danes:

> The spectacle was lamentable and well calculated to rouse every feeling of sympathy. Many houses were still smouldering, and in part crumbled to the ground; mothers were bewailing the melancholy fate of their slaughtered children, and there was not one but deplored the loss of some fondly beloved relative or dearly valued friend. Yet they received us with dignified, though cool courtesy . . .[3]

The insurance claims for buildings came to 2.5 million rigsdaler, injury and loss of personal possessions adding up to another 6.5 million rigsdaler; indeed, the total private losses were put at over 10 million rigsdaler.

One Norwegian eyewitness wrote home:

> It is difficult to think of anything more frightful and terrible than this bombardment, and nobody who was not there can have any real idea of

---

1 Leach, p. 35.
2 Carr-Gomm, p. 85
3 Blakeney, p. 12.

A contemporary print showing the destruction of a hull on the slipway.

the horror of it. Imagine the air filled with rapidly moving . . . shooting
stars . . . imagine them flying along with a piercing scream and crashing
down into a house and smashing roofs, ceilings, beams and floors and
several storeys to pieces with a shocking din and exploding with a dreadful
bang, then flames breaking out through windows, ceilings, doors etc, and
this will give you a vague picture of the sight we have witnessed almost
every second. To this must be added that with almost every bomb we saw
people either killed or with injuries to arms and legs . . . [1]

The historian Arnold Harvey has calculated that three times as much
gunpowder was used during the bombardment of Copenhagen than was used
at the Battle of Waterloo.[2]

A report in one European newspaper stated that:

Besides the principal church, several streets in the northern quarter of
the town are mostly in ashes; there is scarcely a house that is not damaged.
According to report, the bombs, grenades, and rockets thrown into the
town, exclusive of cannon shot, exceed 2,000 in number. Fifteen hundred

---

1 Glenthoj and Ottesen, p. 42.
2 Glenthoj and Ottesen, p. 42.

burgers and inhabitants have lost their lives; and four hundred wounded persons, of both sexes, have been carried to Frederick's Hospital.[1]

The populace of Copenhagen were certainly very unhappy with the actions of the British, but they did cooperate passively. Wellesley wrote to Lord Hawkesbury on 8 September:

> They certainly are much irritated against us, so much so that the Danish officers who settled the capitulation apprehended a riot among the sailors and the Burgher militia on account of the cession of the fleet; and the officers of the navy in particular were likely to be much irritated.[2]

The real danger of unrest led to an agreement that no British troops would be billeted in the city or allowed to enter unless on official business for a few days to allow things to settle, so the gates of the city were therefore left under the control of the Danish forces. The postal service was also allowed to resume, but everything going in or out had to go through the citadel, so that it could be vetted.

Because of the severe economic downturn that followed, it took over two decades to make good the damage to the city. The Church of our Lady was only rebuilt in 1829 and it was not until 1836 that the main university building was fully repaired.

On 7 September, Admiral Gambier wrote his official dispatch but one sentence in it was removed when sent to the printers and was not published in the *London Gazette*. 'As few of the ships are in any considerable progress of equipment, it will require some time to complete them for sea, but not a moment will be lost in bringing the whole of them to England.' This embarrassingly proved that there had been no preparations made to get the Danish fleet ready for sea, just as the Danes had said; it could not therefore be published.

The dockyards of Chatham and Sheerness were warned to prepare to receive the captured Danish ships. Trinity House at London, Leith and Hull were ordered to furnish masters and pilots who were well acquainted with the navigation of the North Sea, to pilot the Danish fleet to England. The government offered £2 10 shillings plus the pay of an able seaman to the crews of Greenland-men just arrived back, to proceed to Denmark to assist in the safe navigation of the ships to England, with the assurance of being sent back home free of charge at the end of the mission. It was reported that well over 2,000 men took advantage of this opportunity.

---

1 *The Naval Chronicle*, Vol. IV, p, 48.

2 Supplementary Despatches of the Duke of Wellington Volume VI page 22.

The Capitulation of Copenhagen 1807 – contemporary print.

The British only had six weeks to get the large number of Danish vessels ready for sea and as much of the immense naval stores on board the transport ships before the deadline of 19 October expired. Vice Admiral Stanhope and Rear Admiral Sir Samuel Hood were given joint responsibility for preparing the captured Danish ships for their voyage to Britain. Two ships of the line and two frigates deemed unserviceable were destroyed. As for the rest, each British ship's crew was allocated their own Danish vessel to prepare for sea and to embark the naval stores on each. This system engendered a friendly rivalry between the crews, each vying to be the first to have their ship ready. Despite some wild estimates by some of those present, with figures in the millions bandied about, the naval stores were eventually calculated for prize money at around £320,000, or about £15 million in today's terms.

Wellesley was aware that the British public would not be particularly pleased with the outcome and would criticize ministers for this questionable act. He wrote 'Our friends in England will certainly be disappointed whatever may be the ultimate result & I am in some degree the cause of their disappointment.' Wellesley sailed home in the *Prometheus* on 18 September,[1]

---

1 It is often mistakenly thought that Wellesley brought a horse back home with him, which he named 'Copenhagen'. The horse Copenhagen which he rode throughout his military career was not foaled until 1808 in England and was simply named in commemoration of the campaign. Wellesley, or the Duke of Wellington as he then was, only bought the horse in 1813 from Sir Charles Vane, who had brought the horse out to Spain with him.

landing at Yarmouth on the 28th. He rushed on to the capital and he met both Castlereagh and Canning in London soon after. He did help to satisfy them of the impossibility of keeping Zealand over the winter and then travelled on to Dublin to take up his post again.

The army supplied large numbers of men to help in the process of preparing the ships, who provided a great deal of much-needed brawn even if they didn't know one end of a ship from the other. Captain George Bowles[1] recorded that 'a working party of 6,000 of the army, exclusive of sailors, have been constantly employed, from daylight till dark, ever since the surrender, loading the ships, and a great deal still remains. The Danes themselves value all that we have taken at ten million's sterling.'

After only nine days fourteen of the line had been warped out of the harbour, fully ready for sea, even though some of them had required major repairs. Within the six weeks, sixteen of the line, eleven frigates and twelve lesser vessels, plus twenty-six gunboats were successfully prepared to sail and all of the spare spars and masts loaded on board the *Leyden* and *Inflexible*. The general naval stores were loaded on ninety-two merchant vessels allocated for this purpose.[2] The weight of the stores embarked exceeded 20,000 tons, a remarkable feat. Wellesley had claimed 'every stick' and it appears that they took him at his word, taking even the stoves, the office furniture, books and maps. Three ships were found partly built on the stocks, two were completely dismantled and all of the useful timbers loaded to transport them to Britain, the third being quite near to completion, but impossible to finish within the six weeks, was sawed through at various locations and allowed to fall over and broken up. Everything went well, apart from one mishap, when a guard from the 32nd Regiment, whose duty was to keep watch on a magazine, incautiously set it ablaze whilst he was smoking. He and three others were killed and a few storehouses badly damaged, but the fire was contained before it caused further serious damage.

There was one moment of a potentially serious nature when Cathcart received a letter from Canning, who now wanted even more. Despite the agreement having already been signed, Canning began to seek advice and support for the idea of retaining the island of Zealand and defending it

---

1 In his letter written on 5 October.

2 It is often stated that these ninety-two ships were Danish merchant vessels which were in harbour and were taken to carry the stores, which is seen as a further hostile act against Denmark. However, Admiral Gambier makes it clear in his despatch of 20 October 1807, that the 20,000 tons of additional shipping required to remove all of the naval stores were chartered for this specific purpose. *Naval Chronicle*, Vol. IV, p. 107.

against France.[1] It had, he claimed, the added benefit of giving free access to the Baltic for British merchant shipping. This was being considered, despite the unequivocal evidence from numerous senior naval officers that the Belt would freeze in winter or at least be infested with icebergs, preventing the navy from patrolling the channel and leaving the island very vulnerable to attack. Sweden was approached, however, in the quest for more soldiers to garrison the island, as it was deemed necessary to have a garrison of at least 30,000 men to hold Zealand. Cathcart was aware of the discussions, but realized that it couldn't succeed and he bravely continued to embark the entire expedition and sailed for England as per the agreement that had been signed, fully prepared to answer the criticism of government ministers on his return. Luckily for him, the Cabinet had eventually concluded that they should not breach the armistice, no matter what provocation they could invent, 'to preserve our character for good faith untainted'.[2] This view was particularly laughable, given that Britain's reputation was already in tatters as far as Europe was concerned over its treatment of Denmark and it really could not sink any lower. The British government did toy later with leaving 15,000 troops in Swedish Scania over the winter, which would have given them the opportunity to re-invade Zealand in the spring, but the Swedish king, afraid that supplies for the British troops would seriously denude the area, politely refused the offer.

Incredibly, the British government then mooted the idea of retaining joint control of Denmark with the Danes – who were already officially at war with Britain! Needless to say, it did not receive a favourable reply, but the British government did not give up the idea entirely until well after the fleet had sailed for home. Jackson had tried to negotiate on these terms, gaining a passport from Peymann to travel home via Nyborg. He was granted the passport but on arrival off the harbour, he was refused entry and he eventually sailed for Britain on 14 September. The government sent another emissary, Anthony Merry, who had served at Copenhagen in 1800 and had maintained friendly relations with the Danes: he was even allowed to broach the subject of compensation for private individuals who had suffered in the bombardment. Britain would prefer an alliance but would accept continued Danish neutrality; if not, Denmark would see her remaining overseas possessions taken from her and its merchant fleet decimated. It was sure to fail.

---

1 Because of the British agreement to leave Copenhagen after six weeks, Canning suggested that the fleet sailed, so as to fulfil the wording of the agreement and then to return the following day to take Zealand. Such an underhand ploy was certainly not in the spirit of the agreement even if it was technically acceptable.

2 *Correspondence of Castlereagh*, Vol. VI, p. 184

The embarkation of the British troops began on 13 October, with the embarkation of all eight line battalions of the KGL at the Arsenal. The following day the two KGL light battalions and Macfarlane's brigade consisting of the 7th and 8th Foot embarked in the same transports they had sailed over on and the whole sailed for Hull. These, with the sick and wounded of the army, had filled all the available troop transports. All of the outlying advance posts were called in, taking up to three days to march in to Copenhagen.

The embarkation of the siege guns and stores had continued separately from the Lime Kilns jetty, which was to continue for some time longer. Over the next few days the cavalry and KGL artillery was embarked from the dockyard in the horse transports. The remainder of the British infantry regiments then embarked gradually from the citadel and were distributed amongst the British warships.

By the afternoon of Sunday, 18 October, all that remained ashore were the Brigade of Guards at the Palace of Frederiksberg; with one British artillery battery and the flank companies of the 32nd, 50th and 82nd Foot in the Arsenal under General Spencer; and the 4th Foot and some British artillerymen in the Citadel under Lieutenant Colonel Wynch. This rearguard was commanded by Lieutenant General Sir George Ludlow.

As a gale blew for the next twenty-four hours, the final embarkation was postponed causing the deadline of the 19th to be missed. The British and Danish authorities agreed to a short extension, but the Danes did complain that the citadel was not returned to them. The Guards Brigade had marched to Hellerup and on the morning of 20 October, Spencer's force rowed out of the Arsenal, moving along the coast to join the Guards. The 4th Foot marched out of the citadel and marched to Hellerup as HMS *Rosamond* sailed out of the harbour, finally bringing the British possession of Copenhagen to an end. At Hellerup a floating battery and prame had been beached and planked over to form a jetty from which the troops could embark in boats and move to the warships, the jetty being set alight as they rowed away. Everything passed off peacefully and the Danish people were civil as the troops passed through, although the loss of the fleet had to hurt. The Danes also lost a huge number of guns to the British, causing a great shortage and the need for a rapid expansion in production of new ones.[1]

As the ships sailed for Britain, they had first to pass Cronborg Castle, whose guns remained silent by prior agreement. The royal family of Sweden came down to Helsinborg to view the passing of this huge fleet of over a thousand

---

1 The Danes calculated that the British had taken 2,041 long guns, 202 carronades and 222 mortars. See James, Vol. IV, p. 212.

ships, whilst Cathcart and Gambier both landed to pay their respects and were very well received.

As the ships began sailing into the North Sea, however, they ran into stormy weather; one Danish battleship, the *Neptunus*, was lost and all but three of the gunboats sank. Private Andrew Watt of the 92nd Foot was on the ship when she foundered:

> The Neptuna man of ware [*sic*] which we took from the Danes I was on board of and which unfortunately ran on a bank in the Baltick and there remained until destroyed. We was then sent to an iland (of Hewan) [*sic*] belonging to Sweden until there were transports got to carry us home.[1]

The Danes were perversely delighted to hear of these ex-Danish ships that foundered, viewing it very much as 'God's punishment.' Later the Danes were able to re-float six gunboats and a gun platform, which were returned to the Danish navy.

The huge fleet crossed the North Sea in safety, but the KGL troopships were ordered to sail into the Channel to land at Portsmouth and Ramsgate. Unfortunately, these ships ran straight into a second storm, with terrible consequences. The *Endeavour* transport struck on Goodwin Sands and twenty-four men of the 3rd Light Dragoons KGL and twenty-three horses perished. The *Providence* transport ran foul of an East Indiaman which carried away her stern, but by extreme good luck all but the horses survived, the *Shorn* losing another nineteen horses; the *Hope* transport was lost with forty sick of the 2nd KGL Light Dragoons and the *Eagle* went down with eight officers and 172 men of the 7th KGL Line Battalion: the chaplain and his family were all lost. The *Augustus Caesar* transport became fouled by HMS *Inflexible* and lost her masts. Many men successfully scrambled on board the warship, but she was driven onto the Dutch coast and despite being in clear distress, the ship was fired on by the Dutch. Colonel Ompteda and eight other officers with 200 men of the 1st KGL Line Battalion were made prisoners. Worst of all was the loss of the transport *Salisbury* which ran onto a bank and had to endure constant huge breakers crashing over her. Help came but was unable to save many before the ship broke up with the loss of nine officers, 212 men and five children of the 2nd KGL Line Battalion. The King's German Legion had suffered just over 1,000 killed and wounded in the expedition, most drowning on their return journey.

The British celebrated this victory with a little more gusto than they had in 1801 and the most senior officers received rewards. What it had achieved

---

1 Hewison, p. 210.

for the British was the virtual blowing open of the gates to the Baltic and giving them easy access and almost unchallenged control of that sea. Lord Cathcart, who was already Baron Greenock, was made Viscount Cathcart of Renfrewshire. Admiral Gambier was made Baron Gambier of Iver in Buckinghamshire. Vice Admiral Edwin Stanhope, Lieutenant General Sir Harry Burrard and Major General Blomefield (who commanded the artillery) were all made baronets. Captain Collier of the *Surveillante*, who carried the dispatches, was knighted. Lieutenant Cathcart (the son of Lord Cathcart), who carried the military dispatches was made a captain. Interestingly, Arthur Wellesley and the other divisional commanders did not receive any honours for Copenhagen.

The King and many others had deep reservations over the whole thing, however, George III going as far as to say that it was 'a very immoral act'.[1] Perhaps tellingly, no medals were issued for Copenhagen in 1807 by either side; and the British did not even issue a bar to the newly-inaugurated General Service Medal and Naval General Service Medal in 1848 for the few veterans who were still alive.

Cathcart came away with his reputation with ministers seemingly intact, but it seems that there was a very different view in the army. Major John Macdonald, his own Military Secretary, noted that:

> We have all been grievously disappointed in our man, and we are anxiously looking to a speedy termination of our present uncomfortable situation. For my own part I would not be obliged to do business again with Lord C[athcart] in the field for any consideration upon earth, and my colleagues about him are all of the same feeling. You have no conception of the state of his temper or of the uncertainty and irregularity of doing business with him.[2]

His view was fully endorsed by Pine Coffin, the Assistant Quarter Master General:

> However, I might have heretofore disliked the conduct of Lord C[athcart] as a man, I had always given him credit for being one of the best officers in our service, but I am now convinced that there is scarcely one that is worse, and I believe I am correct in saying that there is hardly a general officer that has served with him on this expedition would consent to do so upon another.[3]

---

1 Letter of George III to Canning dated 26 August 1807.
2 Undated letter in the Ward papers quoted in Muir, p. 204.
3 Letter of Pine Coffin dated 9 November 1807.

The prize money for Copenhagen was quite substantial, First Lieutenant George Browne of the 23rd Foot received £97 (about £3,500 today) for his 16 shares, meaning that an ordinary private received just over £6 (£250) for their single share and Cathcart would have received a healthy £4,800 (£180,000) z for his 800 shares. The figures of prize money for the navy appear to be smaller, the naval pot being shared by the crews of no less than 126 ships. The *London Gazette*[1] records that able seamen received £3 8 shillings (£150), whilst petty officers received £22 11 shillings (£800), which presumably means that Gambier received £2,720 for his share (£100,000).

As for Denmark, the outcome was not so rosy – for hell hath no fury like a prince scorned. The Crown Prince was apoplectic with rage when he heard on 11 September of the capitulation and that the fleet had not been destroyed, as he had ordered; he was in no mood to accept excuses. Poor Peymann of course stood to face the brunt of his anger, the Prince being unaware that he had never been told of the plan.

The Prince refused to respond to the reports sent from Copenhagen and when General Walterstorff arrived at Kiel – being one of the signatories of the capitulation – he was promptly placed under arrest. Steen Bille was the only commander not to feel the Prince's wrath, his artful subterfuges having obscured his involvement and the Prince summoned him to Kiel as the only man he trusted to give him a faithful report of what had transpired.

Frederick believed that Peymann had overstepped his authority: he was governor of Copenhagen and Elsinore only, but had signed a treaty for the entire island of Zealand. The Prince was however forced to concede the point and to honour the capitulation, including suspending attempts to land troops in Zealand. He did, however, organize Castenchiold's troops on Lolland and moved those on Langeland and Fehmarn to join them, giving him a force of 9,000 militia, ready to land on Zealand as soon as the terms of the armistice were fulfilled.[2]

Frederick was particularly worried how Napoleon would react to the news and he urgently dispatched a letter written in his own hand, addressed to Napoleon personally. He explained that the navy was ordered to be destroyed rather than handed over to the British and stated that he would never negotiate with 'their common enemy'. Meanwhile, Count Bernstorff had met with Marshal Bernadotte, asking for the assistance of a French auxiliary corps on the island of Funen to act as a reserve to the Danish army once it had crossed the Great Belt onto Zealand. In fact, Napoleon was quite lenient,

---

1 *The London Gazette*, 11 July 1809.

2 The Danish newspapers claimed that the 1st and 3rd Jutland Infantry and Horzen's Dragoons had already landed in Zealand during the siege. See James, Vol. IV, p. 211.

but took steps to ensure that Denmark was firmly on his side. The Danes waited until after the British evacuation to publicly declare their decision – an emphatic no to Britain's proposals – and Denmark signed a formal treaty of alliance with France at Fontainebleau on 31 October 1807, which did require Denmark to support any future war against Sweden; Denmark was now in thrall to Napoleon for the foreseeable future. As part of the agreement, the French hinted at the loan of two ships of the line and two frigates to Denmark, to be manned by the Danes but retained under French control. The crews, numbering nearly 2,000 seamen, were sent to the Scheldt in April 1808 to man the ships, but constant bickering over who would command them and how they would pass through the English Channel, led to them never going anywhere. Napoleon ordered the ships to Brest in 1809, but the crews were very close to open mutiny and finally in late 1813, having achieved nothing, Frederick ordered the crews home. A rebellion had also broken out in December 1810, when seamen at Christiansand in Norway were conscripted for the French fleet in the Scheldt.

The Tsar was horrified by Britain's actions against Denmark. He had initially offered to mediate, but when that came to nothing, Russia declared war on Britain on 8 November and the following day an embargo was placed on all British shipping in Russian ports. Realizing that the embargo was imminent, the British merchant ships had hurriedly sailed and only four ships were still at Cronstadt when the sanction was imposed. Prussia followed suit on 1 December, leaving Sweden as Britain's only ally in the Baltic and unfortunately their king was mentally deranged!

When Prince Frederick returned to Copenhagen in November, he discovered one vessel left by the British. It was a yacht originally gifted by George III to his nephew Frederick in 1785. The Crown Prince ordered that it should be crewed by sixteen British prisoners of war under the command of a British merchant captain and sent back to Britain. Peymann, his senior officers and the three others who had signed the capitulation were all placed under arrest and tried by court martial for dereliction of duty. It took a year before the sentences were published on 16 November 1808. Peymann and Bielefeldt were found guilty and sentenced to 'forfeit their honour and lives'; whilst Gedde was sentenced to death but did not forfeit his honour; those who simply signed the capitulation were cleared. Steen Bille was not charged and only attended the event as a witness.

King Christian VII died in March 1808 and the Crown Prince was now on the throne as King Frederick VI.[1] The sentences had made their point and Frederick exercised mercy, commuting the death sentences to dismissal from

---

1 He was crowned king on 16 March 1808.

the army without a pension. General Peymann retired to Holstein, but his rank and pension was fully restored in 1816. He died seven years later.

Denmark could never really recover from the loss of her fleet. It was an abject disaster and led to dreadful economic collapse. Britain suffered no real punishment for her actions: this in fact strengthened her hand in the Baltic significantly and the anger of Russia would only last for five short years, until Napoleon marched on Moscow.

Chapter 20

Danish Losses Further Afield

Copenhagen and her crown jewels – the fleet – were not the only losses that Denmark had to endure this year. Whilst Denmark's entire focus was on Zealand, Britain had the power to act on numerous fronts across the world at the same time. Her first act, however, was more of a surprise than the rest.

The tiny island of Heligoland – only half a square mile in area – lies twenty-nine miles off the North Sea coast of Germany, but is perfectly placed as a base from which to watch over the shipping emerging from a number of North German rivers. Captain Charles Lord Falkland[1] of HMS *Quebec* had already summoned the small garrison on 30 August, but this had been rejected by the governor. Vice Admiral Russel then arrived off the Danish island on board the 74-gun *Majestic* on 4 September at 2:30 p.m., expecting to meet with a small squadron there. Although alone, the admiral began making immediate preparations for a landing in preparation for an immediate storming of the defences by a party of marines and sailors. These hostile preparations were very obvious to the defenders and at 6 p.m. the governor of Heligoland – the garrison consisting of only twenty-six invalids – sent a deputation out to treat for a formal capitulation.

Lieutenant D'Auvergne, First Lieutenant of the *Majestic*, was sent ashore the following morning to discuss terms. The deputation returned with the lieutenant at 2 p.m. with the agreed treaty, which Russel ratified. D'Auvergne was appointed as acting governor until another could be appointed by the government. On the morning of 6 September, the missing squadron, consisting of the *Explosion*, *Wanderer* and *Exertion*, did eventually appear from the north.

Admiral Russell explained the importance of the island, stating that

---

1 Captain Charles John Cary, 9th Viscount Falkland. He was mortally wounded in a duel two years later.

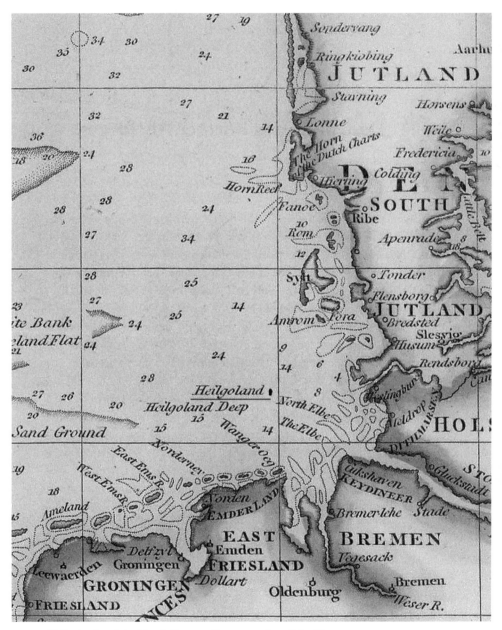

Heligoland and the North German Coast – section of the Thompson map.

With a small expense, this island may be made a little Gibraltar, and a safe haven for small craft, even in the winter; it is a key to the rivers Ems, Weser, Jade, Elbe and Eider, [and forming] the only asylum at present for our cruisers in these seas.

The British government agreed, and they maintained a small garrison on the island;[1] Denmark formally ceded Heligoland permanently to Britain in the Treaty of Kiel on 14 January 1814 and this was ratified at the subsequent Treaty of Paris on 30 May. Britain retained the island, although never using it as a forward naval base as the Royal Navy deemed it too vulnerable, until 1890, when it was ceded to Germany in exchange for Zanzibar.

Another embarrassing incident for Denmark occurred in June 1809, when a Danish sailor, Jorgen Jurgensen,[2] landed on the Danish-controlled island of Iceland and launched a coup d'etat with his ship's company, arresting the Danish governor, Frederick, Count of Trampe, declaring a 'Protectorate' and promising to restore the *Althing*, the ancient Icelandic parliament, with the ultimate aim of a free Iceland. Strangely, HMS *Talbot* arrived in Reykjavik on 14 August and promptly arrested Jurgensen for having broken his parole, having originally been captured by HMS *Sapho*. The Danish governor was restored and the British ship sailed away with her prisoner. All very odd given that Britain was then at war with Denmark! Jurgensen was tried for breaking his parole and gaoled, but was finally freed in 1811. He became a drunk and a gambler, was frequently arrested for debt, became a British spy and was eventually transported to Australia where he died in 1841.

Admiral Sir Alexander Cochrane, commanding the West Indies Station, had received warning in early September, that Britain and Denmark might soon be at war. In October, British naval vessels began capturing Danish merchant ships as prizes and in December, they turned to the Danish islands, which had been returned to the Danes in 1802.

HMS *Fawn* arrived at Barbados on 15 December 1807, bringing official notification of war with Denmark and the British forces – already expecting the news – sprang into action. Admiral Cochrane proceeded to sail with his flagship HMS *Belleisle* in company with a large squadron comprising four other ships of the line, seven frigates and ten brigs.[3] The troops embarked were under the command of General Henry Bowyer and chiefly consisted of detachments of the 70th and 90th Regiments.

Initially, on 21 December, the admiral summoned the governor of St Thomas, St John and their dependencies, a General von Scholten, who the

---

1 Throughout the rest of the war, the garrison consisted consistently of some 50 Royal Artillerymen and 350 men of the 8th Royal Veteran Battalion.

2 He changed his surname to Jorgensen in 1817.

3 The squadron consisted of *Prince George* 90, *Belleisle* 74, *Canada* 74, *Northumberland* 74, *Ramillies* 74, *Blonde* 38, *Latona* 38, *Ethalion* 36, *Cerberus* 32, *Circe* 32, *Galataea* 32, *Rosario* 20, *Melville* 18, *Thais* 18, *Favourite* 16, *Fawn* 16, *Saint Christopher* 16, *Hart* 16, *Lilly* 16, *Haughty* 14, *Swinger* 14 and *Pultusk* 10.

following morning agreed to sign the surrender after three of his officers had been provided with clear evidence of the size of the force about to land. A garrison of 300 men of the 70th Foot and a detachment of Royal Artillery were left on the islands and the remainder moved on to Santa Cruz. Admiral Cochrane had already sent the *Ethalion* ahead, carrying a summons to surrender and she returned on the 24th with a letter from the governor, offering to surrender as soon as three of his officers had visited the ships to ascertain the strength of the British force was as large as it was claimed to be. This was permitted and once these Danish officers reported to the governor, he sent a letter on 25 December, offering to surrender. The Danish West Indian islands had been lost without a single shot fired.

In the East Indies, the British also conquered Tranquebar[1] without a shot on 13 February 1808 when HMS *Russell* landed a detachment of the 1/14th Foot and the Honourable East India Company Artillery and then retained it and Serampore until the end of the war, only returning these possessions following the Treaty of Kiel in 1814.

It is almost universally stated that the Danish navy only possessed one ship of the line after the seizure of Copenhagen in 1807 and that ship was subsequently captured the following year, but this is not entirely correct. Two Danish ships of the line escaped the clutches of the British, the *Prinds Christian Frederik* of 66 guns and the *Prindsesse Lovisa Augusta* of 64 guns, both being in Norway at that time. In March 1808, reports of a British frigate anchoring off Sprogoe in the Great Belt caused some consternation in Copenhagen as its presence would seriously hamper the transfer of Spanish units from the French corps being transported from the mainland to Zealand in readiness for the planned attack on Sweden. Frederick had become King of Denmark on 17 March with the death of Christian and in one of his first acts on the following day, he ordered Captain Jessen and the *Prinds Christian Frederik* to destroy or at least drive the British frigate off, being the only ship available, as the *Prindsesse Lovisa Augusta* was in dry dock at Copenhagen undergoing repairs. The *Prinds Christian Frederik* was not in the best of shape, having been at sea continuously for a considerable period of time and with a third of her crew suffering from typhus. In fact, the only reason that she was still at sea, anchored off Cronborg Castle, was because of the ice which prevented her reaching Copenhagen. Replacement crew were sent to relieve the sick, and having been resupplied, the ship sailed on 21 March.

A British squadron under Commodore George Parker had sighted the Danish ship on 10 March, proceeding to Copenhagen, when they were then ice-bound off Gothenburg. By 21 March the British ships had cut themselves

---

1 Present-day Tharangambadi.

free and were determined to catch up with the *Prinds Christian Frederik*. Captain Jessen was aiming to sail round the south of Zealand to avoid the squadron of British ships known to be in the Kattegat, however, a change in the wind direction forced him to sail around the north of Zealand, hoping to avoid the British ships. However, when Commodore George Parker anchored his vessels that evening off Hornbaek, the local Swedish fishermen told him of the Danish ship's recent passage to the west. Giving immediate chase with his entire squadron of three ships of the line and four smaller ships,[1] they sought to hunt down the Danish ship.

Early on 22 March, HMS *Quebec* spotted *Prinds Christian Frederik* near Sejero Island and was soon joined by the *Falcon*. Captain Jessen looked to engage the two sloops and he moved eastwards into open waters, only to discover at 4 p.m. the *Stately* and the *Nassau* to the north-east and they entered the chase. By 8 p.m. the *Nassau* had come alongside and was exchanging broadsides with the Danish ship. After forty minutes of a severe fire, the *Nassau* looked to forge ahead of the Dane, to allow *Stately* to engage whilst also possibly trying to cross her bows to rake her. With two assailants engaging her, disaster now struck the *Prinds Christian Frederik* as she drove hard onto a shoal and stuck fast, 300 yards from shore and leaving her completely at the mercy of the British ships; she struck her colours. During the 23rd the boats of the squadron transported her crew to the British ships as prisoners and once everyone had been removed, the ship was set on fire. The fire in the hulk blazed into the late evening and then vanished in a great explosion. The *Stately* had lost four killed and thirty-one wounded and the *Nassau* one killed and seventeen wounded. The *Prinds Christian Frederik* lost much more severely, with fifty-five killed and eighty-eight wounded. Thus ended the Danish battleship war, the only remaining Danish ship of the line remaining safely ensconced in Copenhagen for the rest of the war. This is known to Danes as the Battle of Sjaellands Odde or Zealand Point and is particularly remembered for the death of a Danish hero of the Battle of Copenhagen of 1801, Sub-Lieutenant Peter Willemoes who had so valiantly commanded *Fleet Battery No. 1* that day. He was killed outright by a musket ball in the head.

There was also a long-term change of attitudes in Norway, which was originally very sympathetic to the plight of Copenhagen. The Norwegians viewed the defeat of the Swedish invasion of 1808 as a completely Norwegian victory and this saw the emergence of a separate Norwegian identity and the seeds of a national political struggle were sown this year. As time went on and the economic woes of Denmark bit hard, Norwegians began to be more

---

1 The squadron consisted of the *Vanguard* 74, *Stately* 64, *Nassau* 60, the frigate *Quebec* 32, the sloops *Falcon* 16 and *Lynx* 16, and the brig *Constant* 12.

inward-looking and tended to consider Norway separately from Denmark; the close bond of two countries viewing themselves as one nation were straining and were soon broken irrevocably.

The Danish populace came out of this latest event with a very poor view of the Danish military in general. There had been wholesale desertions and a number of those who were caught in the act were summarily shot. By far the worst was the Danish Marine Regiment, of which no less than 1,100 men, or 89 per cent of the corps, changed sides and joined the British: other units suffered but nowhere near as much as this unit. The King and the Royal Family generally were also low in public opinion, the people of Copenhagen unimpressed that they had not stayed to share their trials: Bernstorff was particularly vilified. To the public, the army remaining in Holstein had simply left Copenhagen defenceless and the Prince had just abandoned them. Knowing the poor opinions of the Prince being expressed at Copenhagen, the Crown Prince forbad all communication between Zealand and the rest of Denmark and he had all mail from Zealand opened at Kiel and examined in great detail. One civil servant concluded from the mail that:

> The mood in Copenhagen is extremely unfavourable. People heap abuse on the government, on the Crown Prince and on the ministries. The great merchants are so English-minded that they wish nothing more than to be under English rule. The common man also likes English guineas and curses their bombs. The better half are in the minority and are obliged to hold their tongues, at least while the English are there.[1]

A Patriotic Appeal was eventually launched with collections made for those injured or bereaved, those who had lost their homes and possessions and to help in the rebuilding of the fleet. On 8 April 1808, the funds were amalgamated into one and was further subsidised by the state, helping over 8,000 people in the first three months. New taxes were also raised and income tax was raised for the first time with the aim of paying off the national debt.

---

1 Glenthoj and Ottesen, p. 47.

Chapter 21

The Gunboat War, 1808–1809

Strenuous attempts had been made by Denmark to maintain her battle fleet at all costs, but now with its total loss, a radical rethink was required. Even before 1807, the Danish army had been calling for greater numbers of heavily-armed and shallow-draught gunboats which would allow the navy to support the army in the shallow waters which surround much of Denmark. Many towns and cities offered to raise funds for the building of ships to restore the navy, the pride of the nation, but rather than trying to go back to the very expensive and very lengthy process of building new ships of the line – which would always remain dangerously vulnerable to a return visit by the British to carry them off again – it was decided to concentrate on the production of hundreds of gunboats, which could be manufactured at a great rate. In the shoal waters of the Baltic, where in summer there are often dangerous calms which prevent sailing vessels moving, oared gunboats were a serious threat to even the largest and most powerful ships in the right conditions, particularly when working in groups. When these advantages were not available to them, the gunboats could also easily retire into shallow inlets where they were virtually unreachable. The gunboats were a brilliantly-conceived alternative strategy and they soon became a serious threat to British shipping in the Baltic, both merchant and naval.

The Danes began a rapid programme of gunboat building across the country, although the majority were built in the boatyards of Copenhagen. During the winter of 1807/8 all building work on merchant shipping was suspended, by order of the Crown Prince, to maximize gunboat production. They were mass-produced to a standard design, mostly of two main types, carrying powerful guns; although two other versions carrying mortars were produced but in much smaller numbers. Steen Bille was the only senior officer to emerge from the 1807 campaign with any credit, at least in the eyes of the king, and he was given the task of overseeing this massive operation. The largest gunboat design, and the most numerous, was known as the 'Kanonchaluppen', which carried two 24-pounder cannon and also four 4-pounder howitzers with crew of around seventy men. A smaller type, known as the 'Kanonjollen', carried only one stern-facing 24-pounder and the same four 4-pounder howitzers and was manned by about forty men. A small number of large 'Mortarchaluppen' were built, which carried a huge 100-pounder mortar and two 4pdr mortars with a crew of forty men. Finally, there was the smaller 'Morterbarkasserne', which carried a single mortar and had a crew of only nineteen men. These gunboats did carry a mast and sails, but operated best under oars which made them extremely manoeuvrable. No less than 173 gunboats were built in Denmark during the next six years and another one hundred in Norway. Ten larger schooner-rigged gunboats were also constructed at Bergen and Trondheim over a three-year period, capable of withstanding the rougher weather on the Norwegian coast. To put this into perspective, only four frigates and one ship of the line[1] were built in the same period. The gunboats were not very seaworthy and could only operate in sheltered coastal waters in near calm conditions when they had a distinct advantage over sail. The gunboats were to act like a swarm of hornets, gathering around a prey, military or merchant and overpowering it with numbers. Rarely did they act against larger British warships, whose firepower could devastate the Danish gunboats, which were liable to be destroyed by a single hit or their tightly-packed crews wiped out. There were two principal squadrons, one based at Copenhagen to watch the Sound and the other at Nyborg to cover the Great Belt.

This threat was further bolstered by the encouragement of privateering, some entrepreneurs operating small fleets which not only preyed on British and Swedish shipping, but sometimes took Prussian and Russian vessels, causing a storm of protest. Between 1807 and 1809, the Norwegians alone fitted out no less than 166 privateers and in 1810 there were still 108 in operation, although the profits declined markedly as the war progressed and the British adopted effective countermeasures.

The British were forced to maintain a large fleet in the Baltic each summer to counter the threat from not just the Danish gunboats, but from the Russians as well. Because of the constant risk of attacks, a convoy system was set up and these huge convoys, often including hundreds of merchant ships, required a large number of frigates, brigs and sloops, to ensure their safe passage.

In Britain, ships bound for the Baltic would form up at four locations for convoy, the Nore (which picked up those at Yarmouth en route), the Humber, Leith and the Orkneys. For ships requiring escort through Danish waters, they formed at Vinga Sound off Gothenburg and for those travelling out of the Baltic they formed up off Karlskrona (this changed to Hano Bay when

---

1 The 60-gun *Phoenix*, completed in 1811.

Britain went to war with Sweden later). The convoy system was not completely foolproof and the Danes did see some successes, but in overall terms the losses were insignificant. In fact, between June and November 1809, 2,210 merchant ships were convoyed in and out of the Baltic without a single loss to enemy action. Some historians point to the fact that insurance rates for the Baltic were two and sometimes three times higher than the average for any other destination between 1808 and 1813, but investigations of insurance ratings show that the dangers of navigation in the winter storms and the dangers of confiscation in European ports was deemed much higher than elsewhere and far higher than the risk from Danish gunboats and privateers.

In early January 1808, Captain George Parker of the 64-gun *Stately* was ordered to take a small squadron into the Baltic to deliver the latest instalment of the Swedish subsidy.[1] The following month, the British government were considering sending a fleet of twelve or thirteen warships, under the command of Admiral Sir James Saumarez, to attack the Russian fleet at the port of Cronstadt. This became of greater urgency when Russia invaded Swedish Finland on 21 February and had such success that within six weeks the country had been incorporated into the Russian Empire, although the Tsar granted it the status of a Grand Duchy.

Denmark sought to take advantage of the situation and joined Russia in declaring war on Sweden on 14 March, in the hope of recovering the lands ceded to the Swedes some 150 years ago in the treaties of Bromsebro and Roskilde. The Swedes had reacted by launching an invasion into Southern Norway on 1 April by an army under General Armfelt and this caused Napoleon to send aid to Denmark, with 32,000 of Marshal Bernadotte's troops moving into Zealand, Funen and Jutland. It was proposed by Napoleon that a joint French and Danish attack should be made against Sweden, but the ice melted before they could cross and soon Saumarez and his ships were blocking the passage, as by the April, the British naval role had now changed to cooperation with the Swedes. The Swedish forces enjoyed early success at the Battle of Lier on 18 April, and the Swedes moved towards the fortress of Kongsvinger. The Swedes were then defeated at the Battles of Trangen and Midtskogen, halting their advance. Prince Christian August successfully prevented Swedish reinforcements reaching the main army and eventually the Swedish general decided to retire back into Sweden to concentrate on the planned joint invasion of Zealand with the British troops on their way under General Sir John Moore. Gustav was unhappy with Armfelt's decision, wishing to retain control of the areas captured from the Norwegians. Many

---

1 The other ships in the squadron were *Nassau* 60 (the old Danish *Holsteen*), *Quebec* 32 and *Lynx* 16.

Danish gunboats attacking a British convoy – contemporary print.

modern Swedish historians view the attack on Norway, whilst the fighting continued in Finland, as madcap. However, Norway was blockaded by the British fleet and would soon suffer severely, being totally reliant on Denmark for its food supply. Norway was weak and could expect no military support from Denmark or France because of the British control of the Baltic. In fact it had every sign of being an opportunist masterstroke, but was handled so badly that their obvious advantages were lost.

Saumarez had been given a long list of instructions by the British government. He was specifically ordered to prevent troops passing from the mainland to Zealand in preparation for an invasion of Sweden, and particularly to prevent any proposed attack on Swedish Scania; to watch the ports of Jutland for any signs of French troops being transported to Norway and to prevent any such attempt; to re-establish Anholt lighthouse by any means necessary; to coordinate with the Swedish fleet; to observe the Russian movements in Finland and into Sweden; and to attack Cronstadt, whilst not forgetting convoying merchant vessels safely through the Baltic, but it would be July before he was on station.[1]

Even with all of these precautions, the Danes achieved some notable successes when they took advantage of the local conditions. Their gunboats

---

1 Instructions by the Lords Commissioners of the Admiralty dated 16 April 1808, Ryan, *Saumarez Papers*, pp. 11–12.

regularly worked out of the tiny islands of Christianso, Frederiksholm and Grasholm, usually collectively referred to as Ertholmene. The Danes did not have it all their own way, however, the British navy regularly intercepting, destroying or capturing Danish merchant vessels, privateers, brigs and gunboats, even islands. The most significant actions on both sides include:

- The Danish privateer *Admiral Jawl* of 28 guns was captured by the *Sapho* off Flamborough Head on 2 March 1808.
- On 14 March 1808, the 14-gun HMS *Childers* engaged the stronger 20-gun *Lougen*, the British ship being forced to break off and retire to Leith for repairs having lost two killed and nine wounded. That same month Admiral Sir James Saumarez finally arrived in the Baltic with a large fleet to ensure the free flow of British merchant shipping alongside a number of other tasks already mentioned, including a blockade of Norway, which was quick to cause severe food shortages.[1]
- HMS *Daphne*, *Tartarus* and *Forward* encountered a large convoy of ships taking supplies to Norway on 22 April 1808, driving them ashore. A cutting-out operation successfully captured ten Danish vessels for the loss of only five wounded.
- On 3 May, a large fleet of forty transports carrying General Moore's troops to Sweden to support the Swedes in a possible attack on Zealand passed through the Sound in two divisions and although escorted by two brigs were engaged by the Danish gunboats, but there were no particular losses on either side. The fleet of nine ships of the line, five frigates, six sloops and thirteen brigs anchored off Stockholm on 7 May and the troop transports arrived safely five days later. Gustav viewed the British troops as reinforcements to help him finally conquer Norway, but this was the last thing the British government wanted them to be used for. Having had a difficult interview with the insane King of Sweden, Moore was arrested although he escaped, his 11,000 troops leaving the Baltic to be redeployed in Portugal.
- HMS *Tartar* attempted to attack shipping in Bergen on 15 May 1808, but was attacked by the Danish *Odin* and five gunboats. She was forced to make a hasty escape having lost both her captain and a seaman killed and twelve others wounded. One gunboat was sunk during the exchange. A Danish cutter blew up whilst in action with the *Swan* on 24 May.
- On 4 June 1808 four Danish gunboats attacked HMS *Tickler* in a calm, and after a heavy cannonade of four hours, the British ship was forced to haul down her colours with fourteen men dead and twenty-two wounded

---

1 This included seven ships of the line, the 74s *Vanguard* and *Minotaur* and the 64s *Standard*, *Ardent*, *Dictator*, *Ruby* and *Africa*.

out of a crew of fifty. The Danes only suffered one man wounded, showing how well gunboats could operate in perfect conditions.

- The *Turbulent* of 16 guns was also captured by the Danes on 9 June 1808. She was with the *Thunder* escorting a convoy of seventy merchant ships off Malmo when they became becalmed. Seventeen of the merchantmen were also captured.

- The *Euryalus* and *Cruizer* successfully cut out one gunboat and sank two troop transports on 11 June 1808, the Danes losing seven men killed and twelve wounded for the loss of only one man slightly wounded.

- The 16-gun HMS *Seagull* took on the Danish *Lougen* of 20 guns near Christiansand on 19 June, but was then assailed by four gunboats which joined the fray, raking the British brig and forcing her to surrender having had five guns dismounted, eight men killed and twenty wounded. She sank soon afterwards, but was raised again and joined the Danish navy.

- Admiral Saumarez eventually entered the Baltic on 18 July with a squadron of eight ships of the line[1] and spent the late summer and autumn in attempting to make an attack on the Russian ports but with little real success.

- HMS *Tigress*, a 12-gun brig, was cornered near Agerso in the Great Belt on 2 August, by no less than sixteen Danish gunboats and forced to surrender, with the loss of two killed and eight wounded.

Soon after the loss of the Danish fleet, Marshal Bernadotte began to move some of his motley crew of Portuguese, Spanish, Dutch and German troops into Holstein and then onto the Danish islands in preparation for the projected invasion of Sweden.[2] In August 1808, Rear Admiral Keats began to secretly correspond with the commander of the Spanish troops based in Zealand, the Marquis de la Romana, via a German-speaking Irish Benedictine monk named James Robertson, whom Wellesley had recruited.[3] After a series of adventures,[4] Robertson was able to meet Romana, pretending to be a cigar salesman. He gave him the news from Spain and offered him an evacuation of his Spanish troops on British ships, which Romana agreed to, but only after some deliberation. These Spanish troops, with which Napoleon garrisoned

---

1 It consisted of the *Victory* as flagship, *Centaur, Implacable, Mars, Dictator, Africa, Goliath* and *Superb*.

2 It is sometimes claimed that the shock of seeing foreign troops on Danish soil led to the sudden death of King Christian VII from a stroke.

3 Robertson claims that he was the third or fourth agent to try to accomplish this mission, the others having been caught and shot as spies.

4 His adventures, true or not, were published as a *Narrative of a Mission to Denmark in 1808* in 1863.

Jutland and Zealand, with detachments on the islands of Funen and Langeland were keen to return to their homeland.

Spain had declared war on France on 24 May 1808, following the abduction and forced abdication of the Spanish royal family. An appeal sent to the Spanish troops on 5 August was followed up by a letter two days later, sent personally to Romana, suggesting how the troops could position themselves ideally so that the British ships could collect them. The Spanish troops were ordered to swear allegiance to the new King Joseph of Spain (Napoleon's elder brother) and the two regiments[1] at Roskilde on Zealand mutinied and were forcibly disarmed after they had fired on the French General Frison, killing one of his aides de camp. Romana felt that his commander Marshal Bernadotte was getting suspicious and he took control of Nyborg on 9 August, the local Danish troops choosing not to intervene. Once the guns of the shore batteries were spiked, however, two Danish vessels tried to bar access to the port, but were taken after a short fight. The boats of HMS *Edgar* were sent into the port of Nyborg and captured the Danish *Fama* of 10 guns and the Royal Yacht *Soe-Ormen*, for the loss of Lieutenant Harvey of the *Superb* killed and two men wounded; whilst the Danes lost seven dead and thirteen wounded.

The Royal Navy embarked 6,000 of Romana's men troops between 9 and 11 August,[2] using fifty-seven small vessels found in the harbour to transport the troops out to the waiting ships of the line.[3] Another 2,000 Spanish troops commandeered ships and sailed from Funen to join the squadron,[4] whilst one regiment of Spanish infantry[5] secured the island of Langeland to ensure it was completely safe as a base for all of the Spanish troops, but one regiment stationed on Jutland[6] could not get to the appointed place and was forced to surrender. All told, 9,000 veteran troops[7] were transported back to join the fight in Spain[8] whilst the remaining 4,000 men were disarmed by the French. Bernadotte had effectively lost all 13,000 Spaniards from his corps, ruining any real prospect of success for the projected attack on Sweden. The loss of the Spanish troops did produce one major benefit for cash-strapped

---

1 The Asturias and Guadalajara Infantry Regiments.

2 These consisted of the Princessa and 1st Barcelona Infantry Regiments and the Almanza and Villaviocosa Light Dragoons.

3 These small ships were allowed to go free once the embarkation was complete.

4 Consisting of the Zamora Infantry Regiment and the El Rey and El Infante Dragoons.

5 The 1st Catalonia Regiment.

6 The Algarve Regiment of Dragoons.

7 Plus 116 women and 67 children.

8 They landed at Santander on 9 October 1808 and immediately joined the war.

Denmark, however, as it removed the heavy financial burden of having to feed all of these troops.

Two British brigs, the *Kite* and *Minx,* were attacked at the end of August by twenty-one gunboats; both got away but the *Kite* was badly damaged. One particularly audacious attack by the Danes was against a British merchant convoy of 137 ships on 20 October. Caught in a dead calm, HMS *Africa* of 64 guns, the escort ship, was attacked by twenty-five gunboats and seven armed launches and was fortunate to escape during the night, having suffered no less than nine killed and fifty-one wounded. Four merchantmen ran aground, one being captured by the Danes and the others were burned.

A temporary armistice was cobbled together in the autumn between the Norwegians under Prince Christian August and the Swedish army, the troops on both sides being exhausted, poorly supplied and extremely sickly. Norway was also suffering from rapidly-depleting food stores, caused by a series of bad harvests in Denmark and the British blockade – a cessation of hostilities was agreed on 7 December. Denmark tried to help the suffering Norwegians, but without the ability to break the British blockade, they could achieve little. The Norwegians felt abandoned by Denmark, whilst the Danes felt that the Norwegians did not understand their difficulties, even today these attitudes colour each country's view of the history of this period. It got so bad at one stage that senior Norwegian officials actually discussed with Prince August signing a separate peace with Britain to save Norway.

Saumarez had taken his battleships to the east to help the Swedes as Russia continued to advance in Finland, but despite some local successes, the British fleet could not get at the Russian fleet which remained safely ensconced in its harbours. He eventually sailed home for the winter in November 1808, taking a few of the ships of the line with him, particularly those that required major repairs. A very large number of ships, however, remained in the Baltic throughout the winter under Rear Admiral Keats.[1] A late convoy, sailing from Karlskrona on 22 December, found passing through the Sound in early January fraught with danger from ice. Nine out of the twelve merchant ships, a Swedish escort and the brig *Magnet* were lost.

King Frederick still had the idea of invading Swedish Scania from Zealand with 30,000 Danish troops, proposing to march them over the winter ice, whilst the British navy could not prevent them. Had the ice been thick enough to safely move across it, the army would have crossed the Sound, but it was less likely that the ice would remain long enough to allow them to safely return

---

1 Keats retained the *Superb, Brunswick, Orion, Edgar, Dictator, Salsette, Tribune, Magnet, Ranger, Ariel, Prometheus, Lynx, Kite, Erebus, Gorgon, Proselyte, Fury, Tartar, Fama, Snipe, Minx, Hearty, Earnest, Wrangler* and *Charger*.

and then they would be trapped in Sweden. The ice never really became thick enough to risk it and the march was postponed several times; realistically Frederick did not have the nerve to gamble with such high stakes – he was no Napoleon!

Admiral Saumarez was back in the Baltic in January 1809 when he immediately resumed command. Rear Admirals Keats and Hood were superseded by Dixon and Pickmore, whilst Rear Admiral Bertie retained command in the Sound. The number of convoys sailing for the Baltic in the coming year was itemised in a letter from William Pole at the Admiralty.[1] The first convoy of the year would leave the Nore for Gothenburg on 1 April and from then on, a convoy would set out from the Nore and another from the Humber and Leith every fortnight after that, until the last convoy of the year sailed on 15 October. Ships sailing into the Baltic were escorted all of the way to their destination ports, except those sailing further eastward of Bornholm Island, when the escorts would part company 50 miles to the east, leaving the merchant vessels to complete their journeys alone.

Outgoing convoys would form off Karlskrona or Gothenburg and would be allocated escorts to sail on as soon as possible, the last convoy of the year leaving on 15 November. The decision as to whether to sail through the Sound or the Great Belt would be made by the local naval commanders, based on the latest intelligence. A large number of cruisers were placed in areas where numerous privateers were known to operate from, especially off Danzig and the Island of Gotland. HMS *Egeria* captured the Danish privateer *Aalborg* on 2 March 1809 as it escorted a Danish convoy.

The loss of Finland resulted in an army-led coup in Sweden and the slightly unhinged King Gustav IV Adolf was deposed and was replaced temporarily by his aging uncle as Charles XIII.[2] Charles was childless and given his advanced age, it was unrealistic to presume that he would now sire one. The leader of the coup, Georg Aldersparre, had initially sought to appoint King Frederick of Denmark as heir, which would have reunited Denmark, Norway and Sweden as in ancient times, but Frederick refused the offer very undiplomatically, exclaiming 'any negotiation is difficult with a nation that has to be regarded as nothing but insurgents'. He probably feared that Sweden would prove dominant in such an arrangement. The Danish Prince Christian August of Schleswig-Holstein was therefore officially chosen as heir to the Swedish throne, despite the fact that the prince had successfully

---

1 Ryan, *Saumarez Papers*, p. 66.
2 Gustav wrongly believed that he was standing down to allow his son Gustaf Gustafsson, Prince of Vasa, to reign, but the army banned his entire direct family from retaining the crown – fearing reprisals against those who had led the coup.

repelled a small-scale invasion of Norway by the Swedes the previous year and was made a field marshal and governor general of Norway in 1809. He now renamed himself Charles August in preparation for his anticipated succession to the Swedish throne.

On 18 May 1809, a party of marines and seamen from the 64-gun HMS *Standard* and the 36-gun frigate *Owen Glendower*,[1] with the *Avenger, Ranger, Rose* and *Snipe*, landed on the tiny island of Anholt in the Kattegat. The party was commanded by Captain William Selby of the *Owen Glendower*. The Danes had 170 men in garrison on the island, which included the local militia; they put up a short but stiff resistance which led to the death of a British marine and the wounding of two others before they surrendered. The principal aim of the attack was to reinstate the lighthouse on the island, which the Danes had extinguished, to help British shipping navigate safely through these dangerous waters. A permanent British garrison of 500 men was set up on the island and defences constructed, as it proved to be a safe anchorage and an excellent source of fresh water for the fleet.

The *Melpomenne* frigate was attacked by up to twenty Danish gunboats during the night of 23 May, having four men killed and twenty wounded, but she succeeded in protecting her convoy, whilst the *Ardent*, having landed a large watering party on Romso Island, had eighty men captured, when surprised by Danish troops. The privateer *Christianborg* was taken by the *Cruizer* off Bornholm on 31 May. On 9 June 1809, a Danish gunboat flotilla of twenty gunboats and seven mortar boats attacked a British convoy of seventy vessels near Saltholm Island. The 12-gun brig HMS *Turbulent* and thirteen merchant vessels were captured.

The strength of the Danish gunboats increased markedly in the Great Belt. Admiral Dixon wrote to Saumarez on 5 July requesting that two ships of the line were positioned there to ensure the safe passage of the convoys. This was in addition to the two warships stationed at the northern and southern entrances of the Belt, to meet convoys as they arrived. It was estimated that convoys would average around six weeks to traverse the Belt, because of the problems of contrary winds and of the long nights when it was unsafe to sail with the safety markers removed.

The Danes recaptured the 18-gun *Alaart*,[2] when she found herself pursued by eight Danish gunboats on 10 August and after a two-hour cannonade she struck, having lost one man killed and three wounded. On 12 August 1809, HMS *Monkey* drove three Danish luggers ashore, which were captured and

---

1 Saumarez states that a party of fifty marines from the *Victory* also participated. Ryan, *Saumarez Papers*, p. 81
2 Taken at Copenhagen in 1807.

re-floated. HMS *Minx* of 14 guns was captured on 2 September 1809, by six Danish gunboats, whilst acting as a lightship off the Scaw. In October, the Danish privateer *Dorothea Catherine* was captured by the *Strenuous* and the following month the *Christiania* was taken by the *Snake*. The same month, the Danish garrison on Ertholmene mutinied and Admiral Saumarez sent two ships of the line and three bomb vessels in an attempt to take advantage of the situation and capture this haven for gunboats and privateers, but they were beaten off by the heavy fire maintained by a number of Danish forts on the islands.

Due to the immense number of ships travelling in the Baltic, the last convoy left Gothenburg on 15 December and much of the squadron returned to Britain with the convoy for the winter.

The Danish war against Sweden saw few major incidents in 1809, with Christian August being pushed to make an attack on Sweden on 10 July. It was, however, a lacklustre affair and the attack was abandoned after a defeat at Harjedalen on 24 July, both sides too weak to seriously continue the fighting. Finally, sense prevailed and the war ended with the Treaty of Jonkoping on 10 December 1809, which left both sides without any gains from the fighting.

Chapter 22

The Swedish Question

Saumarez continued in command for the following year, but some of his subordinates changed again, Rear Admiral Reynolds replaced Pickmore, but Dixon and Bertie remained.

In 1810 the supply of corn to Zealand proved difficult with most Danish ships being captured by the British. The Danes reverted to using only small shallow-draught vessels which could sail inside Mon Island, where they remained safe. Four Danish gunboats captured the British gunboat *Grinder*, armed with one 24-pounder and a 24-pounder carronade, on 13 April 1810, with the loss of two killed and two wounded.

The Admiralty ordered Saumarez to blockade Cronborg Castle in May 1810, both to prevent the Danish treasury receiving valuable customs dues and also to help prevent the Danes confiscating ships or cargoes on questionable grounds, something that appeared to be on the increase.

Sweden was thrown into crisis on 28 May, when the heir to the throne, Charles August, fell from his horse during a military exercise and expired immediately. The autopsy showed that the Prince had suffered a severe stroke, but rumours that he was poisoned led to the unfortunate lynching of Count Axel von Fersen, which actually occurred during the Prince's funeral procession; he was wrongly believed to have been the murderer. The army was keen to offer the position of heir to the throne to the French Marshal Bernadotte, who had attained a fearsome reputation as a soldier, but he had also previously apparently shown great kindness to Swedish prisoners in Lubeck.

Baron Karl Otto Morner unilaterally offered the position to Bernadotte, who referred the offer to Napoleon. The French Emperor failed to take it seriously, but his indecision allowed Bernadotte to send a reply indicating that he would accept 'if' elected. The Swedish government had Morner arrested on his return for his effrontery, but they did offer Bernadotte the position of Crown Prince, which he instantly accepted, becoming a Lutheran to be accepted for the post. Being a French officer, the British government were rightly concerned by his appointment, particularly as the infirm king soon granted Bernadotte control of the army and the state. His arrival in Sweden was blocked initially by the British fleet, but having dined with King Frederick of Denmark at Copenhagen, he was allowed to sail unchallenged through the British ships to take up his new position by the authority of Admiral Saumarez; a clear demonstration of British dominance of the Baltic and one not lost on Bernadotte, or Crown Prince Charles John as he now became known. Napoleon insisted that Sweden declare war on Britain and at least nominally agree to join the Continental System, but few seriously believed that this would lead to any fighting or end the lucrative trade with Britain, although it was reduced by more than half its previous extraordinarily high levels. Charles John had one great ambition, to win Norway for Sweden, but he was fully aware that the Norwegians were not keen and that an invasion was unlikely to succeed. He therefore launched a charm offensive to win the Norwegians over and constantly looked for opportunities to enhance his claims: he was prepared to play a long game. Officially there were no longer any friendly ports for British merchants in the Baltic, but the trade did not falter, false papers and corrupt officials allowing their contraband goods to flow unchecked into mainland Europe on a massive scale.

On 19 July, the gunbrig *Forward* reported that the convoy of forty-seven merchantmen it was escorting to Leith was attacked by five large Norwegian gunbrigs and two schooners under the command of Commodore Lorentz Fisker and the entire convoy of merchantmen was captured.[1]

At the Battle of Silda on 23 July, HMS *Belvedira* and *Nemesis* attacked the pilot station on that island and engaged the Danish schooners *Odin*, *Tor* and *Balder* and the gun barge *Cort Adeler*, capturing them all.

French troops now garrisoned all of the Prussian ports on the Baltic coast, in order to stem the flow of British goods, and a number of merchant ships had to sail without cargoes to escape capture. Some of these ports then became havens for privateers.

Two gun sloops and four Danish gunboats captured a becalmed HMS *Alban* on 12 September 1810 after a four-hour battle, having lost her captain and one other man killed and three men wounded.

Saumarez had wintered in England again and the 1811 campaign began with the same subordinate admirals in post. The Danes made a very determined effort to wrest back the island of Anholt from its British garrison on 27 March 1811. Nearly 1,500 Danish troops were transported on to the island, with twelve gunboats involved in the attempt in support. The attack

---

1 Ryan, *Saumarez Letters*, p. 141.

on Anholt resulted in a terrible defeat for the Danes, who were unable to recapture the island and retired having suffered serious losses. The British garrison of 350 marines and seamen was commanded by Captain Maurice of the Royal Navy, the same who had so distinguished himself in the defence of the Diamond Rock at Martinique in 1805. The British had prior knowledge of the attempt and on their first appearance, 200 men with a battery of howitzers moved into position to oppose their landing, but soon discovered that they had already landed in the darkness. Heavily outnumbered, the British troops fell back and as the Danes followed up they were caught in a heavy crossfire of grape shot from Fort Yorke and the Massarene Battery, which forced the Danes to retire into the shelter of some sandhills. With daylight, it was discovered that the Danish gunboats had manoeuvred into a position where they could fire on the works, but all attempts by a Danish infantry column to take the battery failed with great loss. One final attack by the Danes was driven off and on their retiring to the sandhills again for shelter, they now found the *Anholt* schooner, commanded by Lieutenant Baker, in position to fire on them. At the same time, the Danish flotilla had been forced to retire from the heavy fire of Fort Yorke. Seeing no way out, the Danes appealed for terms and were told that only an unconditional surrender would be accepted and they then capitulated. The British lost only two killed and another thirty wounded; whereas the Danish troops lost no less than their commanding officer and three other officers and fifty men killed, whilst another fourteen officers and 504 men were wounded or captured along with three guns! During the retreat of the remainder, they were attacked by the *Sheldrake* and *Tartar*, who captured two gunboats and another 250 men.

Three Danish gunboats attacked the *Swan* near Sunnigesunde on 23 April. A lucky shot from one of the gunboats holed the *Swan* causing the powder magazine to flood and rendering her defenceless. The *Swan* surrendered, having lost two men killed, but she sank soon after off Uddevalla in Sweden.

On 11 May 1811 HMS *Rifleman* recaptured the *Alban* from the Danes off Shetland. HMS *Safeguard* was engaged by four gunboats off Jutland and struck after about four hours.

The *Sheldrake* captured four gunboats on 5 July, having previously captured two on 27 March during the action at Anholt. HMS *Brevdrageren* of 14 guns and the 10-gun *Algerine* encountered the Danish 20-gun *Langeland*, the 18-gun *Lugum* and the 16-gun *Kiel* off Norway on 31 July 1811, which heavily outgunned the British ships who made good their escape.

HMS *Manly* of 12 guns was attacked by the Danish 18-gun brigs *Lolland*, *Alsen* and *Samso* on 2 September, whilst escorting a convoy near Arendal in Norway and captured, having half of her guns disabled and having lost one man killed and three wounded. The *Swan* was captured the same day by Danish gunboats. Two Danish gunboats were taken by the boats of the *Victory* in Wingo Bay on 20 September.

The last convoy of the year was unfortunately a terrible disaster, storms leading to the loss of three British ships of the line[1] and the deaths of some 2,000 seamen all told.

---

1 The 98-gun *St George* and the 74-gun *Defence* and *Hero*.

Chapter 23

The Final Years

Saumarez continued to command the Baltic station in 1812, but Rear Admirals Dixon and Reynolds were replaced by Martin and Morris respectively.

In January 1812, France seized Pomerania because it was being used as a base for smuggling British goods into mainland Europe. This led to an irrevocable breakdown of Franco-Swedish relations, but it also meant that Sweden was now untouchable, lying wholly beyond the Baltic Sea where the French could not get at them. It was also becoming apparent that Russia was clearly moving away from her friendship with France and relaxing its strict controls on the import of British goods as its economy had gone into sharp decline since the imposition of the Continental System. Russia had effectively abandoned the System as early as January 1810 and this was now becoming a serious point of conflict with Napoleon, leading ultimately to invasion. Sweden and Russia signed a peace treaty at St Petersburg on 5 April 1812, by which Sweden guaranteed to accept Russian control of Finland and promised not to invade whilst Russia was fighting France, in lieu of Russian support for the Swedish annexation of Norway.

Following Napoleon's invasion of Russia this year, the British government was not slow to meet with the plenipotentiaries of both Sweden and Russia and to agree peace treaties with both on 18 July. This dramatically changed British fortunes in the Baltic and was doubly fortuitous, having occurred precisely at the time when Britain found itself at war with the fledgling United States of America. Admiral Martin became heavily involved in the defence of Riga but another proposed assault on Denmark could not be launched without the support of Sweden and Russia, which was not forthcoming and was therefore eventually shelved.

On 6 July 1812 two small squadrons engaged each other at Lyngor in Norway. The Danish squadron consisted of the newly-built frigate *Najaden* and the three brigs *Lolland*, *Samsoe* and *Kiel*. The much more powerful British squadron, consisting of the 64-gun *Dictator* and the three brigs *Calypso*, *Podargus* and *Flamer*, eventually withdrew having achieved their main goal, the destruction of the *Najaden*. The Danes lost 127 killed and 88 wounded.

The boats of HMS *Horatio* captured two Danish vessels (*Schooner No. 114* and *Cutter No. 97*) and their American prize on 2 August 1812, the British losing nine men killed and sixteen wounded, whilst the Danes lost ten killed and thirteen wounded. A Danish lugger (*No. 28*) was taken by a boat from the *Dictator* on the same day. HMS *Attack* was captured on 19 August 1812 after a two-day engagement with fourteen Danish gunboats. *Attack* lost fourteen men killed and wounded.

In November 1812, the *Naval Chronicle* recorded that the present size of the Danish navy was four ships of the line, two frigates and around 120 gunboats. That same month Russia and Sweden demanded that Denmark give up Norway in exchange for lands in Germany and Holland as compensation, if and only if they joined the Allied cause, but Frederick remained constant in his support of the treaty with France. Admiral Saumarez went home at the end of this convoy season and was never to return to the Baltic, indeed he never served at sea again. Rear Admirals Hope and Morris continued the role, which was now downgraded by the Admiralty. The number of naval incidents certainly reduced dramatically in these later years.

The Danish *Unge Troutman* and *Liebe* were taken by the boats of HMS *Blazer* and *Brevdragen*, on 21 March 1813. In August 1813 Rear Admiral Graham Moore (brother of Sir John Moore) arrived to replace Hope. His flagship, HMS *Warrior*, captured a Danish gunboat on arrival in the Kattegat. The very last convoy of the year, with no less than 231 merchant ships, was still constantly harassed by the Danes, leading to the loss of five of them.

Between 1807 and 1814 it is estimated that the amount of trade that flowed through Copenhagen halved and that is probably a generous and over-optimistic figure. The failed harvests, restrictions on even fishing during the war and the financial instability eventually led to Denmark being declared officially bankrupt in January 1813. This forced the monetary system to be changed, with the end of the rigsdaler and the introduction of the new Danish dollar.

In early 1813, Britain became involved in the negotiations with Denmark, but the British government were not keen on Sweden gaining Norway and they were also no longer very keen on making any promises regarding the Danish ships taken in 1807. The Danish king responded by sending his son and heir, Prince Christian August, to Norway, where he arrived on 21 May 1813. His tour was a triumph, with the Norwegians enthusiastically cheering him everywhere he went and thus damaging the hopes of Charles John in Sweden. King Frederick was so buoyed by the reaction, that he continued to make insane plans for an invasion of southern Sweden by Danish militia units, which he believed would be enthusiastically supported by the Norwegians. But his son had other ideas, wanting to consolidate his hold on Norway, not to get involved in a hopeless war in Sweden.

As Denmark continued to refuse to join the allies, by the autumn of 1813 she effectively stood alone with France, against the rest of Europe. The king's popularity was at an all-time low at home, with speeches and posters being published, condemning the government and the recent monetary crisis. Until the French evacuation of Hamburg in March 1813, relations remained cordial with the Danes. Danish troops had even been called into the city to help quell disturbances in late February and the Danish troops had colluded in a number of executions. The French eventually left Holstein for good that summer and they emptied the banks as they left, including all of the deposits of the Danish Bank of Altona (held in Hamburg), which helped to further the financial collapse of Denmark. However, Frederick's Danish Auxiliary Corps continued to fight on in alliance with the French, despite huge internal pressures for Denmark to change sides before it was too late. The king however, seemed incapable of changing, he blindly refused to concede an inch of Norway or turn against France. Denmark was in fact, the very last of Napoleon's allies to abandon his cause in 1814, the Danes finally signing a peace treaty with Sweden and Britain at Kiel on 14 January.

The terms of the peace included the restoration of Danish possessions except for Heligoland, all prisoners of war to be released, Denmark to furnish 10,000 men to the Allied armies in exchange for a British subsidy of £400,000 that year,[1] Pomerania to be ceded by Sweden to Denmark, in lieu of Norway which went to Sweden, Stralsund would remain a depot for British merchandise, Denmark would help to abolish the slave trade and Britain would mediate peace between Denmark and the other allies. Norway was not happy with this deal and rose up against the Swedish troops, whilst the British navy blockaded the Norwegian coast to force them to succumb to the new situation. Norway declared their independence on 17 May 1814, but Swedish forces invaded Norway on 27 July and an armistice was concluded at Moss on 14 August. By this convention Norway joined in a union with Sweden as its own state, with its own constitution and institutions, the formal union being ratified on 4 November 1814 and Charles XIII of Sweden was elected King of Norway as well.

---

1 Approximately £16 million today.

Overview

So how should we look on Britain's involvement with Denmark during the Napoleonic Wars, in particular, regarding the twin attacks on Copenhagen?

Britain's response to the Armed Neutrality in 1801 could and should have been predicted. Such a challenge from the Baltic countries to Britain's vital naval supplies could not possibly have ended in any other way. It was obvious that the largest navy in the world would inevitably flex its muscles and seek to dominate the Baltic, whilst conveniently destroying any potential pretenders to their throne.

Nelson's ships had secured a great success in defeating the Danish defence line, but it cannot be seen as anything but a strategic failure. The Danish fleet remained undamaged and safely ensconced within Copenhagen harbour and although they were unable to operate against the British fleet until the end of the fourteen-week armistice, the British admiral could have been in a very awkward position indeed. If by mid-July they had not been able to crush the Russian fleet, they would have been surrounded, with a superior joint Swedo-Danish fleet barring their way out of the Baltic. There is an air of British arrogance and invulnerability in the attack, which the brave and dogged Danish defence betrayed as a dangerous mirage. The fortunate and timely death of Tsar Paul papered over the cracks in the great British adventure into the Baltic and in all honesty, they were very lucky to get away with it. It must be accepted that the failure to destroy the Danish fleet proper in 1801 led unavoidably to the attack in 1807 when the British government was forced, by new and even more dangerous circumstances, to ensure that this sizeable fleet could not be used by an all-conquering Napoleon.

The second attack on Copenhagen has to be seen in a very different light. Britain in 1807 felt herself to be in a very precarious position, with almost all of Europe allied against her, the dominance of her navy being the only thing that continued to guarantee her survival. No one therefore could be surprised, that Britain looked to take all measures possible to prevent Napoleon dramatically boosting his potential naval forces. It was for this reason that in 1807 Britain ensured the safety of the Portuguese navy, eliminated the threat of the Russian Mediterranean fleet and chose to remove the Danish ships before the French Emperor could get his hands on them. In a more modern scenario, the act was similar to the British attack on the navy of Vichy France at Mers el Kebir on 3 July 1940, for very similar reasons.

Britain's attack on Denmark in 1807 must be seen overall as a great strategic success, removing the fifth largest fleet in the world from Napoleon's potential grasp. It must however, also be accepted that it was a publicity disaster and that Britain was consequently demonised throughout Europe, but in war such acts rarely linger long in the memory. It did also potentially put thousands of trained seamen into Napoleon's hands, but that was only relevant had he possessed the ships for them to man.

The loss of the Danish fleet seriously downgraded the country's status as a major power and the government and people were combined in their desire to replace it. The Danes did see some success on a localized basis during the 'Gunboat War', but these were little more than pinpricks against the might of the British navy. They served to boost the morale of Danes and even today this war retains something of an almost mythical status in Denmark – as a just revenge on the perfidious British. In reality, it had very little effect on the bulk of trade flowing in and out of the Baltic and was seen by the British navy as no more than an inconvenience rather than as a crisis. The Baltic, despite the best efforts of the Danes, actually proved between 1808 and 1813 to be the largest open breach in Napoleon's Continental System. The preferred route for British convoys became the Belt, which took five to six days to traverse, but it offered far fewer opportunities for Danish gunboats to ambush convoys and was also deep enough throughout to allow the British to utilize their far more powerful line of battle ships to help protect the convoys.

Once safely within the Baltic, the British merchantmen would split up for their destination ports, almost all of which were officially closed to British trade of any description. Armed with forged documentation, all too often customs officials and even French consuls turned a blind eye to the trade for a handsome bribe and the goods were successfully taken into the European continent. Where this approach failed, smuggling was rife; in fact this became a major industry in its own right and a very lucrative enterprise at that. To take advantage of this huge level of trade which was ripe for attack, it is estimated that up to 900 Danish privateers were fitted out during the war to prey on British merchant ships, some 600 in Denmark and 300 in Norway.

Danish ship losses during the Gunboat War total some 1,400 vessels, which equates to the loss of a Danish or Norwegian vessel every other day throughout the entire war. All told, 7,000 seamen – around 5,000 of which were Norwegians and 2,000 Danes – were captured and held as prisoners of war in Britain, most being held on the infamous hulks in the upper reaches of many coastal estuaries.

As for the Danish army, its best units were mostly deployed in Holstein and the British had little more to face than at best second-line infantry. The

British infantry were not therefore seriously challenged, but the British troops recognized the innate bravery of the Danes and they certainly never despised them. Captain Henry Ross-Lewin of the 32nd Foot, perhaps summed it up best: 'Their troops did not want for bravery, but were quite inexperienced, and required a campaign or two to make them soldiers.'[1]

The greatest disaster for Denmark, however, was not the loss of her neutrality and hence her trade, but the fact that she now felt compelled to fasten herself firmly to Napoleon's carriage and then waited way too long before recognizing that they were backing the wrong side. The inability of King Frederick to recognize when was the opportune moment to switch loyalties ultimately cost the Danes dearly.

With the permanent loss of Norway, Denmark was never in a position to regain her previous status. Her retention of Schleswig and Holstein led to continuous flare-ups with rapidly-expanding Prussia and the eventual inevitable loss of these provinces further reduced the status of the country significantly.[2] She was now relegated to the third tier of nations in Europe and had to cut her cloth appropriately. Denmark sought to remain neutral in both World Wars, but it was overrun in 1940 by the Germans, although they allowed the Danish parliament and police force to continue to operate. The Danish government resigned en masse in 1943 and resistance to the German occupation grew as the war continued, to the point that the Germans found the country very difficult to control. After the Second World War, Denmark has been a member of NATO and of the European Union and has generally prospered. The Danes, however, have maintained a healthy distrust of the European Union, just like the British and it will be interesting what Denmark does in the future following the British decision to leave.

Perhaps the greatest tragedy of the two British attacks on Copenhagen is that it pitted two like-minded, independent thinking, feisty and determined peoples, who are both at their best when their backs appear to be against the wall and who recognize these similar traits within each other. For too many who fought on either side in the actions described in this book, the fighting felt far too much like a Civil War – almost brother fighting brother – and few Britons celebrated or enjoyed either of the victories they gained at Copenhagen.

Perhaps these two episodes can best be described as unfortunate family squabbles that are now best understood for what they were – necessary evils – and forgiven, rather than prolonging the pain and bitterness of two centuries ago. Britons and Danes are kindred spirits and long may it remain so.

---

1 Ross-Lewin, p. 73.
2 Denmark finally lost these provinces in 1864 in the Second Schleswig War.

Visiting the Scenes Today

Visiting Copenhagen is always a delight, but it is a much greater joy when you realize how much evidence of these events 200 years ago can still be traced today.

The city has of course expanded greatly, particularly to the west, where the earthen ramparts and wet ditch have been removed, although traces of them can be still observed in the Orstedsparken, the Royal Library Garden and the Ostre Anloeg behind the National Gallery of Denmark, but the three large water reservoirs which stood outside the ramparts remain intact today. The ramparts on the eastern side, in Christianshavn, are still largely intact and give a very good impression of what the defences looked like. The Citadel (or Kastellet) which completes this defensive ring is still in excellent condition and is very much worth a visit. The positions of the British gun batteries established in 1807 are now largely built over, but they can be traced and their positions in modern Copenhagen are identified in Appendix 22. Finally, regarding the 1807 attack on Copenhagen, the site of Frederiksberg, where the Guards were based, can still be visited, or at least the extensive gardens, as the bulding is now a naval college.

As regards the attack in 1801, it can be a little more difficult to view things exactly as they were 200 years ago, with the harbour having been driven further out by land reclamation since the battle. It is, however, possible to visit the Trekroner Battery by boat and this is well worth the effort. During this boat trip, it is possible to view the Middle Ground where the action took place and you pass part of the naval dockyard which is still used by the Danish navy to this day. Ashore you can also view the sailors' terraced houses of Nyholm still standing in the shadow of the citadel and the Holmen cemetery nearby, where you can see the mound where the Danish dead were buried and the carved stones with the names of the fallen set into the earth.

The Royal Danish Arsenal Museum is also well worth a visit, with a particularly fine selection of artillery pieces on display (although very dusty). One tip – walk right to the back of this long hall and on the right is a superb original example of a British Royal Horse Artillery gun and its original carriage, with original leatherwork etc, a real and unexpected treat! The Danish naval museum has just moved to take the upper floor of the museum, which houses a number of excellent exhibits including artefacts from both attacks.

Further afield, the Castle of Cronborg is well worth a visit, but unfortunately it is difficult to see anything of the 1807 campaign at Kioge or Roskilde at Frederiksvaerk a still-working gunpouder works can be visited, which is highly interesting.

Appendices Relevant to the Battle of Copenhagen 1801

1. Return of the Number of Army Personnel Embarked for the Danish Expedition and the Ships They were Allocated To

2. Full List of the British Ships involved in the Expedition to Denmark in 1801

3. Arrangement for Attack and Line of Battle off Copenhagen, 1 April 1801

4. The Danish Defence Line

5. Report of the Battle of Copenhagen by Nelson

6. Danish Losses at Copenhagen 1801

7. Admiral Sir Hyde Parker's Official Dispatch

8. Letter from Captain Fremantle to his wife Betsey Wynne

9. Sir Hyde Parker's Dispatch Regarding the Official Treaty

Appendix 1

Return of the Number of Army Personnel Embarked for the Danish Expedition and the Ships They were Allocated To[1]

Embarkation Return 28 February 1801

William Stewart, Lieutenant Colonel Commanding
49th Foot on HMS *Bellona*, *Ramillies*, *Saturn*, *Warrior*, *Defiance*, *Ganges*, *Russell*, *Monarch*, *Elephant*, *Edgar* and *Isis*
Rifle Company on *St George*
One platoon of Rifles on *London*
Lieutenant Colonel Brooke commanded the 49th Regiment

Corps	Lt Colonels	Majors	Captains	Lieutenants	Ensigns	Paymaster	Adjutant	Surgeon	Ass. Surgeon	Sergeants	Drummers	Armourer	Rank & File	Total
49th Foot	2	2	6	15	3	1	1	1	1	36	22	0	692	781
Rifles	1	0	1	2	1	0	0	0	0	5	2	1	101	114
Total	3	2	7	17	4	1	1	1	1	41	24	1	793	895

NB.1 – Staff Surgeon (Mr William Ferguson[2]) not included in the above.

NB.2 – 7 Rank & File put on shore at Yarmouth of the 49th Foot.

NB.3 – Captain Doyle 108th Foot was allowed to serve with the infantry detachment, having volunteered.

NB.4 – Captain Frazer Royal Artillery sailed with the Engineer's stores.

---

1 The source of this return is based on the Cumloden Papers, *Stewart's Journal*, Edinburgh, 1871, p.1, although the present author has added further information to correct it.

2 William Ferguson was a Staff Surgeon from 4 April 1800, he served at Copenhagen and in September 1805 he became Deputy Inspector of Hospitals.

Appendix 2

Full List of the British Ships involved in the Expedition to Denmark in 1801[1]

Nelson's Squadron

Ships	Guns	Captain
Elephant	74	Captain Thomas Foley (Nelson's flagship)
Defiance	74	Captain Richard Retalick (Admiral Graves's flagship)
Edgar	74	Captain George Murray
Monarch	74	Captain James Mosse
Bellona	74	Captain Sir Thomas Thompson
Ganges	74	Captain Thomas Fremantle
Russell	74	Captain William Cuming
Agamemnon	64	Captain Robert Fancourt
Ardent	64	Captain Thomas Bertie
Polyphemus	64	Captain John Lawford
Glatton	54	Captain William Bligh

Frigates

Ships	Guns	Captain
Isis	50	Captain James Walker
Amazon	38	Captain Henry Riou
Desiree	36	Captain Henry Inman
Blanche	36	Captain Graham Hammond
Alcmene	32	Captain Samuel Sutton
Shannon	32	Captain Charles Dudley Pater

---

1 This does not agree exactly with any source that the author has discovered as they all vary slightly, but this is correct to the best of his knowledge.

Sloops

Jamaica	24	Captain Jonas Rose
Hyaena	24	Captain David Lloyd
Squirrel	24	Captain John Hamstead
Arrow	28	Captain William Bolton
Dart	18	Captain John Devonshire
Cruizer	18	Captain James Brisbane
Harpy	18	Captain William Birchall
Pylades	16	Captain James Boorder

Bomb Vessels
Discovery, Explosion, Hecla, Sulphur, Terror, Volcano and *Zebra*

Fire Ships
Otter and *Zephyr*

Gun Vessels
Teazer, Sparkler, Tigress, Bruiser, Blazer, Hasty, Biter and *Pelter*

Hired Brigs
Eling, Rover and *Lark*

Ships Remaining with Sir Hyde Parker

London	98	Captain William Domett (Sir Hyde Parker's Flagship)
St George	98	Captain Thomas Hardy
Warrior	74	Captain Charles Tyler
Defence	74	Captain Lord Henry Paulet
Saturn	74	Captain Robert Lambert
Ramillies	74	Captain James Dixon
Raisonable	64	Captain John Dilkes
Veteran	64	Captain Archibald Dickson

William Stewart lists a number of other ships as being involved, but they were in the additional force sent later under Admiral Totty.

> 21 April 1801 – departed North Yarmouth this morning a squadron for the Baltic under the command of Admiral Totty in the *Zealous*, with the *Powerful*, *Vengeance*, 74s; *Ruby*, 64; *Alkmaar*, Hospital Ship; *Pomone*, Frigate; *Vesuve*, *Wrangler, Ready, Safeguard, Pincher, Eclipse, Boxer, Plumper, Griper, Adder* and *Cracker* Gun Vessels; *Drake*, cutter; *Prince William*, Hired Armed Ship.

Admiral Totty had originally sailed in the *Invincible* which ran aground off Yarmouth and broke up, with the loss of 400 lives, 183 escaped; Totty was one of those who survived.

Arrangement for Attack and Line of Battle off Copenhagen, 1 April 1801

The arrangement of the attack is as follows, but as the Vice Admiral Lord Nelson cannot with precision mark the situation of the different descriptions of the enemy's floating batteries & smaller vessels lying between their two decked ships & hulks, the ships which are to be opposed to the floating batteries & such will find their stations by observing the stations of the ships to be opposed to the two decked ships and hulks.

Line of Battle

These ships are to fire in passing to their stations	*Edgar* *Ardent* *Glatton* *Isis* *Agamemnon* *Bellona* *Elephant* *Ganges* *Monarch* *Defiance* *Russell* *Polyphemus*	Line to lead in succession & take their stations and anchor as is prescribed by the following arrangement

The *Edgar* to anchor abreast of No. 5 (a 64–gun ship hulk).
The Ardent to pass the *Edgar* and anchor abreast of No's 6 & 7.
The *Glatton* to pass the *Ardent* and anchor abreast of No. 9 (a 64–gun ship hulk).
The *Isis* to anchor abreast of No. 2 (a 64–gun ship hulk).
The *Agamemnon* to anchor abreast on No. 1.

Memo No.1 begins with the enemy's first ship to the southward.

No.	Rate	Supposed No. of Guns mounted on one side	Station of the line as they are to anchor and engage	Notes
1	74	28	*Agamemnon*	This division is to follow the
2	64	26	*Isis*	*Agamemnon* & rake No. 1
3	Low floating batteries	10		It is hoped the *Desiree*'s fire will not only rake No. 1 but also rake the two floating
4	Ship rigged lay without the line	10		batteries. Capt. Rose is to place the 6 gun brigs so as to rake them also
5	64	27	*Edgar*	
6	Pontoon	10	)	
7	Frigate Hulk	12	) *Ardent*	
8	Small no guns visible		)	
9	64	30	) *Glatton*	
10	Ship gunboat of 22 guns	11	)	To give her attention
11	) Pontoons or	12	) *Bellona*	to the support
12	) Floating batteries	9	)	of the *Glatton*
13	74	36	*Elephant*	
14	) Pontoons or	12	)	
15	) Floating batteries	12	) *Ganges*	
16	64	30	*Monarch*	
17	64	30	*Defiance*	
18	64	30	*Russell*	
19	64	30	*Polyphemus*	
20	A small ship supposed a bomb	11		

The six gunboats Captain Riou is to place with the *Jamaica* to make a raking fire upon No. 1. The gunboats it is presumed may get far enough in shore of No. 1 to rake No.'s 3 & 4 & Captain Riou is to advance with the ships & vessels under his orders to the northward as he may perceive the British fire to cease, where he is first stationed.

No.'s 1, 2, 3 & 4 being subdued, which is expected to happen at an early period, the *Isis & Agamemnon* are to cut their cables & immediately to make sail & take their stations ahead of the *Polyphemus* in order to support that part of the line. One flat boat manned & armed is to remain upon the off side of each line of battle ship. The remaining flat boats with the boats for boarding which will be sent by Admiral Sir Hyde Parker under the command of the First Lieutenant of the *London*, are to keep as near the *Elephant* as possible, but out of the line of fire & to be ready to receive the directions of Lord Nelson.

The four launches with anchors & cable which will be sent by Admiral Sir Hyde Parker, under the command of a lieutenant of the London, to be as near to the *Elephant* as possible, out of the line of fire, ready to receive orders from Vice Admiral Lord Nelson.

The *Alcmene, Blanche, Arrow, Dart*, & the *Zephyr & Otter* fire ships are to proceed under the orders of Captain Riou of the *Amazon* to perform such services as he is directed by Lord Nelson.

Nelson & Bronte

Appendix 4

The Danish Defence Line

Ship	Guns	Men[1]	Description	How Disposed
Blockship *Provestenen*	56	529	Old cut-down 3-decker	Burnt
Blockship *Wagrien*	48	361	Old 2-decker	Burnt
Prame *Rendsborg*	20	211	Cavalry transport	Burnt
Prame *Nyborg*	20	221	Cavalry transport	Escaped/Sank
Blockship *Jylland*	48	371	Old 2-decker	Burnt
Radeau *Svaerdfisken* (platform)	20	176	Floating battery	Burnt
Blockship *Cronborg*	22	223	Old Frigate	Burnt
Radeau *Hajen*	20	175	Floating battery (platform)	Burnt
Blockship *Dannebrog*	62	357	Old 2-decker	Blew up
Elven	6	88	Signal repeating vessel	Escaped
Radeau *Grenier* (platform)	24	120	Floating battery	Escaped
Prame *Aggerhuus*	20	213	Cavalry transport	Escaped/Sank
Sjoelland	74	553	Old 2-decker	Burnt

1 These figures are slightly different to those normally published but conform to Dudley Pope's meticulous official counts (except for *Wagrien*, which he puts at 261, which seems far too low for the size of ship and would appear to be a misreading of the figures – all other sources quote 361).

Blockship *Charlotte Amalie*	26	241	Old East Indiaman	Burnt
Radeau *Sohesten*	18	126	Floating Battery (platform)	Burnt
Holstein	60	400	A 2-decker in good repair	Taken away
Blockship *Infodsretten*	64	394	Old 2 decker	Burnt
Hjaelperen	20	269	Frigate in good repair	Escaped

11 Gunboats of Steen Bille's 2nd line (all with 2 guns in bow)

Aalborg, Ahrendahl, Christiansund, Flensborg, Langesund, Nakskov, Nykobing, Odense, Stavaern, Stege and *Viborg.*

Ships of the Defence Line in the Harbour Mouth

Danmark	74	2-decker	Unharmed
Trekroner	74	2-decker	Unharmed
Elefanten	70	Old 2-decker	Unharmed
Mars	64	Old 2-decker	Unharmed
Iris	36	Frigate	Unharmed
Sarpen	16	Brig	Unharmed
Nid-Elven	16	Brig	Unharmed

List of Remaining Warships in Danish Fleet

(Most of which would have been within Copenhagen Dockyard — those known to be elsewhere are annotated as such.)

Christian VII, 90 (discarded in 1801)
Neptunus, 80
Valdemar, 80
Prinsesse Sophie Frederik, 74
Justitia, 74
Arveprins Frederick, 74
Kronprins Frederick, 74
Fyen, 74
Odin, 74
Skjold, 74
Kronprinsesse Marie, 74
Norge, 74

Nordstiernen, 74
Prinsesse Louise Augusta, 64
Ditsmarken, 64
Sejeren, 64 (Mediterranean)
Oresund, 60
Prinsesse Vilelmine Caroline, 60

Frigates
Pommeren, 42
Thetis, 40 (Mediterranean)
Rota, 38
Havfruen, 36 (Mediterranean)
Freya, 36 (Mediterranean)
Venus, 36
Najaden, 36 (Mediterranean)
Frederiksvaern, 32
Triton, 28
Frederikssteen, 28
St Thomas, 22
Little Belt, 20
Fylla, 20
Lougen, 20 (West Indies: captured 28 March)

Brigs
Elven, 16
Glommen, 16
Delphinen, 16
Coureer, 16
Brevdrageren, 16
Flyvendefiske, 14
Anne Marie, 14
Den Aavaagne, 14 (West Indies: captured 28 March)
Forsvar, 14
Iresine, 12 (West Indies: captured 28 March)

Gunboats
Six more with two guns in the bow: *Corsoer, Dragoe, Kioge, Nysted, Praesto* and *Wardoehuus*.

Fifteen with one gun in the bow, and one in the stern: *Kallundborg, Helsingoer, Nestved, Roeskilde, Saltholmen, Frederiksund, Stubbekjobing, Rodbye, Nysted, Svendborg, Faaborg, Holbek, Middelfart, Assens, Kjerteminde.*

Kragero galley and *Lindormen* xebec.

Appendix 5

Report of the Battle of Copenhagen
by Nelson

Elephant, off Copenhagen 3 April 1801

Sir,

In obedience to your directions to report the proceedings of the squadron named in the margin[1] which you did me the honour to place under my command, I beg leave to inform you, that having, by the assistance of that able officer Captain Riou, and the unremitting exertions of Captain Brisbane, and the Masters of the *Amazon* and *Cruizer* in particular, buoyed the channel of the Outer Deep, and the position of the Middle Ground, the squadron passed in safety, and anchored off Draco the evening of the first; and that yesterday morning I made the signal for the squadron to weigh, and to engage the Danish line, consisting of six sail of the line, eleven floating batteries, mounting from twenty-six 24 pounders to eighteen 18 pounders, and one bomb ship, besides schooner gun-vessels.

These were supported by the Crown islands, mounting 88 cannon, and four sail of the line, moored in the harbour's mouth, and some batteries on the island of Amak.

The bomb-ship and schooner gun vessels made their escape; the other seventeen sail are sunk, burnt, or taken, being the whole of the Danish line to the southward of the Crown islands, after a battle of four hours.

From the very intricate navigation, the *Bellona* and *Russell* unfortunately grounded, but although not in the situation assigned them, yet so placed as to be of great service. The *Agamemnon* could not weather the shoal of the Middle, and was obliged to anchor; but not the smallest blame can be attached to Captain Fancourt; it was an event to which all the ships were liable. These accidents prevented the extension of our line by the three ships before mentioned, who would, I am confident, have silenced the Crown islands, the two outer ships in the harbour's mouth, and prevented the heavy loss in the *Defiance* and *Monarch*, and which unhappily threw the gallant and good

---

1 *Elephant, Defiance, Monarch, Bellona, Edgar, Russell, Ganges, Glatton, Isis, Agamemnon, Polyphemus, Ardent, Amazon, Desiree, Blanche, Alcmene*, sloops *Dart, Arrow, Cruizer*, and *Happy*, fire ships *Zephyr* and *Otter*, and bombs *Discovery, Sulphur, Hecla, Explosion, Zebra, Terror* and *Volcano*.

Captain Riou (to whom I had given the command of the frigates and sloops named in the margin[1] to assist in the attack of the ships at the harbour's mouth) under a very heavy fire: the consequence has been the death of Captain Riou, and many brave officers and men in the frigates and sloops.

The bombs were directed and took their stations abreast of the *Elephant*, and threw some shells into the arsenal.

Captain Rose, who volunteered his services to direct the gun-brigs, did everything that was possible to get them forward, but the current was too strong for them to be of service during the action; but not the less merit is due to Captain Rose, and, I believe, all the officers and crews of the gun-brigs for their exertions.

The boats of those ships of the fleet, who were not ordered on the attack, afforded us every assistance; and the officers and men who were in them merit my warmest approbation.

The *Desiree* took her station in raking the southernmost Danish ship of the line, and performed the greatest service.

The action began at five minutes past ten. The van, led by Captain George Murray of the *Edgar*, who set a noble example of intrepidity, which was as well followed up by every captain, officer, and man in the squadron.

It is my duty to state to you, the high and distinguished merit and gallantry of Rear Admiral Graves.

To Captain Foley, who permitted me the honour of hoisting my flag in the *Elephant*, I feel under the greatest obligations; his advice was necessary on many and important occasions during the battle.

I beg leave to express how much I feel indebted to every captain, officer, and man, for their zeal and distinguished bravery on this occasion. The honourable Colonel Stewart did me the favour to be on board the *Elephant*; and himself, with every officer and soldier under his orders, shared with pleasure in the toils and dangers of the day.

The loss in such a battle has naturally been very heavy. Amongst many other brave officers and men who were killed, I have with sorrow to place the name of Captain Mosse, of the *Monarch*, who has left a wife and six children to lament his loss; and among the wounded, that of Captain Sir Thomas B. Thompson, of the *Bellona*.

I have the honour to be, &c Nelson and Bronte.

Losses British[2]

Edgar	First Lieutenant Edmund Johnson, 24 seamen,
	Marine Lieutenant Benjamin Spencer,
	2 marines and 3 privates 49th Foot killed;
	Lieutenants Joshua Johnson and William
	Goldfinch, Midshipmen Thomas Gahagan,
	William Whimper, John Ridge, Peter Procter

---

1 *Blanche, Alcmene, Dart, Arrow, Zephyr* and *Otter*.

2 The Return has been reordered to show the ships in the order they engaged, which then matches their listing in the Casualty Return which follows.

and William Domett, 79 seamen, 17
Marines and 8 privates 49th Foot wounded.

Ardent   Midshipman George Hoare, 29 seamen and
                    marines killed; 64 seamen and marines wounded.

Glatton   The pilot, 17 seamen and marines killed;
                    Lieutenant William Tindall, Masters Mate
                    Robert Thompson, Midshipman John Williams,
                    34 seamen and marines wounded

Isis   Master Daniel Lamond, Midshipmen George McKinlay and
                    Thomas Ram, 23 seamen, 4 marines, Lieutenant Grant 95th
                    Rifles and 2 privates 49th Foot killed; Lieutenant Richard
                    Cormack, Midshipmen Reuben Pain, Simon Frazer and Charles
                    Jones, 69 seamen, 13 marines and 2 privates 49th Foot wounded

Desiree   Lieutenant Andrew King and 3 seamen wounded

Bellona   9 seamen and 2 marines killed; Captain Southey and Thomas
                    Wilks, Masters Mate James Emmerton, Midshipmen John
                    Anderson, Edward Daubenny, William Sitford and William Fig,
                    48 Seamen, Marine Captain Alexander Sharp, ten marines and
                    five privates 49th Foot wounded

Russell   5 seamen and 1 marine wounded

Elephant   Masters Mate Henry Yaulden, 4 seamen, 3
                    marines, Captain Sharpe 49th Foot and
                    1 private 49th Foot killed; Midshipmen Robert
                    Gill and Hugh Mitchel, 8 seamen, 1 marine
                    and 2 privates 49th Foot wounded

Ganges   Master Robert Stewart, 6 seamen killed; the pilot wounded

Monarch   Captain Mosse, 35 seamen, 12 marines and 8
                    privates 49th Foot killed; Lieutenant William
                    Minchin, Boatswain William Joy, Midshipmen
                    Henry Swimmer, William Bowes, Thomas
                    Harlowe, George Morgan and Philip le
                    Vesconte, 101 seamen, Marine Lieutenant
                    James Marrie, 34 marines, 1 infantry
                    Lieutenant[1] and 20 privates 49th Foot wounded

---

1 Possibly Lieutenant Bowden (Cornish Miners) who had volunteered to join the
   49th on the expedition and was killed.

Defiance	Lieutenant George Gray, the pilot, 17 seamen, 3 marines and 2 privates 49th Foot killed; the boatswain, Midshipman James Gallaway, the Captain's clerk, 36 seamen 5 marines and 7 privates 49th Foot wounded
Polyphemus	Midshipman James Bell, 4 seamen and 1 marine killed; Boatswain Edward Burr, 20 seamen and 4 marines wounded
Amazon	Captain Riou, Midshipman the Honourable George Tucket, Captain's Clerk Joseph Rose, 10 seamen and a marine killed; Master's Mates James Harry and Philip Horn, 16 seamen and 5 marines wounded
Blanche	6 seamen and 1 marine killed; 7 seamen and 2 marines wounded
Alcmene	5 seamen killed; Lieutenant Henry Baker, Boatswain Charles Church, Master's mate George Spearing, the pilot, 12 seamen 1 marine lieutenant and 2 marines wounded
Dart	First Lieutenant Richard Sandys and 2 seamen killed; 1 seaman wounded

Total 254 killed, 667 wounded

Total loss of 49th Foot 16 killed, 44 wounded

Table of Losses per ship[1]

Ship	Average Crew	Killed	Wounded	% Casualties
Edgar	600	31	111	23.7
Ardent	450	30	64	20.8
Glatton	400	18	37	13.8
Isis	350	33	88	34.6
Desiree	250	0	4	1.6
Bellona	600	11	71	13.7
Russell	600	0	6	1.0[1]
Elephant	600	10	13	3.8[2]
Ganges	600	7	1	1.3

1 This did not form part of Nelson's Return.

Monarch	600	56	144	33.3
Defiance	600	24	51	12.5
Polyphemus	450	6	25	6.9
Amazon	250	13	23	14.4
Blanche	250	7	9	6.4
Alcmene	250	5	19	9.6
Dart	150	3	1	2.7
Total	**6,950**	**254**	**667**	**13.3**

1 *Russell* was aground throughout the action as well as *Bellona*: the latter would appear to have been under a significantly heavier fire.

2 It is quite surprising how few casualties *Elephant* and *Ganges* suffered in the middle of the line, *Monarch* seeming to have drawn all the fire.

Appendix 6

Danish Losses at Copenhagen 1801

I have been unable to discover an original source for the losses by individual ship. However, figures are produced by Dudley Pope and I have re-used these as a basis here with some amendments. Any Danish ships not listed below did not return any casualties.

Ship	Crew	Killed	Fatally Wounded	Wounded	Missing	% Casualties
Provestenen	529	40	8	27	0	14.2
Wagrien	361[1]	21	7	35	0	17.5
Rendsborg	211	28	0	43	7	37.0
Nyborg	221	28	0	30	0	26.2
Jylland	371	28	7	36	0	19.1
Svaerdfisken	176	18	4	15	0	21.0
Cronborg	223	18	2	17	0	16.6
Hajen	175	7	0	6	0	7.4
Dannebroge	357	53	3	48	0	29.1
Elven	88	9	1	6	0	18.2
Fleet Battery 1 (Grenier)	120	12	6	28	0	38.3
Aggerhuus	213	19	13	41	0	34.3
Sjoeland	553	39	17	108	20	33.3
Charlotte Amalie	241	19	2	18	0	16.2
Sohesten	126	12	7	14	0	26.2
Holstein	400	12	4	49	0	16.3
Infodsretten	394	21	6	35	0	15.7
Hjaelperen	269	0	3	3	0	2.2
Danmark	600	1	0	0	0	0.1
Stavaern gunboat	70?	0	0	1	0	1.4
Viborg gunboat	70?	3	0	0	0	4.3

---

1 Pope states 261 but all other sources say 361 and I believe given the size of vessel that Pope has misread the figure.

Reinforcements from shore	171?[1]	?	?	33[2]	0	19.3
Total	**5,939**	**388**	**90**	**560**	**27**	**17.96**[3]

Total losses in King's Deep	Killed	388
	Fatally Wounded[4]	90
	Wounded	560
	Total	1,065
Prisoners of War		1,779
Missing		205

---

1 This is the best figure we can come up with, it might have been higher.

2 This represents killed and wounded: I have been unable to separate them.

3 If those ships only engaged slightly (*Hjaelperen*, *Danmark*, *Stavaern* and *Vib*org) are removed the average percentange of casualties is 21.5.

4 Recorded as wounded on 2 April but died in the coming days and weeks.

Appendix 7

Admiral Sir Hyde Parker's Official Dispatch

Published in the *London Gazette* of 15 April 1801

To Evan Nepean Esq
Copenhagen Roads 6 April

Sir,

You will be pleased to acquaint the Lords Commissioners of the Admiralty, that since my letter of the 23rd of March, no opportunity of wind offered for going up the Sound until the 25th, when the wind shifted in a most violent squall from the S.W. to the N.W. and N. and blew with such violence, and with so great a sea, as to render it impossible for any ship to have weighed her anchor. The wind and sea were even so violent as to oblige many ships to let go a second anchor to prevent them from driving, notwithstanding they were riding with two cables and end; and, by the morning, the wind veered again to the southward of the west.

On the 30th of last month, the wind having come to the northward, we passed into the Sound with the fleet, but not before I had assured myself of the hostile intentions of the Danes to oppose our passage, as the papers marked Nos I, II, III and IV [not included] will prove: after this intercourse, there could be no doubt remaining of their determination to resist.

After anchoring about five or six miles from the Island of Huin, I reconnoitred, with Vice Admiral Lord Nelson and Rear Admiral Graves, the formidable line of ships, radeaus, pontoons, galleys, fire-ships, and gun-boats, flanked and supported by extensive batteries of the two islands called the crowns; the largest of which was mounted with from 50 to 70 pieces of cannon: these were again commanded by two ships of 70 guns, and a large frigate in the inner road of Copenhagen, and two 64-gun ships (without masts) were moored on the flat, on the starboard side of the entrance, into the arsenal.

The day after, the wind being southerly, we again examined their positions, and came to the resolution of attacking them from the southward.

Vice Admiral Lord Nelson having offered his services for conducting the attack, had, some days before, we entered the Sound, shifted his flag to the *Elephant;* and after having examined and buoyed the outer channel of the Middle Ground, his lordship proceeded with the twelve ships of the line named in the margin,[1] all the frigates, bombs, fire-ships, and all the small vessels; and that evening anchored off Draco Point to make his disposition for the attack, and wait for the wind to the southward.

It was agreed between us, that the ships remaining with me should weigh at the same moment his lordship did, and menace the Crown batteries, and the four ships of the line that lay at the entrance of the arsenal; as also to cover our disabled ships as they came out of action.

I have now the honour to enclose a copy of Vice Admiral Lord Nelson's report to me of the action on the 2nd instant. His lordship has stated so full the whole of his proceedings on that day, as only to leave me the opportunity to testify my entire acquiescence and testimony of the bravery and intrepidity with which the action was supported throughout the line.

Was it possible for me to add anything to the well-earned renown of Lord Nelson, it would be by asserting, that his exertions, great as they have heretofore been, never were carried to a higher pitch of zeal for his country's service.

I have only to lament that the sort of attack, confined within an intricate and narrow passage, excluded the ships, particularly under my command, from the opportunity of exhibiting their valour: but I can, with great truth, assert, that the same spirit and zeal animated the whole of the fleet; and I trust, that the contest in which we are engaged will, on some future day, afford them an occasion of showing that the whole were inspire with the same spirit, had the field been sufficiently extensive to have brought it into action.

It is with the deepest concern I mention the loss of Captains Mosse and Riou, two very brave and gallant officers, and whose loss, as I am well informed, will be sensibly felt by the families they have left behind them; the former a wife and children, the latter an aged mother.

From the known gallantry of Sir Thomas Thompson on former occasions, the naval service will have to regret the loss of the future exertions of that brave officer, whose leg was shot off.

For all other particulars, I beg leave to refer their lordships to Captain Otway, who was with Lord Nelson in the latter part of the action, and able to answer any questions that may be thought necessary to put to him. A return of the killed and wounded you will receive herewith. I have the honour to be, &c H. Parker

P.S. The promotions and appointments that have taken place on this occasion will be sent by the next opportunity that offers; but I cannot close this without acquainting their lordships, that Captain Mosse being killed very early in the action, Lieutenant John Yelland continued it with the greatest spirit and good conduct: I must, therefore, in justice to his merit, beg leave to recommend him to their lordships favour.

---

1 *Elephant, Defiance, Monarch, Bellona, Edgar, Russell, Ganges, Glatton, Isis, Agamemnon, Polyphemus* and *Ardent.*

Appendix 8

Letter from Captain Fremantle to his wife Betsey Wynne

Ganges off Copenhagen

4th April [1801]

My dearest Betsey,

I send you for the information of your County acquaintance a plan of our mode of attack with the orders given by Nelson; he had conducted himself towards me with the same kindness he ever did and made the *Ganges* his second in the action. We anchored where we were directed and Lord Nelson himself hailed me when to let go my anchor. We have been more fortunate than any ship that was so long in action and I can account for it in no other way than by saying that the vessels we were opposed to did not hold us much more than ¾ of an hour. The two ships immediately ahead of us, the *Monarch* and *Defiance* were exposed to the Crown batteries, which made dreadful slaughter on board those ships, but the most remarkable part of the whole business is that one man only, the Pilot, should be wounded before we anchored. The Master was killed and the Pilot lost his arm, so that I was obliged to con the ship myself. Our masts and rigging are very much cut indeed, but I am in hopes to keep them together with the assistance of some good fishes which the carpenters are putting up. Every merit is due to Lord Nelson for his policy as well as bravery on this occasion; as soon as the ships abreast of the *Elephant* and *Ganges* had struck, he hailed and desired I would come on board. I found him talking with some Danes in his cabin and telling them how he longed to see the Russians down; at the same time he was sending an officer with a flag of truce on shore to tell the Prince that if he did not cease firing from the batteries, he should be under the necessity of burning all the ships with the people in them. This produced a cessation to the very severe battle, which was certainly as convenient for us and the Enemy, as we had several ships on shore and most of the ships engaged so completely crippled that it was with difficulty they could sail out.

Lord Nelson has been on shore with the Prince; he was received by the multitude with cheers and *Viva Nelson*; on his going to the palace they were more loud in their applause, so much so that the *Government* did not seem well pleased with it; he embarked in the same way and is the life and soul of the squadron. The signal is made for letters. I am well and am busy as a man can well be. I have daily every reason to be more satisfied with my ship and ship's company, and I do not think there is a probability of the *Ganges* returning to England before we have settled with this Northern Confederacy. God bless you and the children. I write another letter for *yourself* by this conveyance. Ever yours most Affectionately, Thomas Fraser Fremantle

Appendix 9

Sir Hyde Parker's Dispatch Regarding the Official Treaty

Letter from Sir Hyde Parker to Evan Nepean Secretary of the Admiralty, dated onboard His Majesty's Ship, *London*, in Copenhagen Road, 9 April 1801

Published in the *London Gazette* on 21 April 1801

Sir,

The honourable Lieutenant-Colonel Stewart having volunteered his services by being the bearer of these dispatches, I have accepted thereof, on a belief that it will be more expeditious than by sea.

I have the pleasure to transmit an armistice concluded between the court of Denmark and myself.

I mean, as soon as the disabled ships are refitted, and the worst of the wounded moved into the *Holstein* Danish ship of the line, which I have commissioned as an hospital ship, to proceed over the Grounds into the Baltic, to put into execution the remaining part of my instructions.

The *Isis* and *Monarch* being found in so bad a state from the late action, as to render it necessary to send them to England, to have their damages repaired; I shall send them home for that purpose with the *Holstein* hospital ship, which has the wounded and sick on board.

The Danish government on the one hand, and Admiral Sir Hyde Parker, knight, Commander-in-Chief of His Britannic Majesty's forces in the Road of Copenhagen, on the other, being, from motives of humanity, equally anxious to put a stop to the farther effusion of blood, and to save the city of Copenhagen from the disastrous consequences which may attend a farther prosecution of hostilities against that city, have mutually agreed upon a military armistice or suspension of arms.

His Danish majesty having for that purpose appointed Major-General Ernest Frederick Walterstorff, chamberlain to His Danish majesty, and colonel of a regiment, and adjutant General Hans Lindholm, Captain in his Danish majesty's navy, his commissioners for agreeing about the terms of the said armistice; and Admiral Sir Hyde Parker, knight, having, with the same view, duly authorized the right hon. Horatio Lord Nelson of the Nile, knight of the most honourable order of the Bath, Duke of Bronte, in Sicily, Knight of the Grand Cross of the Order of St Ferdinand and of Merit, and of the Imperial Order of the Crescent, Vice Admiral in the fleet of his Britannic majesty, and the honourable William Stewart, Lieutenant Colonel in his Britannic Majesty's service, and commanding a detachment of his Britannic Majesty's forces embarked; these said commissioners have met this day, and having exchanged their respective powers, have agreed upon the following terms.

Art I. From the moment of the signature of this armistice, all hostilities shall immediately cease between the fleet under the command of Admiral Sir Hyde Parker, and the City of Copenhagen, and all the armed ships and vessels of his Danish Majesty in the road or harbour of that city, as likewise between the different islands and provinces of Denmark, Jutland included.

Art II. The armed ships and vessels belonging to his Danish Majesty shall remain in their present actual situation as to armament, equipment and hostile position; and the treaty commonly understood as the treaty of armed neutrality shall, as far as relates to the co-operation of Denmark, be suspended while the armistice remains in force.

On the other side, the armed ships and vessels under the command of Admiral Sir Hyde Parker, shall in no manner whatsoever molest the City of Copenhagen, or his Danish Majesty's armed ships and vessels on the coasts of the different islands and provinces of Denmark, Jutland included; and in order to avoid everything which might otherwise create uneasiness or jealousy. Sir Hyde Parker shall not suffer any of the ships or vessels under his command, to approach within gun-shot of the armed ships or fort of his Danish Majesty in the road of Copenhagen. This restriction shall not, however, extend to vessels necessarily passing or re-passing through the Casper or King's Channel.

Art III. This armistice is to protect the City of Copenhagen, as also the coasts of Denmark, of Jutland, and islands included, against the attack of any other naval force which his Britannic Majesty may now or hereafter, during its remaining in force, have in these seas.

Art IV. The fleet of Admiral Sir Hyde Parker shall be permitted to provide itself at Copenhagen, and along the coasts of the different islands and provinces of Denmark and Jutland included, with everything which it may require for the health and comfort of its crews.

Art V. Admiral Sir Hyde Parker shall send on shore all such subjects of his Danish majesty as are now on board the British fleet under his command, the Danish government engaging to give an acknowledgement for them, as also for all such wounded as were permitted to be landed after the action of the 2nd instant, in order that they may be accounted for in favour of Great Britain, in the unfortunate event of the renewal of hostilities.

Art VI. The coasting trade carried on by Denmark, on all such parts of her coast as are included in the operation of this armistice, shall be unmolested by any British ships or vessels whatever and instructions given accordingly by Admiral Sir Hyde Parker.

Art VII. This armistice is to continue uninterrupted by the contracting parties for the space of fourteen weeks, from the signature hereof, at the expiration of which time, it shall be in the power of either of the said parties to declare a cessation of the same, and to recommence hostilities upon giving fourteen day's previous notice.

The conditions of this armistice are upon all occasions to be explained in the most liberal and loyal manner, so as to remove all ground for future disputes, and facilitate the means of bringing about the restoration of harmony and good understanding between the two kingdoms.

In faith whereof, we, the undersigned commissioners, in virtue of our full powers, have signed the present armistice, and have affixed to it the seal of our arms.

Done on board his Britannic Majesty's ship the *London*, in Copenhagen Roads, 9 April 1801

Signed

Nelson and Bronte
William Stewart
Ernest Frederick Walterstorff
Hand Lindholm

In pursuance of my above-mentioned authority, I ratify this document with my hand.

Frederick
Ratified by me

Hyde Parker, Admiral and Commander in Chief of his Britannic Majesty's fleet.

Appendices Relevant to the Siege of Copenhagen 1807

29. List of Danish Ships Captured 1807

30. Report of Admiral Gambier to The Honourable W. Wellesley Pole

31. Letter from General Cathcart to his Troops

32. Report of Transports Lost on Return from Copenhagen

33. Report from Sir William Rule to the Honourable William Pole, Secretary of the Admiralty, dated the 25 January 1808, respecting the general state of the Danish ships

34. Report of the Capture of Heligoland

35. List of Convoys which passed through the Great Belt between 30 May and 4 August 1810

36. The Danish Army in Holstein, 1807

The Copenhagen Expedition, 1807

Naval Forces

Admiral James Gambier, Commander-in-Chief

Vice Admiral the Honourable Henry Stanhope
Rear Admiral William Essington
Commodore Sir Samuel Hood
Commodore Sir Richard Keats
Sir Home Popham, Captain of the Fleet

Ships of the Line Sailed with Admiral Gambier, 26 July 1807		Commanders
Prince of Wales	98	Captain Mackenzie (Gambier's flagship)
Pompee	74	Captain Richard Dacres (Stanhope's flagship)
Centaur	74	Captain William Webley (Commodore Hood's flagship)
Ganges	74	Captain Peter Halkett (Commodore Keats's flagship)
Spencer	74	Captain Robert Stopford
Vanguard	74	Captain Alexander Fraser
Maida	74	Captain Samuel Linzee
Brunswick	74	Captain Thomas Graves
Resolution	74	Captain George Burlton
Hercule	74	Captain John Colville
Orion	74	Captain Sir Archibald Dickson
Alfred	74	Captain John Bligh
Goliath	74	Captain Peter Puget
Captain	74	Captain Isaac Wolley

1 From Anon., *Narrative of the Expedition to the Baltic,* London, 1808, and Clowes' *History of the Royal Navy* with a large number of amendments.

Ruby	64	Captain John Draper
Dictator	64	Captain Donald Campbell
Nassau	64	Captain Robert Campbell

Joined 5 August off Elsinore

Superb	74	Captain Donald McLeod

Joined 7 August off Elsinore

Minotaur	74	Captain Charles Mansfield (Rear Admiral Essington's flagship)
Valiant	74	Captain James Young
Inflexible	64	Captain Joshua Watson
Leyden	64	Captain William Cumberland
Defence	74	Captain Charles Ekins
Mars	74	Captain William Lukin

Joined 12 August

Agamemnon	64	Captain Jonas Rose

Frigates

(Most of these smaller ships sailed with Gambier)

Hussar, 46	*Cambrian*, 40	*Africaine*, 40	*Surveillante*, 40
Sybille, 38	*Leda*, 38	*Nymphe*, 36	*Gloire*, 36[1]
Franchise, 36	*Astraea*, 32	*Banterer*, 24	*Comus*, 22
Cyane, 22	*Cossack*, 22		

Sloops

Alert, 20	*Wanderer*, 20	*Combatant*, 20	*Valorous*, 20
Lightning, 20	*Leveret*, 18	*Mosquito*, 18	*Bonetta*, 18
Pandora, 18	*Valorous*, 18	*Sappho*, 18	*Bellette*, 18
Rosamond, 18	*Cruizer*, 18	*Pelican*, 16	*Alacrity*, 16
Goshawk, 16	*Orestes*, 16	*Paulina*, 16	*Railleur*, 14
Arrow, 14			

Gun Brigs

Mutine, 18	*Kite*, 18	*Hebe*, 18	*Procris*, 18
Halcyon, 16	*Forward*, 14	*Mariner*,	14 *Basilisk*, 14
Minx, 14	*Flamer*, 14	*Fearless*, 14	*Gallant*, 14
Urgent, 14	*Safeguard*, 14	*Desperate*, 14	*Pincher*, 14

---

1 Admiral Gambier calls her the *Gloria* in a letter, but there was no such ship in the navy.

Richmond, 14	*Fearless*, 14	*Mariner*, 14	*Safeguard*, 14
Intelligent, 12	*Fury*, 12	*Turbulent*, 12	*Indignant*, 2
Acute, 12	*Tigress*, 12	*Surly*, 10	*Quail*, 4
Pigeon, 4			

Fire Ships

Lightning, 20	*Prometheus*, 16	*Tartarus*, 16

Bombs

Thunder, 8	*Zebra*, 12	*Vesuvius*, 10	*Aetna*, 8

Land Forces

Lieutenant General Cathcart, Commander-in-Chief
Lieutenant General Burrard, Second-in-Command

Right Division

Lieutenant General Sir G. Ludlow KB

Major General Finch
1st Battalion Coldstream Guards   Lieutenant Colonel Armstrong
1st Battalion 3rd Foot Guards   Lieutenant Colonel Stopford

Brigadier General Warde
1st Battalion 28th Foot   Lieutenant Colonel Johnson
79th Foot   Lieutenant Colonel Cameron

Left Division
Lieutenant General Sir David Baird K.B.

Major General Grosvenor
1st Battalion 4th Foot   Lieutenant Colonel Wynch
1st Battalion 23rd Foot   Lieutenant Colonel Jones

Major General Spencer
1st Battalion 32nd Foot   Lieutenant Colonel Hinde
1st Battalion 50th Foot   Lieutenant Colonel Walker
1st Battalion 82nd Foot   Lieutenant Colonel Smith

Brigadier General Macfarlane[1]
1st Battalion 7th Foot   Lieutenant Colonel Packenham
1st Battalion 8th Foot   Lieutenant Colonel Horton

---

1 This brigade did not sail to Denmark from Britain until 8 August so was not present
   during the early operations.

Reserve
Major General Sir Arthur Wellesley K.B.

Acting Brigadier General, Colonel Stuart
1st Battalion 43rd Foot	Major Arbuthnot
2nd Battalion 52nd Foot	Lieutenant Colonel Gyfford
1st Battalion 92nd Foot	Lieutenant Colonel Napier
1st Battalion 95th Foot 5 comps	Lieutenant Colonel Beckwith
2nd Battalion 95th Foot 5 comps	

Royal Artillery
Major General Bloomfield
Lieutenant Colonel Harding
Lieutenant Colonel Cookson

10 companies of Royal Artillery

Royal Engineers
Colonel D'Arcey
Major Fletcher

Staff
Colonel Hope	Deputy Adjutant General
Lieutenant Colonel Murray	Deputy Quarter Master General
Major Macdonald	Military Secretary
Mr Smith Esquire	Pay Master General
Mr Kennedy Esquire	Commissary General

Staff of the German Legion
Lieutenant General the Earl of Rosslyn
Major General von Drechsell
Brigadier General von Decken

Major General von Linsingen commanding the cavalry
1st Regiment of Light Dragoons KGL
2nd Regiment of Light Dragoons KGL
3rd Regiment of Light Dragoons KGL

1st Brigade
Colonel du Plat
6th Line Battalion KGL
7th Line Battalion KGL
8th Line Battalion KGL

2nd Brigade
Colonel von Drieberg
3rd Line Battalion KGL
4th Line Battalion KGL
5th Line Battalion KGL

3rd Brigade
Colonel Barsse
1st Line Battalion KGL
2nd Line Battalion KGL

4th Brigade
Colonel von Alten
1st Light Battalion KGL
2nd Light Battalion KGL

Major Rottiger commanding KGL Artillery

Captain A. Sympher's horse artillery battery KGL
Captain Gesenius' foot artillery battery KGL
Captain Tieling's foot artillery battery KGL
Captain Heise's foot artillery battery KGL

Appendix 11

Declaration of King Christian VII

Gluckstadt, 16 August

We Christian the Seventh, by the Grace of God, King of Denmark, Norway, of the Wends and Goths, Duke of Schleswig, Holstein and Ditmarshen, and also of Oldenburg &c &c &c. do hereby make known, that, whereas by the English Envoy, Jackson, it was made known to us, the 13th of this month, that hostilities against Denmark would be commenced; and whereas, at the same time, he demanded a passport for himself and suite; consequently the war between England and Denmark, may be considered as having broken out: Therefore we hereby call on all our faithful subjects to take up arms, whenever it shall be required, to frustrate the insidious designs of the enemy, and repel hostile attacks.

We further hereby ordain, that all English ships, as well as all English property, and all English goods, shall everywhere be seized by the magistrates and others, particularly by the officers of customs, wherever they may be found. It is further our will, that all English subjects, until pursuant to our orders they can be sent out of the country, shall, without exception, be arrested, as enemies of our kingdom and country; which is strictly to be carried into execution by all magistrates, as well as by all subordinate officers, duly to be instructed by them for that purpose; and it is a matter of course that all English ships and boats which approach our coast, shall be considered and treated as hostile.

It is also our will, that all suspicious foreigners be watched with the greatest attention: and that all magistrates, as well as all subordinate officers, shall use their utmost efforts to discover all spies.

Lastly, we find it necessary to ordain, that, immediately after the publication hereof, all correspondence with English subjects shall entirely cease; and that no payment shall be made to them, on any ground whatsoever, until our further orders, on pain of severe punishment in case of contravention. For the rest, we rely on the justice of our cause, and the courage and tried fidelity of our beloved subjects.

Given under our Royal Seal, in our fortress of Gluckstadt, the 16th of August 1807

C L Baron v Brockdorf

J C Moritz

Appeal by Admiral Gambier and General Cathcart for the Surrender of the Danish Fleet

18 August 1807

Whereas the present treaties of peace and the changes of government and of territory, acceded to by so many powers, have so far increased the influence of France on the continent of Europe, as to render it impossible for Denmark, though it desires to be neutral, to preserve its neutrality, and absolutely necessary for those who continue to resist the French aggression, to take measures to prevent the arms of neutral powers from being turned against them: In this view the King cannot regard the present position of Denmark with indifference; and his Majesty has sent negotiators with ample powers, to his Danish Majesty, to request, in the most amicable manner, such explanations as the times require, and a concurrence in such measures, as can alone give security against the farther mischiefs which the French meditate, through the acquisition of the Danish Navy.

The king, our Royal and most gracious master, has therefore judged it expedient to desire the temporary deposit of the Danish fleet, in one of his Majesty's ports. This deposit seems to be so just, and so indispensably necessary, under the relative circumstances of the neutral and belligerent powers, that his Majesty has further deemed it a duty to himself and to his people, to support the demand by a powerful fleet, and by an army amply supplied with every preparation necessary for the most active and determined enterprise.

We come therefore to your shores, inhabitants of Zeeland, not as enemies, but in self-defence, to prevent those who have so long disturbed the peace of Europe, from compelling the force of your Navy to be turned against us. We ask deposit; we do not look to capture; so far from it, the most solemn pledge has been offered to your government, and is hereby renewed in the name, and at the express command of the king our master, that, if our demand be amicably acceded to, every ship belonging to Denmark shall, at the conclusion of a general peace, be restored to her in the same condition and state of equipment, as when received under the protection of the British flag.

It is in the power of your government, by a word, to sheath our swords, most reluctantly drawn against you: But, if on the other hand, the machinations of France render you deaf to the voice of reason, and the call of friendship, the innocent blood that will be spilt, and the horror of a besieged and bombarded capital, must fall on your heads, and those of your evil advisors.

His Majesty's seamen and soldiers, when on shore, will treat Zeeland, as long as your conduct to them permits it, on the footing of a province of the most-friendly power in alliance with Great Britain, whose territory has the misfortune to be the theatre of war. The persons of all those who remain at home, and do not take an hostile part, will be held sacred. Property will be respected and preserved, and the most severe discipline will be enforced. Every article of supply furnished or brought to market will be paid for at a fair and settled price: but as immediate and constant supplies, especially of provisions and forage, fuel and transports, are necessary to all armies, it is well known that requisitions are unavoidable; and must be enforced: much convenience will arise to inhabitants and much confusion and loss to them will be prevented, if persons in authority are found in the several districts to whom requisition may be addressed, and through whom claims for payment may be settled and liquidated.

If such persons are appointed and discharge their duty, without meddling in matters that do not concern them, they shall be respected, and all requisitions shall be addressed to them, through the proper channel, and departments of the Navy and Army: but, as forbearance on the part of the inhabitants is essential to the principal of those arrangements, it is necessary that all manner of civil persons should remain at their respective habitations; and any peasant or others found in arms, singly or in small troops, or who may be guilty of any act of violence, must expect to be treated with rigour.

The government of his Danish Majesty, having hitherto refused to treat this matter in an amicable way, part of the army disembarked, and the whole force has assumed a warlike attitude, but it is not yet too late for the voice of moderation to be heard.

Given in the Sound, under our hands and seals this 18th day of August 1807

Gambier

Cathcart

Commanders in Chief of his Majesty's forces by sea and land, employed in the expedition

Reaction of the Danes

General Peymann to Prince Frederick

The admonitions and the menaces contained in the summons, are not unusual in similar circumstances; but if the English thought to make any impression upon me, they have been strangely deceived. You may be assured, my gracious Sovereign, that consistent with my duty, I shall defend myself to the uttermost: and that, under my command, Copenhagen shall never fall into the hands of an enemy otherwise than by storm; even though the force brought against me was greater than the present. I shall endeavour to defend our honour, and to end my days as a brave soldier.

Appendix 13

Summons by General Cathcart

18 August 1807

Sir,

I cannot omit requesting your Excellency, as well in my own name, as in that of the Admiral who commands his Majesty's fleet. To take into your most serious consideration, the present situation of the city of Copenhagen, which is brought into a dreadful crisis. If this city, the capital of Denmark, the residence of the King and that of all the Royal Family, and of the government; the seat of the sciences and commerce, and full of inhabitants of all ranks, of every age and sex; if this city should determine to abide the horrors of a siege, then the same shall be annoyed, by every possible means of devastation. As soon as ever the order shall be issued for this purpose, the officers who are intrusted with them, will no longer have any choice left them, of exerting every means in their power to make themselves master of the place. An assault made upon a place so full of men and treasure, must, in the issue, involve the inhabitants in ruin and the loss of their property, as an unavoidable consequence.

Should Denmark refuse to join us in a friendly alliance, the most absolute orders are given by our government to attack this city by land and sea. The preparations for this purpose are in a state of greater forwardness than you are willing to believe.

For God's sake, Sir, consider coolly whether resistance will not be the ruin of the place which you wish to defend; and whether, under the circumstances of the present contest, an exhibition of your valour, which certainly no man will dispute, will not involve the capital in that ruin, which is always the result of a siege; and the final issue of which will be the loss of your fleet and arsenal, both of which may now be prevented.

All the property without the city has been hitherto respected. I must also avail myself of this occasion to inform you, that objects of the greatest consequence and importance to Denmark are in my power, and that I have also hitherto respected them: this state of things cannot endure long.

I will not offend your Excellency by any kind of menace; but I request you, and your advisers, most earnestly, to think of the irreparable injury which may be caused, by the operations of a few days; and that you are still in a situation to avert it.

Cathcart

Appendix 14

Report of General von Decken

To General Cathcart

Jaegersborg. 19 August 1807

My Lord,

After I had the honour to state to your lordship yesterday the capture of six waggons loaded with powder, and also of a considerable quantity of arms at Frederiksborg,[1] which I have sent to Major General Linsingen, I learned that a convoy of 180 waggons, loaded with gunpowder, and escorted by upwards of 500 men, was on its way to Frederiksborg, after having in vain attempted to enter Copenhagen by way of Roskilde. I resolved to attempt to cut it off from Frederiksvaerk, and proceeded for that purpose to Kregme. I was informed here, that the said convoy had passed there two hours before, that the escort was very much fatigued, and had begun to desert. I was told that Frederiksvaerk was a very strong position, defended by a corps called the volunteers of that place, raised by the Crown Prince himself for the protection of the powder mill and arsenal there. Although the horses of my detachment (which was composed of 100 Hussars of the 1st Line [Hussars], (including eighteen dragoons of the 3rd) were very fatigued, yet I thought it advisable to attempt to take the place by surprise. I approached Frederiksvaerk at one o'clock of the morning. Captain Krauchenberg, of the 1st Hussars, succeeded in surprising an advanced picquet of nine men. In arriving near the entrance, where we expected to find a battery, we met an officer, who informed me that the commanding officer was willing to capitulate, if I would grant him honourable terms. After some conversation with Major Tscherning, aide de camp to the prince, and governor of that place, he agreed to surrender with his corps, 860 strong, including officers, under the condition that he and his whole corps should not serve during the war, or until an exchange had taken place.

I found a great quantity of powder (about 1,600 centners[2]), a number of guns and small arms. As I had no means to carry off the powder, and even no time to destroy it, I was obliged to be satisfied with the promise of the major, and all the officers, upon honour, that neither powder nor stores should be issued to the Danes. As there was no means of getting waggons, I was obliged to be satisfied with carrying off the four guns,

---

1 He writes Friedrickstadt, but means Frederiksborg.

2 A unit of weight of 50kg, which means the total weight of gunpowder captured was 80,000kg, or 80 metric tonnes.

and half the arms of the corps which had surrendered, and which I have delivered to Major General Linsingen.

I left Frederiksvaerk this morning at five o'clock, and found myself soon after attacked almost in all the villages by peasants armed with forks, delivered for that purpose by the Danish government, the greater part on foot, but some on horseback. The dragoons took about fifty of these peasants, and five horses, without any loss on our side. On receiving information that all the roads in the woods before and behind Frederiksvaerk, were full of peasants (some of which were armed with rifles), I changed my road by marching to the left, where the ground is open, and I discharged the peasants, after explaining to them the object of our being in this country.

I cannot conclude this long report without certifying to your lordship my great satisfaction with the conduct of the officers and men which I have had the honour to command on this occasion, and to recommend to your lordship's notice Captain Krauchenberg, of the 1st Hussars.

I have the honour to be &c
Friedrich von Decken, Brigadier General

Appendix 15

Admiral Gambier Announces the Commencement of Hostilities

17 August 1807

Hostilities having this day commenced between his Majesty's arms and those of Denmark, by the Danish gunboats having captured and destroyed a British merchant ship, passing Copenhagen: The Flag Officers. Captains, and Commanders of his Majesty's ships and vessels, are hereby authorized and required to use their utmost endeavours to take possession of, and detain any ships or vessels of war belonging to the King of Denmark; or any merchant vessels whatsoever, with their cargoes, belonging to subjects of his Danish Majesty: observing to send all such ships and vessels to me, to be dealt with as circumstances shall require.

Gambier Admiral

And Blockades the Great Belt Passage

21 August 1807

Whereas I have judged it expedient, in conducting the operations of his Majesty's fleet under my command against Copenhagen, to surround the Island of Zeeland, and the other islands contiguous with his Majesty's ships, in order to prevent reinforcements or supplies, of any kind whatsoever, from being thrown into the said islands: I do hereby declare them, as well as the passage of the Great Belt (extending from a bank or shoal named Hasteen's Ground, to the south-east end the Island of Femeren) to be in a state of close blockade: and do also hereby direct the Flag officers, Captains, and Commanders of the said ships, to give notice thereof to any neutral vessels they may find going into any of the ports of the same islands, or into the passage aforesaid; and do request them to desist there from. And in case any neutral vessels, after receiving such notice, shall attempt to enter into any port or place of the same islands, or into the passage aforesaid, the said Flag officers, Captains, and Commanders, are hereby authorized and required to detain such vessels, and leaving their respective masters and a proportion of their crew on board to assist in navigating them, put a careful petty officer, with as many seamen as may be necessary, into them respectively, and send them to me at this anchorage.

Gambier, Admiral

Appendix 16

Return of British Losses during the Disembarkation

General Return of Casualties from the Landing of the troops in the Island of Zealand on the 16th, to the 21st August 1807

Royal Artillery – One officer, one rank & file, 2 horses killed. Four horses wounded.

1st Battalion 92nd – One rank & file killed

1st Battalion 95th – One rank & file wounded

1st Battalion 82nd – One officer killed; one officer wounded

1st Battalion 43rd – One rank & file wounded

Total – Two officers, two rank & file, two horses killed; one officer, one rank & file, four horses wounded

Names of officers killed

Lieutenant Lyons of the Royal Artillery, and Ensign Dixon of the 1st Battalion 82nd.

Name of officer wounded

Captain Hastings of the 1st Battalion 82nd.

Appendix 17

Return of the British Inshore Squadron and Losses

Names of the Vessels forming the Advanced Squadron, with an Account of the Killed and Wounded on 23 August 1807

Hebe armed ship; *Cruizer* and *Mutine* sloops.
Fearless, Indignant, Urgent, Pincher, Tigress, Desperate and *Safeguard* gun brigs;
Thunderer, Zebra, Fury, Aetna and *Vesuvius* bombs;
with three armed transports and ten launches fitted as mortar boats.

Cruizer – Lieutenant Woodford killed
Fearless – 2 Seamen killed; Lieutenant Williams (slightly), 1 Seaman and 4 Marines wounded.
Indignant – 1 Seaman killed; 1 Seaman wounded
Urgent – 1 Seaman and 1 Marine wounded
Valiant's Launch – 3 Seamen wounded
Africaine's Boat – 1 Seaman wounded

Total – 4 killed, 13 wounded

List of Killed and Wounded by the Explosion of the *Charles of Kircaldy* Armed Transport, attached to the Advance Squadron on the 31st August

Belonging to the *Valiant* – 2 Seamen killed; Lieutenant N. Rowe, Mr Phillip Tomlinson, Master's Mate (since dead of his wounds) and 12 Seamen, wounded
Belonging to the Transport – Mr James Moyase, Master, and 7 Seamen killed; and 7 Seamen wounded.

General Wellesley's Report on the Battle of Kioge

To General Cathcart,

Kioge 29 August 1807
My Lord,
According to the intention which I announced to your lordship on the evening of the 27th, I moved to Roskilde Kroe, and placed Colonel Reden at Vallensbrek, and General Linsingen marched yesterday morning to Roskilde; by these different movements, his force became the right instead of the left.

Having had reason to believe that the enemy still remained at Kioge, I determined to attack him this day. I settled with General Linsingen, that he should cross the Kioge rivulet at Lille Salby, and turn the enemy's left flank, while I should move along the sea road towards Kioge, and attack him in front.

Both divisions broke up this morning, and marched according to the plan concerted. Upon my approach to Kioge, I found the enemy in force on the north side of the town and rivulet, and they commenced a cannonade upon the patroles of hussars in my front; they had three or four regular battalions formed in one line, with cavalry on both flanks, and apparently a large body beyond the town and rivulet. At the time agreed upon with General Linsingen, I formed my infantry in one line, with the left to the sea, having the two squadrons of hussars upon the right. There had been some appearance of a movement by the enemy to their left; and I had not any communication with General Linsingen, and was not certain that he had passed the rivulet. I therefore thought it proper to make the attack in an echelon of battalions from the left; the whole covered by the 1st Battalion 95th Regiment, and by the fire of our artillery.

It fell to the lot of the 92nd Regiment to lead this attack, and they performed their part in the most exemplary manner, and were equally well supported by the 52nd and 43rd.

The enemy soon retired to an entrenchment which they had formed in front of a camp on the north side of Kioge, and they made a disposition of their cavalry upon the sands to charge the 92nd in flank, while they should attack this entrenchment. This disposition obliged me to move Colonel Reden's hussars from the right to the left flank, and to throw the 43rd into a second line; and then the 92nd carried the entrenchment, and forced the enemy to retreat into the town in disorder. They were followed immediately, in the most gallant style, by Colonel Reden and his hussars, and by the 1st Battalion 95th Regiment, and afterwards by the whole of the infantry of my corps. Upon crossing the rivulet, we found General Linsingen's corps upon our right flank, and the whole joined in the pursuit of the enemy.

Major General Oxholm, the second in command, who had joined the army with four battalions last night from the southern island, attempted to stand in the village of Herfolge; but he was attacked, briskly by the hussars, with detachments of which were Captain Blaquire, and Captain Cotton of the staff, and by a small detachment of the 1st of the 95th; and he was compelled to surrender with Count Wedel Jarlsberg, several other officers and 400 men.

The loss of the enemy has been very great, many have fallen, and there are nearly 60 officers and 1,100 men prisoners. In their flight they have thrown away their arms and clothing, and many stands of the former have fallen into our hands. I believe that we have taken ten pieces of cannon; but I have not yet received all the reports from the detachments employed in the pursuit of the enemy. I have not seen General Linsingen, as he is still out with his hussars; but I understand that the enemy had destroyed the bridges at Lille Salby, which was the cause of the delay of his operations upon their flank.

I cannot close this letter without expressing to your lordship my sense of the good conduct of the troops; all conducted themselves with the utmost steadiness. But I cannot avoid to mention particularly the 92nd Regiment, under the command of Lieutenant Colonel Napier; the 1st Battalion 95th Regiment under the command of Lieutenant Colonel Beckwith; the British artillery, under the command of Captain Newhouse; the Hanoverian Hussars, under Colonel Reden; and the Hanoverian light artillery, under Captain Sympher; as corps that had particular opportunities of distinguishing themselves. I am much obliged to General Linsingen and to Brigadier General Stewart, for the assistance I received from them in the formation and execution of the plan by which the enemy have been defeated. The officers of the staff have also rendered me much assistance; and I must particularly mention Captain Blaquire and Captain Campbell.

I have the honour to be & c

Arthur Wellesley

P.S. We have taken a large store of powder and other military stores in this town, which I propose to destroy, if I should not be able to prevail upon the captain of one of his Majesty's ships to take charge of them.

Major General Linsingen's Report of the Battle of Kioge

To General Cathcart

Ringsbjerg 31 August 1807

Sir,

The right column consisting of six squadron of the 1st, 2nd and 3rd Hussars, King's German Legion, 5 companies of the 95th, half a battery of horse artillery, the 43rd Foot, and the 6th Line Battalion, King's German Legion, broke up from Roskilde by 5 o'clock on the 29th instant, reached Havdrup by eight o'clock, when two squadrons, that had been sent the night before from Roskilde to Havdrup, did join the division. This detachment, under the command of Major Grote, 1st Hussars, had been sent to Havdrup for the purpose of getting information with regard to the enemy at and in the neighbourhood of Ringsbjerg and Kioge. The major took two prisoners in the night; the one carrying dispatches directed to a Danish general, and detailing all our marches, and ascertaining the strength of our corps. The major likewise took thirty waggons with provisions. The column again, after a short halt, moved towards Ladager, on the road to Ejby; having reached the former place, some armed militia and small detachments were seen towards Ejby.

As it was my intention to cross the rivulet that runs from Gummesmark to Kioge at Vemmedrup or Lellinge Gaard, I detached one squadron, one gun, and two companies of the 95th riflemen, to the right, to reconnoitre either passage, under the command of Major Plessen, of the 1st Hussars. The grounds between Ejby and Dalby being greatly covered with wood, intersected by a large morass, and found impracticable for a column to pass, the passage at Vemmedrup was given up, and that of Lellinge Gaard chosen. The detachment under Major Plessen went along the left bank of the rivulet by Ladager, to protect the right of the column, which moved on by Ejby at about half past nine o'clock a.m. The cavalry being arrived at the banks of the rivulet near Lellinge Gaard, the planks over the bridge had been taken up, and nothing remained for the cavalry and part of the horse artillery, but to ford the rivulet, which they instantly did, and advanced along the right bank of it, halted to await the infantry and the rest of the horse artillery, who by this time had arrived in close column at the bridge. The pioneers of the 6th Battalion of the line repaired it so far, in twenty-five minutes time, that the infantry were enabled to pass by single files (which retarded much the progress of the column) while the rest of the horse artillery passed through the ford. Till now the enemy did not in the least attempt to oppose it. After having passed the bridge, the infantry moved on in close columns, through Lellinge Gaard, on the road to Kioge, between the rivulet and the wood. Here I ordered part of the 95th to clear the woods to the right of the column; the detachment of the 43rd to do the same in front; and forming the 6th Battalion and rest of the 43rd in line, advanced with them, and the horse artillery in the rear of the cavalry, four squadrons of which had already reached the plain at the end of the woods. In the mean while I detached two squadrons in the rear, directing them to cross the wood upon the right, and to advance upon Svansbjerg Syllum to the bridge on the road between Herfolge and Saedder. Major Plessen who took the command, passed the wood, which in the meantime had been cleared by the rifle corps, and some sharpshooters of the 6th Battalion, who met with little opposition, except some platoon firing, occasioned by several divisions of the enemy's infantry retreating out of the woods, the greatest part of whom were either taken prisoners or cut to pieces. It was at this time that Lieutenant Ruedorff, of the 1st Hussars, was dangerously wounded, together with Lieutenant Jance, of the 3rd Hussars, whilst gallantly charging some infantry at the entrance of Kioge.

The cavalry of Colonel Alten having passed the opening between the woods, I ordered the horse artillery to play upon a Danish column of infantry, retreating from Kioge towards the shore, which Captain Wetzleben executed with as much precision as effect; but a few shots were fired by the Danish artillery, the same being soon silenced by the superior firing of the British. The cavalry during this had taken eighteen waggons with ammunition, arms, and accoutrements, and made a few prisoners.

The country being much intersected with high banks and ditches, did not allow the 6th Battalion and 43rd to advance in line: they were obliged to cross them, by firing in divisions, before they could reach the plains before the wood, where they formed the line again. By this time the squadron of Major Plessen having crossed the wood in front of Ashoje, and advanced across the plain, overtook about fifty waggons, partly laden with baggage, ammunition, arms &c and being obliged to leave a good number of men with them and the prisoners, they greatly weakened their strength, and were necessitated to await the arrival of the centre, under Colonel Alten, whom I, after he passed Clemenhap, ordered to advance speedily upon Helfoge, where part of the Danish column of infantry had taken possession of the church yard, Colonel Alten inclined to the right with his squadrons, in order to turn the village; and whilst the light artillery opened a fire upon the church, and some riflemen of the 95th assailed it in flank, he and Lieutenant Schnuring, of the 2nd Hussars, rapidly advanced with 16 hussars, obliged the Danish General Oxholm, four officers, and about 150 privates, to lay down their arms; on this occasion a corporal of the 2nd Hussars was shot, and several horses wounded. The village having been taken, the cavalry, joined by the horse artillery, followed up their advantage, by pursuing the enemy towards Saedder, where many prisoners were made.

The infantry being unable to follow the rapid movements of the cavalry, took a position near Svansbjerg; and perceiving the enemy completely routed, I took the road through the wood by Flojterup, and from thence to Gorslev; in order to pursue the enemy in the right flank, and watch his movements in his retreat, protecting at the same time the flanks of my cavalry that had advanced towards the heights of Saedder, losing sight of the enemy. The cavalry of my division received orders, with the 95th rifle corps, to fall back to us to take a position, with their advanced posts from Lellinge Gaard, by Ashoje, Svansbjerg, Sollerup and Vedskolle, to cover the headquarters at Kioge.

The 6th Battalion, part of the 43rd, some horse artillery, and a few cavalry, followed me to Gorslev, and with some detachments, pursued the retreating enemy towards the plains of Ringsbjerg.

The conduct of both officers and men on this occasion claims my warmest thanks; and I beg leave to bring to your notice Colonel Holmstedt, who commanded the infantry, Colonel Alten, who led the cavalry, and Lieutenant Wade, at the head of the rifle corps and light infantry, who all three, by their zeal and attention, greatly assisted me.

I have the honour to be &c
Linsingen Major General

Appendix 20

General Peymann's Regular Bulletins to the People of Copenhagen

16 August

Hostilities having commenced, I hereby command, in consequence of the order of the King, that all British property be sequestered, and that everyone who is in possession of English money, or property of any kind, shall announce it to the police, who will carry the necessary measure into execution. Everyone who does not act according to this order shall be regarded as a traitor to the country.

17 August

Fellow Citizens! A second time the British Government violates the law of nations and disturbs our peace; a second time do we see our capital attacked in a treacherous manner: our enemies have chosen the period when our brethren in arms are absent, to secure, on the Banks of the Elbe, the peace of our country. But they have miscalculated our strength and means of defence. They have forgotten that we are inspired and animated by the genius of Frederick. Fellow Citizens! I am intrusted with the honourable task to guard our honour, and to fight with you. It is with rapture I witness your ardent love for our country, and your courage. You need no encouragement. I am convinced that our dear Prince Royal, when he rejoins us, will not disown us.

22 August

Fellow Citizens! The sally of our brave troops, according to all accounts, has cost the enemy many men, and he has neither ventured to pursue us on our return to the fortress or to attack our advance-posts. Our loss is not yet considerable; we have at most 21 killed and 58 wounded, both of our sea and land troops. The lakes about the capital are in our possession, and the plan of our defence is laid. The city has a great stock of provisions, and the cattle, corn and forage are brought in security, and conducted in from all the places being in our possession and laying within the boundaries of our advance-posts. The firearms of the manufactory at Cronborg and the greatest part of the gunpowder at Frederiksvaerk are secured; but Frederiksborg and Frederiksvaerk are in the hands of the enemy, and the frigate *Frederiksvaern* has been taken on her way to Norway. Fellow Citizens! Secure in your courage and firmness, you may depend upon the care and vigour, which, on my side, shall ever defend and guard our common wealth.

23 August

Some of the Danish bomb-vessels were ordered to attack several of the enemy's bomb vessels and gun brigs, which had placed themselves on the northern side of the lime-kilns (Kalkbraenderie), in order to destroy a battery, which the enemy had erected by the Swan-mill. At ten o'clock our bomb-ketches began to fire, which was directly returned by the English bomb-ketches and gun-brigs. Notwithstanding these were reinforced, the fire of the enemy declined about one o'clock, and a good many of the enemy's bomb ketches made off with full sails. In order to disturb them in their retreat, the advanced-guard of our cannon-boats pursued them and kept up a strong fire. Our ships continued in the mean time to fire upon the land-battery. In consequence of the reports, which are come in, we have reason to believe, that the enemy had suffered much. Our loss has been 8 or 9 killed and 10 or 12 wounded. Some of the ships have suffered more or less, but they will be repaired again tomorrow. It deserves to be remarked, that the English, besides their bombs, threw a kind of rocket, which civilised nations never made use of before. The latest account received from the Crown-battery, mentions, that they fired this day on the enemy's ships, and from hence one could see with a glass, several of the English ready to sink, and their bomb-ketches in a bad condition.

On this occasion, one of the Danish prames got seven shots in her hull, only one man killed, and three wounded. On the same day a garden-house on the glacis was burnt by the Danes.

The Danish commander in chief sent Lieutenant Cederfeldt to the English general, in order to ask for a pass-port for his Highness Prince Ferdinand, which was immediately granted, and brought by an English officer, who was ordered besides to summon the capital to surrender, declaring that the English had a greater force than the Danes might imagine, but that they would fain spare a capital, which is the chief seat of the arts and sciences and the first city in the kingdom. It was answered 'That the capital would be defended with the most determined resistance, and that every Dane is ready to sacrifice his life for his country'. The English officer returned to the headquarters, attended by several Danish aides-de-camp. All the gates of the town were now shut, except the gate of the Citadel.

26 August

We have had several engagements with the enemy, who have approached us, and frequent skirmishes with his riflemen, in the garden of Mr Classen in front of the citadel. We fired into the garden; which discomposed the English.

During the cannonade on Wednesday, the gun vessel *Stubbekjobing* was blown up by a shell from the enemy's battery at the Swan mill. The commander, Lieutenant Brunn, and sixteen men, were saved; but twelve men were wounded, and thirty-one blown up. A battery erected by the enemy at old Pesthouse [the battery on the right] has suffered much by the fire from the citadel and gun vessels behind the Kalleboe. But, a battery of twelve-pounders and some mortars having now been erected at the Timber yard, which totally commands the enemy's battery and renders it ineffectual, our gun vessels have changed their position: Lieutenant Zeuthen was killed, Lieutenant C. Wulff slightly wounded, and Cadet Bull lost an arm; fifteen of our men were wounded. Premier Lieutenant Brunn, of the Life Riflemen, was killed;

two Life Riflemen wounded, and some killed; Captain Hammel, Lieutenants Friboe, Rothe, and Ellenson of the land artillery, as well as Count Platen of the Danish Life Regiment, were slightly wounded.

29 August

Four or five thousand English troops, attacked the armed peasantry of Zeeland, Lolland, and Moen, near Kioge, about six Danish miles from Copenhagen, under the command of General Castenskiold. But the greatest part of these peasants wanting regular arms, as well as artillery, and being totally untrained, the consequences were very unfortunate for the Danes. One hundred and fifty men were wounded; and General Oxholm, as well as fifty-six officers of different ranks, and seventeen or eighteen hundred men, were made prisoners. The whole engagement could not be regarded as a regular battle. We slightly pass over this affair, for the whole conduct of these peasants deserves no consideration.

31 August

Finding it necessary to reconnoitre the garden of Mr Classen, to learn whether the enemy had begun to erect a battery on that spot, a sally was made today at four o'clock by the Norwegian Life Regiment, under the command of Colonel Beck. The force consisted of three battalions of the infantry, the riflemen or chasseurs of the King's Life Guard, and the riflemen of other regiments, and the huntsman from the country. This corps was supported by 8 guns. The design of this sally was perfectly attained. The garden being exactly examined, and the riflemen of the enemy driven out, we were convinced that the English had neither erected or begun to erect any battery. All the buildings at that place were burnt, besides a great part of the wood. After that was executed, our troops returned in good order to the citadel, when they saw several large columns of the enemy approaching from Wibenhuus and along the shore. Our brave troops executed this undertaking to my greatest satisfaction. The loss of the enemy we are unacquainted with, but it is supposed to be considerable. On our side we suffered no more than we had to apprehend from the circumstances of the ground. We must lament the loss of from 70 to 80 killed or wounded. I myself have got a musket shot through the left leg, but the wound is not dangerous. During this affair, shells were thrown from our bomb and mortar battery upon the English battery at the Swan-mill, and the enemy's fleet, which was returned. This bombardment was continued after the attack, (which ended at seven o'clock) both from the Citadel and by our bomb-ketches and men of war were driven from the bay of Charlottenlund, and pursued by our gun-vessels; after which time one of the enemy's bomb ketches was blown up, and another sunk. The loss of our brave seamen in this honourable fight consisted but of one man killed and four wounded. Accounts had been received from Dragoe (on the Island of Amack), that the enemy had landed during the former night with some armed shallops, having the design, to burn the unarmed ships, which were laying there and which belong to that place. Fire was set to one galliot, but was soon again extinguished. The enemy was soon driven away by our troops, but continued a good while after this to fire with round-shot and grape on the houses at Dragoe, on which occasion a blind man was killed in his bed, and the houses were injured.

Second British Summons and Reply by General Peymann

British Headquarters 1 September 1807

Sir,

We the Commanders in Chief of his Majesty's sea and land forces now before Copenhagen, judge it expedient, at this time, to summon you to surrender the place, for the purpose of avoiding the further effusion of blood; by giving up a defence which, it is evident, cannot long be continued.

The King our gracious Master, used every endeavour to settle the matter now in dispute, in the most conciliating manner, through his diplomatic servants.

To convince his Danish Majesty, and all the world, of the reluctance with which his Majesty finds himself compelled to have recourse to arms: we, the undersigned, at this moment when our troops are before your gates, and our batteries ready to open, do renew to you the offer of the same advantageous and conciliatory terms, which were proposed through His Majesty's Ministers to your court. If you will consent to deliver up the Danish fleet, and to our carrying it away, it shall be holden in deposit for his Danish Majesty, and shall be restored, with all its equipments, in as good a state as it is received, as soon as the provisions of a general peace shall remove the necessity which has occasioned this demand.

The property of all sorts which has been captured since the commencement of hostilities, will be restored to its owners; and the union between the United Kingdoms of Great Britain and Ireland, and Denmark, may be renewed. But if this offer is rejected now, it cannot be repeated. The captured property, public and private, must then belong to the captors; and the city, when taken, must share the fate of conquered places. We must request an early decision, because, in the present advanced position of the troops so near your glacis, the most prompt and vigorous attack is indispensable, and delay would be improper.

J. Gambier, Cathcart

Copenhagen 1 September 1807

My Lords,

Our fleet, our own indisputable property, we are convinced, is as safe in his Danish Majesty's hands, as ever it can be in those of the King of England, as our master never intended hostilities against yours. If you are cruel enough to endeavour to destroy a city, that has not given any the least cause for such a treatment at your hands, it must submit to its fate: but honour and duty bid us reject a proposal unbecoming an independent power; and we are resolved to repel every attack, and defend to the utmost the city and our good cause, for which we are ready to lay down our lives. The only proposal in my power to make, in order to prevent further effusion of blood, is to send my Royal Master, for learning his final resolution, with respect to the contents of your letter, if you will grant a passport, for this purpose.

Peyman

Headquarters before Copenhagen 2 September

Sir,

It is with regret that we acquaint you, that it is not in our power to suspend our combined operations during the time necessary for consulting your government. We have done the utmost within the limits of our authority, in offering to you, at this moment, terms as advantageous as those which were proposed to prevent a rupture. We shall deeply lament the destruction of the city, if it is injured; but we have the satisfaction to reflect, that, in having renewed to you, for the last time, the offer of the most advantageous and conciliatory terms, we have done our utmost to save the effusion of blood, and prevent the horrors of war.

Appendix 22

Positions of British Batteries (present-day locations)

1. At the old Pesthus (junction of Valdemarsgade/Istedgade)
    6 x 24pdrs commanded by Captain Bolton.

2. Behind the Gardener's Garden (Valdemarsgade /Istedgade)
    4 x 10in mortars commanded by Lieutenant Stewart.

3. In front of The Shooting Range (Absalonsgade/Svendsgade)
    4 x 8in mortars and 2 x 8in howitzers commanded by Captain Broome.

4. In Svanholm's Garden (Gammel Kongevej/Vodroffsvej)
    4 x mortars and 2 x howitzers.

5. In Vordroff's Garden (Vodroffsvej/Martinsvej)
    8 x 24pdrs.

6. By Ladagardvejen in front of the farm of Roelighed (Åboulevarden/
    Bûlowsvej/Rolighedsvej)
    2 x 13in and 8 x 10in mortars commanded by Captain Sandham.

7. In Blaagaads Garden (Stengade/Korsgade)
    8 x 24pdrs.

8. In Toxveds Garden (Mollegade/Peter Faber's Gade)
    2 x 13in and 8 x 10in mortars commanded by Captain Franklyn.

9. In the redoubt by Saltpeterværket (north of Triangle)
    2 x 13in and 8 x 10in mortars, 2 x 8in howitzers commanded by Captain May.

10. Sailors Battery (Viborggade/Nøjsomhedsvej)
    Never used.

11. At the New Lime Kiln (Vordingborggade/Ostebanegade)
    Never used.

    12 & 13. At Swan Mill (Strandvejen/Strandvaenget)

    11 x 24pdrs and 2 x 10in mortars, 1 x 8in howitzer commanded by Captain Meadow.

    Fleche: 3 x 24pdrs and 1 x 8in howitzer commanded by Lieutenant Lord.

Rocket Positions

1. Behind St Hans Hospital (Jacob Dannefaerds Vej)
2. Behind Scrubland on right of Gammel Kongevej (Henrik Steffens Vej)
3. To right of Frederiksberg Alle (Edisonvej)

Note. On only one of the copies of the Fadden maps at the National Archives showing the positions of the siege batteries, one has an additional notification for the three rocket positions with blue circles marked R. I produce below a copy of this section of the unique map.

Appendix 23

Garrison of Copenhagen – Dispositions

West Gate

The troops in these bastions commanded by Colonel Beck

Holkens Bastion	1 Battalion of Marines
Gyldenhoves Bastion	1 Battalion of Marines
Schakens Bastion	1 Landvaern Battalion
Helmers Bastion	1st Battalion of Norwegian Life Guard Regiment

North Gate

The troops in these bastions commanded by Major General Lemming

Hahnens Bastion	1 Landvaern Battalion
Ahlefeldts Bastion	1 Landvaern Battalion
Stadtsbristen Bastion	Garden Corps
Rosenborg Bastion	1 Landvaern Battalion

East Gate

The troops in these bastions commanded by Major General Walterstorf

Quitzows Bastion	2nd Battalion of Danish Life Regiment
Peucklers Bastion	1 Landvaern Battalion
Rosenkrants Bastion	1st Battalion of Danish Life Regiment

Life Jaeger Corps, Herregardesskyttern, Danish Shooting Company at Schakens, Ahlefeldts and Rodsenkrants Bastions which flanked the three gates.

Crown Prince's Life Corps of eight companies, two companies on the three adjoining courtiner and two as a reserve at North Gate.

Jaeger Company of Landvaern under Captain Wildenrath, in reserve at Christianshavn near Langebro.

In the lunette between Langebro and Tommerpladsen was a detachment of 150 men under Captain Restorf of the Danish Life Regiment. Each night a picquet of fifty men were in reserve on the Tommerpladsen, and at the three ravelins outside the gates there was a lieutenant and fifty men to defend outside the gates.

Near West Gate a field battery of eight guns and near Rosenborg the same, and some amusetter (1pdr guns) with four Landevearn guns outside the East Gate.

Appendix 24

Final Exchange Before Capitulation

Copenhagen
5 September 1807

My Lords,
For preventing further effusion of blood, and not exposing the city to the sad consequences of a longer bombardment, I propose an armistice of twenty-four hours, in order to come to an agreement that may lead to the settling of the Preliminary articles of Capitulation.

It is with the highest personal consideration,
I have the honour to be, &c
Peymann

Headquarters before Copenhagen
5 September 1807

Sir,
The same necessity which has obliged us to have recourse to arms in the present occasion, compels me to decline any overture which might be productive of delay only: but to prove to you my ardent desire to put an end to scenes which I behold with the greatest grief, I send an officer, who is authorized to receive any proposal you may be inclined to make relative to Article of Capitulation, and upon which it may be possible for me to agree to any, even the shortest armistice.

I have the honour to be &C
Cathcart Lieutenant General

Copenhagen
5 September 1807

My Lord,
The proposal has been made without any the least dilatory intention; but the night being too far advanced for deliberating upon a matter of such very high importance, with the retrospective departments, a measure necessary on account of his Majesty's absence, and that of the Prince, and my state of health not permitting me to proceed as expeditiously as I wish, I engage to send tomorrow, before twelve o'clock, the Articles relative to the Capitulation: and have, in the meantime, the honour to be, &C

Peymann

Headquarters before Copenhagen
6 September 1807

Sir,

Having communicated to Admiral Gambier your letter received this morning, together with those of last night, I have to acquaint you, that we will consent to treat with you for the Capitulation of Copenhagen, on the basis of your delivering up the Danish fleet. But as you have not forwarded Articles of Capitulation; officers of rank, in the Sea and Land Service of his Britannic Majesty, shall be sent forthwith, to prepare Articles with you, or with the officers you may appoint; and which may, if possible, unite the object you have in view, in regard to the occupation of Copenhagen, with the performance of the service entrusted to us. Cathcart

Lieutenant General

Copenhagen
6 September 1807

My Lord,

I accept of your proposal with respect to delivering up to his Majesty's fleet, as the fundamental basis of negotiations; but with this proviso, that no other English troops enter the city, than those commissaries, officers, and military men, who shall be stipulated and agreed on in the course of the said negotiations.

I have the honour to be, &c
Peymann

Copenhagen
6 September 1807

My Lord,

As soon as you shall be pleased to appoint a neutral place out of the town, where to meet on both sides for regulating the Articles of Capitulation, officers provided with full powers for negotiating shall be sent; and in the interim the armistice is considered as subsisting, till contrary orders should be given.

I have the honour to be &c
Peymann

Appendix 25

General Cathcart's Letter Announcing the Capitulation

Citadel of Copenhagen, 8 September 1807

My Lord,

It has fallen to my lot to have the great satisfaction of forwarding to your lordship the ratified Capitulation of the Town and Citadel of Copenhagen, including the surrender of the Danish Fleet and Arsenal in this port, which are placed at his Majesty's disposal.

The object of securing this fleet having been attained; every other provision, of a tendency to wound the feelings or irritate the nation, has been avoided: and although the bombardment and cannonade have made considerable havoc and destruction in the town, not one shot was fired into it till after it was summoned, with the offer of the most advantageous terms, not a single shot after the first indication of a disposition to capitulate: on the contrary, the firing which lasted three nights from his Majesty's batteries was considerable abated on the 2nd, and was only renewed on the 3rd to its full vigour, on supposing from the quantity of shells thrown from the place, that there was a determination to hold out.

On the evening of the 5th of September, a letter was sent by the Danish general, to propose an armistice of twenty-four hours, for preparing an agreement, on which Articles of Capitulation might be founded. The Armistice was declined, as tending to unnecessary delay, and the works were continued, but the firing was countermanded, and Lieutenant Colonel Murray was sent to explain that no proposal of Capitulation could be listened to, unless accompanied by the surrender of the fleet.

This basis having been admitted by a subsequent letter, on the 6th, Major General Sir A. Wellesley, whom I had sent for, for this purpose, from his command in the country, where he had distinguished himself in a manner so honourable to himself, and advantageous to the public, was appointed with Sir Home Popham and Lieutenant Colonel Murray, to prepare and sign Articles of Capitulation: and those officers having insisted on proceeding immediately to business, the Capitulation was drawn up in the night between the 6th and 7th.

The ratification was exchanged in the course of the morning; and at four in the afternoon of the same day, Lieutenant General Burrard proceeded to take possession.

The British grenadiers present, with detachments from all the other corps of cavalry and infantry, under the command of Colonel Cameron of the 79th Regiment, with two brigades of artillery, marched into the Citadel, while Major General Spencer, having embarked his brigade at the Kalk Brandiere, landed in the dockyard, and took possession of each of the line-of-battle ships, and of all the Arsenal; the Danish guards withdrawing when those of his Majesty were ready to replace them, and proper officers attending to deliver stores as far as inventories could be made up.

The town being in a state of the greatest ferment and disorder, I most willingly acceded to the request that our troops should not be quartered in it, and that neither officers or soldiers should enter it for some days; and having the command of possession from the Citadel whenever it might be necessary to use it, I had no objection to leaving the other gates in the hands of the troops of his Danish Majesty, together with the police of the place.

We have consented to the re-establishment of the post; but all arrivals and departures are to be at and from the Citadel.

The work is in good condition, very strong, and well stored with ordnance and ammunition.

The amount of the garrison of the town is not easily ascertained. The number of regular troops were not numerous; but the number of batteries which fired at the same time, together with the floating defences, prove that there must have been a very great number of Militia and burghers, with other irregular forces; and their ordnance was well served.

Considering the advanced position in which his Majesty's troops have been placed for the last fortnight, our loss (highly as I prize the value of every officer or soldier who has fallen or been wounded) has been comparatively small.

The zeal, spirit, and perseverance of every rank in the army have been truly characteristic of the British nation; and the King's German Legion are entitled to a fair share in this commendation.

All the generals, and indeed each officer, has rendered himself conspicuous in proportion to his command, and the opportunities which have occurred, and opportunities have occurred to all.

The Staff have done themselves the greatest credit, and been of all the service that could be desired in their several departments.

Colonel D'Arcey, the Chief Engineer, and every Engineer under him, have given the most unequivocal proofs of science and indefatigable industry; the works under their direction have gone on with fresh parties without ceasing.

General Bloomfield, and the officer and corps of Royal Artillery, have done great honour to themselves, and to that branch of his Majesty's service, of which their fire upon the gunboats, and the rapidity and success of the mortar practise, afford sufficient proofs, nor is the distribution of battering ordnance, and of so much ammunition at so many points in this extensive line, in so short a period, a small proof of the method and resources of that corps.

Lieutenant Colonel Smith, with the 32nd Regiment under his command, held the post at the windmill on the left, which for the greater part of the time was the most exposed to the gunboats and sorties of the enemy; and the unremitting attentions of that officer claim particular notice.

By the naval blockade, the force opposed to us has been limited to the resources of this and the adjacent islands, separated by only narrow ferries; and almost every wish of assistance has been anticipated, and every requisition of boats, guns, and stores, has been most amply and effectually provided for with the greatest dispatch and the most perfect cordiality; and every possible attention has been paid, and every accommodation given, by every officer in that service, from Admiral Gambier downwards.

A battalion of seamen and marines, with three divisions of carpenters, were landed on the 5th, under Captain Watson of his Majesty's ship *Inflexible;* and had the effort been made, which would have been resorted to in a few days, if the place had not capitulated, their services in the passage of the ditch would have been distinguished.

I send this dispatch by Lieutenant Cathcart, who has become for some time my first Aide de Camp, who has seen everything that has occurred here and at Stralsund, and will be able to give any further details that may be required.

I have the honour to be &c
Cathcart.

List of Army killed, wounded and missing

Killed – Four officers, 1 sergeant, 1 drummer, 36 rank & file and 8 horses.
Wounded – Six officers, 1 sergeant, 138 rank & file and 25 horses.
Missing – One sergeant, 4 drummers and 19 rank and file.

Names of officers killed

Lieutenant Lyons, of the Royal Artillery; Ensign Robert Dixon of the 82nd Foot; Lieutenant Rudoff, of the 1st Regiment of Hussars, King's German Legion; and Ensign Jenning, of the 23rd Foot, or Royal Welch Fusiliers.

Names of officers wounded

Captain Hastings, of the 82nd Foot; Lieutenant Suter, of ditto; Captain During, 1st Battalion King's German Legion; Lieutenant-General Sir David Baird, in the shoulder and hand, slightly; and Ensign Bilson.

Danish Losses at Copenhagen, 1807

Military

Naval force	53 killed (2 officers)	50 wounded (4 officers)
Danish Royal Artillery	10 killed (0 officers)	26 wounded (3 officers)
Cavalry	2 killed (0 officers)	4 wounded (0 officers)
Line Regiments	38 killed (1 officer)	117 wounded (5 officers)
Landvaern	5 killed (1 officer)	11 wounded (1 officer)
King's Life Jaeger Corps	18 killed (1 officer)	47 wounded (0 officers)
Herregaardskyttere	16 killed (0 officers)	32 wounded (0 officers)
City Militia Infantry	16 killed (0 officers)	36 wounded (6 officers)
City Militia Artillery	6 killed (0 officers)	1 wounded (0 officers)
Student Corps	6 killed (0 officers)	3 wounded (0 officers)
Total Military	188 killed (5 officers)	346 wounded (19 officers)

Civilians (Estimated)	450 killed	900 wounded

Lost by desertion   Army 1,186 men (most of these came from the Marine regiment who deserted to the British on a large scale, many not being Danish nationals) Navy 11 artificers and 14 sailors

Appendix 27

Terms of the Capitulation of Copenhagen

Articles of Capitulation for the town and citadel of Copenhagen, agreed upon between Major-Gen the right Honourable Sir Arthur Wellesley, K.B., Sir Home Popham Knt. of Malta and Captain of the Fleet, Lieut-Colonel George Murray, Deputy Quarter-Master General of the British forces; being thereto duly authorized by James Gambier, Esq. Admiral of the Blue, and Commander-in-Chief of His Britannic Majesty's Ships and Vessels in the Baltic Sea, and by Lieutenant-General the Right Honourable General Cathcart, Knight of the Thistle, Commander-in-Chief of His Britannic Majesty's Forces in Zealand and the North of the Continent of Europe, on the one part; – and by Major General Walterstorff, Knight of the Order of Dannebroge, Chamberlain to the King, and Colonel of the North Zealand Regiment of Infantry, Rear-Admiral Luthen, and I.H. Kerchhoff, Aid-du-Camp to His Danish Majesty; being duly authorized by His Excellency Major-General Peymann, Knight of the Order of Dannebroge, and Commander-in-Chief of His Danish Majesty's Forces in the Island of Zealand, on the other part.

Art I. When the Capitulation shall have been signed and ratified, the troops of his Britannic Majesty are to be put in possession of the Citadel.

Art II. A guard of his Britannic Majesty's troops shall likewise be placed in the dock-yards.

Art III. The ships and vessels of war of every description, with all the naval stores belonging to his Danish Majesty, shall be delivered into the charge of such persons as shall be appointed by the Commander-in-Chief of his Britannic Majesty's forces; and they are to be put in immediate possession of the dock-yards, and all the buildings and storehouses belonging thereto.

Art IV. The store-ships and transports in the service of his Britannic Majesty are to be allowed to come into the harbour for the purpose of embarking such stores and troops as they have brought into this island.

Art V. As soon as the ships shall have been removed from the dock-yard, or within six weeks from the date of this Capitulation, or sooner, if possible, the troops of his Britannic Majesty shall deliver up the Citadel to the troops of his Danish Majesty, in the state in which it shall be found when they occupy it. His Britannic Majesty's troops shall likewise, within the before-mentioned time, or sooner if possible, be embarked from the Island of Zealand.

Art VI. From the date of this Capitulation, hostilities shall cease throughout the Island of Zealand.

Art VII. No person whatsoever shall be molested, and all property, public or private, with the exception of the ships and vessels of war, and the naval stores before-mentioned, belonging to his Danish Majesty, shall be respected: and all Civil and Military Officers in the service of his Danish Majesty shall continue in full exercise of their authority throughout the Island of Zealand; and everything shall be done which can tend to produce union and harmony between the two Nations.

Art VIII. All prisoners taken on both sides, shall be unconditionally restored; and those officers who are prisoners on parole, shall be released from its effect.

Art IX. Any English property that may have been sequestered in consequence of the existing hostilities, shall be restored to the owners.

This Capitulation shall be ratified by the respective Commander-in-Chief, and the Ratifications shall be exchanged before twelve o'clock at noon.

Done at Copenhagen, this 7th day of September 1807;

Arthur Wellesley
E F Walterstorff
Home Popham
J Lutken
George Murray
J H Kirchoff
Ratifie par moi Peymann

Appendix 28

Copy of the Official Dispatch of Admiral Gambier as Published in the *London Gazette*

Captain Collier, HMS *Surveillante* arrived in London on 16 September with the following.

To the Hon. William Wellesley-Pole, Secretary of the Admiralty

Prince of Wales, in Copenhagen Road,

7 September 1807

Sir;

The communications which I have already had the honour to transmit to you, will have made the Lords Commissioners of the Admiralty acquainted with the proceedings of the Fleet under my command down to the 2nd instant: I have now to add, that the mortar batteries which have been erected by the army in the several positions they had taken round Copenhagen, together with the bomb-vessels, which were placed in convenient situations, began the bombardment in the morning of that day, with such power and effect, that in a short time the town was set on fire, and by the repeated discharges of our artillery, was kept in flames in different places till the evening of the 5th; when, a considerable part of it being consumed, and the conflagration having arrived at a great height, threatening the speedy destruction of the whole city, the General commanding the garrison sent out a flag of truce, desiring an armistice, to afford time to treat for a Capitulation. After some correspondence had passed between the Danish General, and General Cathcart and myself, certain articles were agreed upon, of which I have the honour to transmit you a copy. From these, their lordships will perceive, that all the Danish ships and vessels of war, (of which I enclose a list) with the stores in the arsenal, were to be delivered up to such persons as should be appointed to receive them, on the part of his Majesty. I accordingly appointed Sir Home Popham for this purpose, and, having made the necessary arrangements for equipping them with the utmost dispatch, I have committed the execution of this service to Vice-Admiral Stanhope, in whose ability and exertions I can place the fullest confidence. *As few of the ships are in any considerable progress of equipment, it will require some time to complete them for sea, but not a moment will be lost in bringing the whole of them to England.*[1]

I am happy on this occasion to express the warm sense I entertain of the cordial co-operation of the army, by whose exertions, with the favourable concurrence of circumstances, under Divine Providence, ever since we left England, our ultimate success has been more immediately obtained. I must also convey to their Lordships, in terms of the highest approbation and praise, the conspicuous zeal and earnest endeavours of every Officer and man under my command, for the accomplishment of this service; and although the operations of the fleet have not been of a nature to afford me a general and brilliant occasion for adding fresh testimony to the numerous records of the bravery of British Seamen and Marines, yet the gallantry and energy displayed by the advanced squadron of sloops, bombs, gun-brigs &c which were employed under the command of Captain Paget, to cover the operations of the left wing of the army from the Danish flotilla, ought not to be passed over in silence. I have beheld with admiration the steady courage and arduous exertions with which, on one occasion in particular, they sustained for more than 4 hours a heavy and incessant cannonade with the Danish batteries, block ships, prames, and gun-boats, in a situation where from the shoalness of the water it was impossible to bring any of the large ships to their support.

I feel it my duty to make a particular acknowledgement of the aid I have derived from Sir Home Popham, Captain of the Fleet, whose prompt resources and complete knowledge of his profession, especially of that branch which is connected with the operations of an army, qualify him in a particular manner for the arduous and various duties with which he has been charged.

I herewith inclose an account of the killed and wounded.

I beg leave to refer their Lordships to Captain Collier, whom I have charged with this dispatch, for any further particulars they may desire to know.

I have the honour to be, &c

J. Gambier.

Total Losses of Royal Navy in entire operation
Killed 14 Wounded 34 Missing 1[2]

---

1 These words in italics were removed from the published version. See 'The Copenhagen Operation 1807', *The Naval Miscellany* Vol. V, p. 323.

2 This was not part of Gambier's report but fits well here so I have added it.

Appendix 29

List of Danish Ships Captured 1807

A List of the Danish Ships and Vessels delivered up by the Capitulation of Copenhagen to his Majesty's forces, September 7, 1807

Ship	No. of Guns	Date Built	Fitted Out By
Christian VII	84	1803	*Pompee*
Neptunus	80	1789	*Minotaur*[1]
Valdemar	80	1798	*Prince of Wales*
Prindsesse	4	1775	*Ganges*
Sophia Frederike			
Justitia	74	1780	*Cambrian*
Arveprinds Frederick	74	1782	*Brunswick*
Kronprins Frederick	74	1784	*Maida*
Fyen	74	1787	*Mars*
Odin	74	1788	*Hercules*
Trekroner	74	1789	Unknown
Skjold	74	1798	*Valiant*
Krondprinsesse	74	1791	*Goliath*
Maria			
Danmark	74	1794	*Captain*
Norge	74	1800	*Centaur*
Prindsesse Caroline	74	1805	*Agamemnon*
Ditmarksen	64	1780	Cut to pieces in dock
Sejeren	64	1795	Unknown
Mars	64	1784	Destroyed*[2]
Frigates			
Perlen	38	1804	*Inflexible*
Rota	38	1801	*Rosamund*
Havfruen	36	1789	*Nymphe*
Freya	36	1793	*Astraea*

1 The *Neptunus* ran aground off Hven Island on the passage to the UK and was destroyed.
2 It is usually only stated that one Danish ship of the line escaped capture in 1807, however the naval records indicate that in fact two escaped, the *Prinds Christian Frederick*, which was later captured in 1808, was at Christiansand and the *Prindsesse Lovisa Augusta*, which continued in the Danish navy until 1829, was at Frederiksvaern. these were Therefore safe at the time of the expedition.

Iris	36	1795	*Africaine*
Venus	36	1805	*Leyden*
Najaden	36	1796	*Ariadne*
Nymphen*	36	1806	Unknown
Frederiksvaern	32	1783	Captured[1]
Triton*	28	1790	Destroyed
Frederikssteen	28	1800	*Surveillante*
St Thomas	22	1779	Destroyed
Little Belt	20	1801	*Gannet*
Fylla	20	1802	*Charger*

Brigs

Elven	16	1800	Unknown
Eyderen	16	1802	Unknown
Gluckstadt	16	1804	Unknown
Sarpen	16	1791	*Prometheus*
Glommen	16	1791	Unknown
Delphinen*	16	1792	*Desparate*
Nid-Elven	16	1792	Unknown
Mercurius	16	1806	*Pompee*
Allart*	16	1806	*Pandora*
Coureer	16	1801	Unknown
Flyvendefiske	14	1789	Unknown
Brevdrageren	16	1801	Destroyed*[2]

Gunboats

Eleven with two guns in the bow:

Ahrendahl, Nykobing, Nakskov, Aalborg, Odense, Langesund, Stavaern, Stege, Christiansund, Flensborg, Viborg.

Fifteen with one gun in the bow and one in the stern:

Kallundborg, Helsingoer, Nestved, Roeskilde, Saltholmen, Frederiksund, Rodbye, Nysted, Svendborg, Faaborg, Holbek, Middelfart, Assens, Kjerteminde*.[3]

Kragero galley?

*These ships do not appear in Gambier's report but were discovered later and added to James' list.

The Naval Stores found in the Arsenal of Copenhagen, are estimated at a value of Two Million, Five Hundred Thousand Pounds.[4]

---

1 Captured by the *Comus* on 14 August 1807.
2 Five other brigs existed in the Danish Navy at this time and served on – these were presumably in Norway during the expedition. They were the *Anne Marie, Fama, Fehmern, Lougen* and *Storen.*
3 Six other gunboats were commissioned in the Danish Navy at this time – these were presumably the six which were refloated after they sank during the British evacuation. They were the *Corsoer, Dragoe, Kioge, Nysted, Praesto* and *Wardoehuus,* and also the *Haien* artillery prame.
4 About £100 million in today's terms.

Appendix 30

Report of Admiral Gambier to The Honourable W. Wellesley Pole

Sir,

I have the honour to acquaint you, for the information of the Lords Commissioners of the Admiralty, that the whole of the Danish fleet being equipped (except two unserviceable ships of the line and two frigates, which have been destroyed) and the Arsenal cleared of stores, the army has been re-embarked, and that I shall proceed with the first favourable wind to carry into execution the instructions I have received from the Lord Viscount Castlereagh.

Having so far accomplished the service on which I have been employed, I feel it my duty to state the great activity, energy, and zeal, which have been shown by the Vice-Admiral Stanhope, and Rear-Admiral Sir Samuel Hood, in superintending the equipment of the Danish ships, and the embarkation of the stores from the Arsenal; nor has the same spirit been less manifest in the Captains, Officers, seamen and marines, who have all executed their respective parts in the general exertion, with a promptitude and alacrity, which has not only entitled them to my warmest thanks and praise, but will, I doubt not, when the aggregate result of their labour is considered, obtain for them the approbation of their Sovereign, and the applause of the nation.

In the space of six weeks, sixteen sail of the line, nine frigates, fourteen sloops of war, and smaller vessels, besides gun-boats, have been fitted for sea, and all the large ships laden with masts, spars, timber, and other stores, from the Arsenal, from whence also ninety-two cargoes have been shipped on board transports, and other vessels chartered for the purpose, the sum of whose burthen exceeds twenty thousand tons. A considerable number of masts and spars, have been put on board the *Leyden* and Inslexible, which were well adapted for this purpose, and some valuable stores on board his Majesty's ships; nor can I forbear to remark, that such was the emulation among the several ships of the fleet, to which the Danish ships were respectively attached for equipment, that within nine days, fourteen sail of the line were brought out of the harbour, although several of them underwent in our hands considerable repairs. Of the three ships on the stocks, two have been taken to pieces, and the useful part of their timbers brought away; and the third, being in a considerable state of forwardness, was sawed in various parts, and suffered to fall over.

On a review of the whole, I think it may be asserted, without derogating from the merit of any former service, that characteristic activity of British officers, seamen, and marines, were never more zealously exerted than on this occasion; but I must not omit at the same time to inform their Lordships, that a very considerable proportion of the labour of the Arsenal has been performed with equal zeal and energy, by large working parties from the army, whose exertions entitle them to the same praise.

I beg leave to express the great satisfaction I have felt, from the zealous and attentive services of Rear-Admiral Essington, to whom the general superintendence of the numerous transports, and the re-embarkation of the army, with all its artillery and stores, has been committed.

I embrace this opportunity to make a particular acknowledgement of the very able and judicious dispositions which Rear-Admiral Keats has made from time to time of the force under his command, for guarding the Belt; and the vigilant attention which his whole squadron have paid to this important branch of the service.

Sir Home Popham has not ceased to manifest his usual zeal and alacrity in the assistance he has rendered me in the various services of the fleet; and I should not do justice to the diligent attention and arduous endeavours of Captain Mackenzie to fulfil the civil duties of the Arsenal, which were committed to his management and superintendence, if I did not, on this occasion, express my warm approbation of his exertions: and I beg leave to recommend him to their Lordship's favourable notice.

I have the honour to transmit herewith a list of the Danish ships and vessels, which have been brought away, and of those destroyed.

The account of the stores shipped from the Arsenal shall also be sent, as soon as the several returns can be collected and arranged.

I have the honour to be, &c,
J. Gambier

Appendix 31

Letter from General Cathcart to his Troops

7 September

The Commander of the Forces cannot delay expressing his best thanks to all the General Officers and Staff, for the great and able assistance he has received from them in their several ranks and stations; ad he feels himself in like manner indebted to all officers commanding brigades and regiments, and to the officers and soldiers under their command. He must, however, be allowed, in a particular manner, to express his thanks to Major General Bloomfield and Colonel D'Arcy; and to the officers and corps of the Royal Artillery and Engineers, whose labours, science, and success, collectively and individually, have been most remarkable, and reflect great credit on that branch of His Majesty's service. The services and perseverance of Lieutenant Colonel Smith, and the 82nd Regiment, in occupying and maintaining the Windmill batteries, have been particularly distinguished, and claim peculiar thanks. The gallant conduct of Lieutenant Light, of the 59th Regiment, in command of a picquet of that regiment on the 31st, was particularly noticed.

Appendix 32

Report of Transports Lost on Return from Copenhagen[1]

Transport Office 1 February 1808

Account of the Transports employed on the Expedition against Copenhagen

	No of ships	Tons
Sailed from England for Copenhagen	377	78,420
Returned from Copenhagen	362	75,294
Wrecked, Captured, and Missing agreeably to the enclosed list	15	3,126

Return of Transports that were lost or missing, by capture, wreck, or otherwise

Transports	Tons	Troops Lost	Troops Saved	Regiments	Seamen Lost	Seamen Saved	Remarks
Augustus Caesar	457		387	1st Line Battalion KGL		27	Dismasted and driven onto coast of Holland
Mary	141		12 Men 18 Horses	British Artillery Drivers		8	Captured by *Decide* French Privateer
King George	141			Naval Stores		8	Captured by *Decide* French Privateer
Bee	157			Naval Stores		9	Captured by Unknown

---

1 From Anon, *Naval Papers respecting Copenhagen.*

Olive *Branch*	112			Opthalmia Patients		7	Captured by Unknown
Hope	176	40[1]		Hospital Ship		10	Wrecked on Return
Hope's *Increase*	197			Naval Stores		11	Wrecked on Return
Emperor of *Russia*	334			Naval Provisions		20	Wrecked on Return
Salisbury	324	200[2]	60	2nd Line Battalion KGL	Un-known had	19 onboard	Wrecked between
Eagle Packet	230	180		7th Line Battalion KGL	14		Yarmouth
Endeavour	167	24 Men 23 Horses		3rd Lt Dragoons KGL		9	&
Providence	112	18 Horses	16 Men	2nd Lt Dragoons KGL		7	The Downs
Shorn	160	19 Horses	20 Men			9	Run down Dover Roads
Avon	160			Naval Stores		9	Missing
Charles	252				Un-known had	15 onboard	Armed with heavy guns, blown up by enemy

1 This box is blank on the form, but Ludlow Beamish states that forty sick men of the 2nd Light Dragoons KGL perished.

2 Beamish states that 221 officers and men perished.

Appendix 33

Report from Sir William Rule to the Honourable William Pole, Secretary of the Admiralty, dated the 25 January 1808, respecting the general state of the Danish ships

Navy Office, 25 January 1808

Sir,

In addition to the Report already sent to their Lordships, stating the age of the Danish ships in Portsmouth harbour, and the time it will require to put them into condition for service, I further beg leave to state, that I consider the ships named in the margin [*Christian VII*, *Princess Carolina*, *Norge* and *Denmark*] to require little more to be done to their hulls than to sheath and copper their bottoms, and to make such internal arrangements for the magazines, store rooms &c as are absolutely necessary in a man of war; the time required for the performance of which has been before stated [6–7 weeks].

The *Waldamar*, *Heir Apparent*, *Frederick*, *Odin*, *and Trekroner*, will require more to be done to them, but may be brought forward after the other ships, and in time before mentioned [8–12 weeks].

The *Venus* and *Frederickssteen* frigates, being coppered and copper-flattened, will require little more to be done to them than to alter their internal arrangements.

The ten aforementioned ships will, in my opinion, when completed, be fit for foreign service.

The *Skiold*, *Princess Sophia Frederica*, *Crown*, *Princess Maria*, *Justitia*, and *Syeren*, will require a longer time to fit them for service, but may be brought forward in the time already mentioned [6–7 months].

The foregoing is the best judgement that can be formed of their condition in their present encumbered state (most of them being full of stores) and which must be subject to correction when the ships are taken into a dock.

I am, sir, your most obedient servant,
W. Rule

Appendix 34

Report of the Capture of Heligoland

Letter from Vice Admiral Russell, to the honourable Wellesley Pole;
Majestic off Heligoland

6 September 1807

I beg you will be pleased to acquaint my Lords Commissioners of the Admiralty, that I arrived at this island, and anchored close to the town, on the 4th instant, at half past two p.m. but did not, as I expected, find the *Explosion*, the *Wanderer*, or the *Exertion*, with which their lordships had intended to reinforce me.

Having found that Lord Falkland had, with his usual zeal and promptness, summoned the garrison on the 30th ultimo, and that his proposals were rejected by the governor, I was making my arrangements to storm him with the marines and seamen of the squadron[1] if he did not instantly surrender; for at this time the value of the island to us is immense.

At six p.m. however, he sent out a flag of truce, desiring that an officer might be sent in the morning to treat on articles of capitulation; and I accordingly, at daylight, yesterday morning, dispatched Viscount Falkland and Lieutenant d'Auvergne (first of the ship) on that service.

At two p.m. the deputation returned with the articles of capitulation, which I immediately ratified.

With a small expense, this island may be made a little Gibraltar, and a safe haven for small craft, even in the winter; it is a key to the River Ems, Weser, Jade, Elbe, and Eyder, the only asylum at present for our cruisers in these seas.

I have appointed Lieutenant d'Auvergne as acting governor until their lordships pleasure is known; and I beg leave to add, that from his perfect knowledge of both services, his zeal and loyalty, and a high sense of honour, I know no seaman more competent to the trust.

T. Macnamara Russell

---

1 From another letter of the same day, he advises that *Explosion*, *Wanderer* and *Exertion* had come in sight from the north of the island that morning.

Appendix 35

List of Convoys which passed through the Great Belt between 30 May and 4 August 1810

Date	No. of Vessels	Where From	Where Bound	Under whose Convoy
30 May	362	England	Baltic	*Princess Carolina*
1 June	145	Baltic	England	*Alexandria* and *Sheldrake*
4 June	35	England	Baltic	*Pyramus*
11 June	76	Baltic	England	*Vanguard* and *Diligence*
13 June	5	England	Baltic	*Africa*
21 June	150	England	Baltic	*Loire* and *Erebus*
27 June	175	Baltic	England	*Solebay* and *Wrangler*
12 July	175	Baltic	England	*Lynx* and *Alonzo*
23 July	332	England	Baltic	*Hussar*
27 July	220	Baltic	England	*Fisgard* and *Reynard*
4 August	140	Baltic	England	*Orion*
Total	**1,815**			

Appendix 36

The Danish Army in Holstein, 1807

Regiment	Organization	Establishment
Life Regiment Ryttere[1]	4 Squadrons	587
Life Regiment Light Dragoons	4 Squadrons	587
Schleswig Ryttere Regiment	4 Squadrons	587
Holstein Ryttere Regiment	4 Squadrons	587
Hussar Regiment	4 Squadrons	587
Field Jaeger	1 Troop	50
Crown Prince Frederick Regiment	2 Battalions	1,539
Prince Christian Frederik Reg	2 Battalions	1,539
Queen's Life Regiment	2 Battalions	1,539
Oldenburg Regiment	2 Battalions	1,539
Holstein Regiment	2 Battalions	1,539
2nd Jutland Regiment	2 Battalions	1,539
3rd Jutland Regiment	2 Battalions	1,539
Funen Regiment	2 Battalions	1,539
Schleswig Regiment	2 Battalions	1,539
Zealand Jaeger	1 Battalion	576
Schleswig Jaeger	1 Battalion	710
1st Zealand Sharpshooters	1 Battalion	548
2nd Zealand Sharpshooters	1 Battalion	548
Schleswig/Holstein Light Battalion	1 Battalion	368

Two Horse Artillery Batteries: 2 x howitzers and 8 x 6-pounders each.

Two Foot Artillery Batteries: 2 x howitzers and 8 x 6-pounders each.

Nine Regimental Artillery Batteries: 2 x howitzers and 8 x 3-pounders each.

---

1 Ryterre cavalry were heavy dragoons.

Bibliography

Archival Material

National Archives	WO 17/1864-68 Returns from Heligoland Garrison 1808–15.
National Archives	ADM 106/2031 In Letters Heligoland 1808–15.
National Archives	MPH 1/617 Fadden Plans of Copenhagen 1807 and Fadden's Accompanying Account of Siege.
National Archives	ADM101/101/3 Medical Journal of HM Hospital Ship *Frederiksvaern*, Copenhagen 1807.
National Archives	MPH 1/557 Fadden Map of Copenhagen 1807.
National Archives	MPH 1/1209 No of Maps of Copenhagen & Fadden's map of Route taken through the Great Belt in 1801.
National Archives	ADM 101/81/1 Medical Journal of Surgeon James Campbell HMS *Aetna*, July 1807–July 1808 including Copenhagen
National Archives	WO 164/527 Prize Records for Copenhagen 1807.

Published Sources

Anon, *British Minor Expeditions 1746-1814*, London, 1884.

Anon, *Cumloden Papers*, Edinburgh, 1871.

Anon, *Journal of an Officer in the King's German Legion*, London, 1827.

Anon, *Letters to Sulpicius on the Northern Confederacy. With an Appendix containing the Treaty of Armed Neutrality, together with other documents relative to the Subject*, London, 1801.

Anon, *Meddelelser fra Krigsarkiverne undgivne af Generalstaben*, Copenhagen, 1883.

Anon, *Narrative of the Expedition to the Baltic with an Account of the Siege and Capitulation of Copenhagen, Including the Surrender of the Danish Fleet, by an officer employed in the Expedition*, London, 1808.

Anon, *Naval Papers respecting Copenhagen, Portugal and the Dardanelles, presented to Parliament in 1808*, London, 1808.

Anon, *Short Sketch of the English Inroad in Sealand 1807*, London, 1808.

Anon, *The Annual Register 1801*, London, 1802.

Anon, *The Annual Register 1807*, London, 1808.

Anon, *The Journal of the Royal Artillery*, Vol. LXXX No. 4 (Woolwich, 1953).

Adams, M., *Admiral Collingwood, Nelson's Own Hero*, London, 2005.

Aspinall, A., *The Later Correspondence of George III 1783-1810*, Cambridge, 1968.

Beamish, L., *History of the King's German Legion* 2 vols, London, 1832.

Blakeney, R., *A Boy in the Peninsular War*, London, 1989.

Buckley, R., *The Napoleonic War Journal of Captain Thomas Henry Browne 1807-16*, London, 1987.

Carr-Gomm, F., *Letters and Journals of Field Marshal William Maynard Gomm from 1799 to Waterloo 1815*, London, 1881.

Clowes, W, *The Royal Navy. A History from the Earliest Times to 1900* Vols IV & V, London, 1899.

Crook, J., *The Very Thing – The Memoirs of Drummer Richard Bentinck, Royal Welch Fusiliers 1807-23*, London, 2011.

Feldbaek, O., *The Battle of Copenhagen 1801*, Barnsley, 2002.

Fjeldborg A, *A Tour in Zealand in the year 1802, with an historical sketch of the Battle of Copenhagen, by a native of Denmark*, London, 1805.

Flamand, L., *Kjobenhavns Bombardement 1807*, Copenhagen, 1860.

Fortescue, J., *A History of the British Army* Vol. VI, London, 1910.

Fraser, A., *Narrative of a Secret Mission to the Danish Islands in 1808 by the Rev. James Robertson*, London, 1863.

Glenthoj, R. and Ottesen, M., *Experiences of War and Nationality in Denmark and Norway, 1807-13*, London, 2014.

Glover, G., *A Guards Officer in the Peninsula and at Waterloo: The Letters of Captain George Bowles, Coldstream Guards, 1807-19*, Godmanchester, 2008.

————, *A Hellish Business: The Letters of Captain Charles Kinloch 52nd Foot*, Huntingdon, 2007.

————, *The Diary of a Veteran: The Diary of Sergeant Peter Facey 1803-19*, Huntingdon 2007.

————, *Seven Years on the Peninsula: The Memoirs of Private Adam Reed, 47th (Lancashire) Foot 1806-17*, Godmanchester, 2012.

Grainger, J., *The British Navy in the Baltic*, Woodbridge, 2014.

Granville, Countess, *Lord Granville Levenson Gower. Private Correspondence 1781-1821* Vol. II, London, 1916.

Gurwood, J., *Duke of Wellington's Dispatches 1799-1818*, London, 1837.

Hamilton, Sir R., *Letters and Papers of Admiral of the Fleet Sir Thomas Byam Martin* Vol. II, London, 1898.

Hewison, W., *Not Born to Drown, an Orkney Soldier in the Napoleonic Wars*, Orkney, 2001.

Hounslow, E., *Nelson's Right Hand Man. The Life and Times of Vice Admiral Sir Thomas Fremantle*, Stroud, 2016.

Howarth, S., *Battle of Copenhagen 1801 200 Years, The Bicentennial International Naval Conference, Portsmouth, England, 19 May 2001*, Shelton, 2003.

Jackson, Lady, *The Diaries and Letters of Sir George Jackson KCH*, London, 1872.

James, W., *Naval History of Great Britain* Vols III and IV, London, 1902.

Jelsdorf, Hans, *Surgeon General and Chief of Defence Health, Rendsborg, 2007*.

Jespersen, K., *The Besieging of Copenhagen in 1807 and the Map in the Governor's Library in Odense*, Odense, 1974.

Kennedy, G., *Captain Bligh, the man and his Mutinies*, London, 1989.

Leach, J., *Rough Sketches of the Life of An Old Soldier*, London, 1831.

Malmesbury, Earl of, *Letters of the First Earl of Malmesbury, His Family and Friends*, Vol. 2, London, 1870.

Muir, Rory, *Wellington: The Path to Victory 1769-1814*, Yale, 2013.

Munch-Petersen, T., *Defying Napoleon. How Britain bombarded Copenhagen and seized the Danish Fleet in 1807*, Stroud, 2007.

Navy Records Society, *The Bombardment of Copenhagen 1807, The Journal of Surgeon Charles Chambers of HM Ship Prometheus. The Naval Miscellany* Vol. III, London, 1928.

_____, *Five Naval Journals 1789-1817*, Greenwich, 1951.

_____, *The Naval Miscellany* Vol. V, London, 1984,

Nicolas, Sir N., *The Dispatches and Letters of Lord Nelson, Volume IV, September 1799-December* 1801, London, 1998.

O'Byrne, W., *A Naval Biographical Dictionary* (3 volumes), London, 1849.

Ompteda, Colonel, *In the King's German Legion*, London, 1894.

Petrides, A and Downs, J., *Sea Soldier, An Officer of Marines with Duncan, Nelson,*

Collingwood *and Cockburn. The Letters and Journals of Major T. Marmaduke Wybourn RM, 1797-1813* (Tunbridge, 2000).

Pope, D., *The Great Gamble. Nelson at Copenhagen*, London, 1972.

Robertson, D., *The Journal of Sergeant D Robertson Late 92nd Foot*, Perth, 1842.

Rodd, T., *The Battle of Copenhagen fought on 2nd April 1801 by Lord Nelson. A Poem with Notes*, London, 1801.

Roeder, J., *Danmarks Krigs – og Politiske Historie, fra krigens udbrud 1807 til Freden til Jonkoping den 10de December 1809* (3 volumes), Copenhagen, 1845.

Ross-Lewin, H., *With the 32nd In the Peninsula and other campaigns*, London, 1834.

Ryan, A., *Documents Relating to the Copenhagen Operation 1807. The Naval Miscellany* Vol. V, London, 1984.

_____, *The Causes of the British Attack on Copenhagen in 1807*, London, 1953.

_____, *The Saumarez Papers 1808-12*, London, 1968.

Schilling, Lieutenant A., *Journal of the hostilities at Copenhagen, 10 August 1807 to 7 September 1807*, n.d.

Sommer, F., *A Description of Denmark; and a Narrative of the Siege, Bombardment, and Capture of Copenhagen, with the Surrender of the Danish Fleet, Arsenals &c to the British Arms on the 7th September 1807*, Colchester, n.d.

Surtees, W., *Twenty-Five Years in the Rifle Brigade*, London, 1833.

Teague, J. and D., *Where Duty Calls Me, The Experiences of William Green of Lutterworth in the Napoleonic Wars*, Kent, 1987.

Tracy, N., *The Naval Chronicle Vol. IV 1807-1810*, London, 1999.

_____, *The Naval Chronicle Vol. V 1811-15*, London, 1999.

Verner, W., *History and Campaigns of the Rifle Brigade 1800-13*, London, 1912.

Wellington, Duke of, *Supplementary Dispatches, Correspondence and Memoranda of Field Marshal Arthur, Duke of Wellington* Vol. VI, London, 1860.

Wolff, Jens, *Sketches on a Tour to Copenhagen through Norway and Sweden*, London, 1816.

Index